"For God sent not His Son into the world
to condemn the world,
but that the world, through Him,
might be saved."

John 3:17

From Ruin to Resurrection

Reflections on the Nature of Man and his Eternal Destiny

by

Al Maxey

© Copyright 2022 by Al Maxey
ISBN: 978-1-63249-441-2
All rights reserved.

Designed and Published by:
Battle Born Digital Media and Marketing
Gold Hill, Nevada 89440
Phone 775-583-8655
sam@battleborndigital.com
www.battleborndigital.com

Proudly Designed and Printed in The United States

To my eleven grandchildren: Alexandria, Cameron, Kain, Katelynn, Chase, Luke, Peyton, Jacob, Emma, Preston, and Addilyn for whom I pray daily that they may grow into godly men and women destined for eternal life.

Table Of Contents

Chapter 1 The Nature of Man: Body, Soul, Spirit	11
Chapter 2 Imago Dei: Created in the Image of God	29
Chapter 3 Qoheleth's Depiction of Man	35
Chapter 4 Defining Death–Physical, Relational, Eternal	49
Chapter 5 How Long is Forever?	63
Chapter 6 Reflecting on Hades	75
Chapter 7 The Rich Man and Lazarus	81
Chapter 8 The Thief on the Cross	95
Chapter 9 Samuel, Saul and the Witch	107
Chapter 10 Preaching to Spirits in Prison	117
Chapter 11 Spirits of Just Men made Perfect	123
Chapter 12 Dead Body – Dead Faith	133
Chapter 13 Three Dead Jewish Patriarchs	139
Chapter 14 Souls Under the Altar	149
Chapter 15 The Consuming Fire	157
Chapter 16 Torture or Termination?	167
Chapter 17 Salted With Fire	177
Chapter 18 Understanding the Undying Worm	191
Chapter 19 Beaten With Fewer Blows	197
Chapter 20 Grace and the Caveman	205

Chapter 21 Baptism for the Dead   223

Chapter 22 A Meeting in the Air   239

Chapter 23 Paradise Regained The New Heavens and Earth 249

Chapter 24 Post-Resurrection Recognition s   259

Chapter 25 Whose Wife will She Be?   269

Chapter 26 Paul's Anticipated Departure   281

Chapter 27 Paying the Penalty for Sin   287

Foreword

Al Maxey is not timid, naturally reticent, or afraid to stand and declare his honest thinking in public. Yet his mind is not set in concrete, and he is both willing and able to learn from others. Our models in this regard are the ancient Bereans who heard "new" preaching from a visitor named Paul. They welcomed his ongoing message tentatively but with an open mind. And each day they determined the truthfulness of what they were hearing by comparing it with the Jewish Scriptures they already knew. For taking that approach, Dr. Luke called the Bereans "noble" (literally: "well-born" or "high-class"), adding that they looked even better when compared to their neighbors over at Thessalonica (Acts 17:11-12).

By this measure, Al is "high-class" too, for the Bereans' behavior as reported by Luke also describes Al's reaction one day in 1986, when a brother in the congregation walked into his office, placed on his desk a copy of the 1982 first edition of my book, *The Fire That Consumes: A Biblical and Historical Study of the Doctrine of Final Punishment*, issued the challenge: "Read this book and then tell me what you think about it," and walked out. The first thing Al did was to read the book cover to cover. Then he read it again. On the third reading, he also looked up every Scripture referenced in the book, checking to see if the book misused or abused any passage of Scripture cited. It did not.

Al's mind was changed concerning the purpose of hell – i.e., it was not intended to torment forever people who can never die, but to destroy finally and forever people who, without God's gift of immortality, cannot possibly continue to live. One thing led to another, and soon Al was rethinking not only hell, but also human nature and immortality, death and life, the so-called "intermediate state" between death and resurrection, judgment, heaven, and much more. He has been preaching, teaching and spreading his understanding of Scripture on these themes ever since, making him perhaps the most influential popular presenter of this "Conditionalist" (biblical) understanding in the Churches of Christ today.

Because of common human frailties, all Bible teachers sometimes will disagree. Given that reality, it would be a very strange thing indeed if Al and I were of one mind on every specific detail in this forest of related subjects – and it would not matter anyway. What *does* matter is that all of us – you and I and Al, and everyone we influence – always have that "Berean spirit." Whatever Scripture teaches is what is ultimately right, and following it we will never go wrong. Thank you, Al Maxey, for demonstrating this so eloquently in your ministry.

Edward William Fudge
Author, *The Fire That Consumes*

Author's Preface

Every now and then something occurs in a person's life that has a lasting impact upon them; having the potential to alter the course of their lives. For me, one of those momentous events took place in Santa Fe, New Mexico in 1986. I was the minister for a little congregation of about 150 members. It was a great group, and my family and I stayed there for eight years (1984-1992). One morning, as I was studying in my office, Dave England, one of the members, walked in, placed a book on my desk, and said, "Would you read this and tell me what you think?" He then turned and walked out, giving me no indication as to his own views of the book. I picked up the book and looked at the cover. It was by Edward Fudge, someone I had never heard of, and the title was "The Fire That Consumes." I set it aside and continued with what I had previously been doing.

Some time later I noticed the book on my desk and picked it up again. As I flipped through it I realized this was a presentation of a position on the nature of man and his eternal destiny with which I was completely unfamiliar, and, frankly, somewhat skeptical. It seemed radically different from what I had always been taught to believe, although I must admit that I had never been completely comfortable with the traditional teaching on this subject, especially the view that God would torture people endlessly and find some satisfaction therein.

Over the next few days I read the book. Then I read it *again*, this time much more carefully. After that, I picked up my Bible and literally went through every verse, from cover to cover, over the next several months, examining the Scriptures to determine if "these things be true" (as did the Bereans in Acts 17:11 with the astounding teachings of Paul). To make a long story short, I could not refute this view of the nature of man and his eternal destiny. Indeed, the more I studied it over the coming years (and I studied it extensively and in great depth), the more convicted I became that Conditionalism (the view that man was by nature mortal, and that immortality was a promised gift conditioned upon being "in Christ Jesus," and that eternal punishment was an everlasting loss of life itself, not just a "life of loss") was a powerful Truth our traditional teaching had tragically subverted.

In the twenty-eight years that followed that encounter in my office in Santa Fe, I have become increasingly vocal in my support of what I am convinced is the biblical teaching on the nature of man and his eternal destiny. I have presented in-depth classes on this view in every congregation with which I have served as minister and elder, and these studies have been well-received. My most recent class, which was a 20 week study from June to October, 2012, was recorded in MP3 format and is available for purchase on a two CD set on my web site. I held a public debate on this subject in 2002, and the full text of "The Maxey-Thrasher Debate" is also available on my web site (which site may be easily found by simply entering my name in any Internet search engine, such as "Google" or "Bing").

For the past twelve years I have been sending out weekly written articles (on a variety of subjects) via email to a growing list of subscribers (now numbering in the tens of thousands all over the world). During those years I have written close to 30 in-depth articles dealing with the nature of man and his eternal destiny. For several years now readers have been requesting that I place these studies in a book. I have finally decided to do so, and they make up the 26 chapters of this present book: "From Ruin to Resurrection," which takes us on a journey from the fallen state of mankind, resulting in death and ruin, to the glorious and everlasting life the Father offers to all through His Son, and which will be fully and finally realized at the resurrection.

The reader will quickly notice that this book consists of independent essays, yet they are tied together by the thread of biblical teaching on man's nature and God's design for our eternal well-being. I have chosen to adopt a somewhat polemic approach in this book, presenting the Conditionalist teaching through what might be perceived as a didactic dialogue. Thus, I begin with a presentation of what I perceive to be the nature of man as presented in the pages of God's Word. "But, what about…?" Such questions then lead to the next essay. Which leads to: "But, what about…?" By the end of the book each of these questions have been addressed in didactic dialogue with this unseen skeptic. The polemic is less "warlike" than many polemical presentations, yet the traditional teaching on man's nature and eternal destiny (of both the righteous and unrighteous) is directly and boldly confronted and refuted with a reasoned and extensive exegesis.

It is my prayer that this work will encourage you to further study of God's revelation regarding this important topic, and to a renewed appreciation of His love, mercy and grace. The journey I began in 1986 has certainly resulted in such for me. Little did I know, when I first picked up that book by Edward Fudge, that three decades later he would be writing the Foreword for my own book on this topic, or that in his third edition of "The Fire That Consumes" he would mention me by name and make reference to my own efforts to promote this biblical Truth. Our God is indeed an awesome God!

Chapter 1
The Nature of Man
Body – Soul – Spirit

"What is man, that Thou dost take thought of him?" (Psalm 8:4). We all know that he is "fearfully and wonderfully made" (Psalm 139:14), but exactly what is the nature of man? Mankind has been asking this question, and seeking the answer, almost from the beginning of time. One of the important truths conveyed in the OT Scriptures, as the nature of man is considered, is that man is a *unified whole*, rather than a loose fusion of separate and disparate entities. It was much later that the pagans began to influence the thinking of the people of God in the direction of two (*dichotomy*) or three (*trichotomy*) distinct parts. This dualistic manner of conceptualizing human beings has persisted throughout most of Christian history, and began in the so-called Intertestamental Period to influence the Jewish thinking as well.

"A human being is a totality of being, not a combination of various parts and impulses. According to the Old Testament understanding, a person is not a body which happens to possess a soul. Instead, a person *is* a living soul. ... Because of God's breath of life, the man became 'a living being' (Genesis 2:7). A person, thus, is a complete totality, made up of human flesh, spirit (best understood as 'the life-force'), and *nephesh* (best understood as 'the total self' but often translated as 'soul')" [*Holman Bible Dictionary*, p. 61]. "The Old Testament truth that people exist as a totality remained firm in New Testament writings" [*ibid*]. "The New Testament illustrates four specific and distinct dimensions of human existence, but the writers of the New Testament affirm with the Old Testament writers that a human being is a totality, a complete whole" [*ibid*].

"In the Bible, a person is a unity. Body and soul or spirit are not opposite terms, but rather terms which supplement one another to describe aspects of the inseparable whole person. Such a holistic image of a person is maintained also in the New Testament even over against the Greek culture which, since Plato, sharply separated body and soul with an analytic exactness and which saw the soul as the valuable, immortal, undying part of human beings. ... According to the Bible, a human being exists as a whole unit and remains also as a whole person in the hand of God after death. A person is not at any time viewed as a bodyless soul" [*ibid*, p. 1295-1296].

Dr. Everett Ferguson, a dear brother in Christ, in his book *Early Christians Speak: Faith and Life in the First Three Centuries* [ACU Press], comments on some statements found in the noted second century work *The Epistle to Diognetus* (in which are found the statements: "The invisible soul is imprisoned in a visible body" and "The immortal soul dwells in a mortal tent"). Dr. Ferguson observes: "From the standpoint of the Biblical doctrine of man, one can fault the author for his Greek distinction between body and soul. The sharp separation he makes is more in accord with Greek philosophy than it is with the Biblical view of the unity of the whole man" [p. 198]. Everett later comments, "The author's anthropology is faulty" [*ibid*].

"The ancient Hebrews did not approach man dualistically as have the Greeks nor, by implication, the general public of contemporary Western society" [Dr. Arnold De Graaff and Dr. James Olthuis, *Toward A Biblical View Of Man*, a paper produced for the *Institute For Christian Studies*, p. 81]. "Man is not a soul imprisoned in a body. Both belong together in a psychosomatic unity. ... There is not dualism in the sense of separation, as though there could be full man either as body alone or as soul alone. ...together they make up the one man" [*International Standard Bible Encyclopedia*, vol. 1, p. 134].

"The English translation ... 'soul' has too often been misunderstood as teaching a bipartite (soul and body: dichotomy) or tripartite (body, soul and spirit: trichotomy) anthropology. Equally misleading is the interpretation which too radically separates soul from body as in the Greek view of human nature. Porteous states it well when he says, 'The Hebrew could not conceive of a disembodied soul.' ... As R.B. Laurin has suggested, 'To the Hebrew, man was not a body and a soul, but rather a body-soul, a unity of vital power'" [*The Zondervan Pictorial Encyclopedia of the Bible*, vol. 5, p. 496]. "What is essential to understanding the Hebrew mind is the recognition that man is a unit: body-soul" [*ibid*, p. 497].

It is important to note the growing number of scholars who have perceived the doctrine of *dualism* to be anti-biblical and totally opposed to the true *holistic* nature of man. This realization is especially vital to our theology, for "what Christians believe about the make-up of their human nature largely determines what they believe about their ultimate destiny" [Dr. Samuele Bacchiocchi, *Immortality or Resurrection? -- A Biblical Study on Human Nature and Destiny*, p. 21]. "A survey of the studies produced during the last fifty years or so, reveals that the traditional dualistic view of human nature has come under massive attack. Scholars seem to outdo one another in challenging traditional dualism and in affirming Biblical wholism. ... Christianity is coming out of a stupor and is suddenly discovering that for too long it has held to a view of human nature derived from Platonic dualism rather than from Biblical wholism" [*ibid*].

Thus, as we examine the "parts" of man (body, soul, spirit) we need to keep in mind that these are not separate living entities that perhaps can survive, and even prosper, apart from one another. Rather, they are integral aspects of the whole man and do not rise to higher, fuller life when freed from one another. Such a concept is pure paganism, and it has no basis in the Scriptures and certainly has no place in the teachings of Christianity.

The *biblical* view of the nature of man is probably best perceived in Genesis 2:7, "Then the Lord God formed man of dust from the ground, and breathed into his nostrils the breath of life; and man became a living being." One could perhaps present this passage as an equation:

$$B + B = B$$

Body + Breath = Being

Let's notice each of these three concepts more closely, especially since some traditionalists see in this verse justification for the doctrine of "immortal soulism."

THE BODY

"Of the thirteen words which refer to the animal or human body, the most frequent is *basar*, 'flesh.' It can designate the body as a whole, but the form or shape of the body or of its parts is not what is important. The focus is on the function or dynamics" [*Holman Bible Dictionary*, p. 202]. The Greek word most often utilized for the body is "*soma*."

The body of man was formed from the physical elements that also make up the earth about us. According to one source on the Internet, "A chemical analysis of man's body reveals that it consists of 72 parts oxygen, 13.5 parts carbon, 9.1 parts hydrogen, 2.5 parts nitrogen, 1.3 parts calcium, 1.15 parts phosphorus, and small amounts of potassium, sulfur, sodium, chlorine, magnesium, iron, silicon, iodine, and fluorine. The first six elements listed in this paragraph, therefore, make up more than 99% of man's body."

Although one might want to verify these figures with those better equipped to know than I, nevertheless the point is made that our human bodies consist of common elements found in the physical creation. Phrased more poetically: *we are formed from the dust of the ground*. In Genesis 3:19 man was informed, "You are dust, and to dust you shall return." Abraham, as he ventured to speak to the Lord, acknowledged, "I am but dust and ashes" (Genesis 18:27). "For He Himself knows our frame (what we are made of); He is mindful that we are but dust" (Psalm 103:14).

Solomon, in speaking of both men and animals, declares, "All came from the dust and all return to the dust" (Ecclesiastes 3:20). He later observes, "Then the dust will return to the earth as it was" (Ecclesiastes 12:7). In Psalm 104, which speaks of the animals, we are informed that the Creator "dost take away their spirit, they expire, and return to their dust" (vs. 29). With regard to the physical composition of man and beast, it is the same. Neither has an advantage over the other in this area (Ecclesiastes 3:19-21). If God should decide to withhold breath/spirit from both, "all flesh would perish together, and man would return to dust" (Job 34:15).

"The wordplay between '*adam*' and '*adama*' (ground, soil) in Gen. 2:7 suggests the relatedness between humanity and the created world" [*Eerdmans Dictionary of the Bible*, p. 615]. "There is a wordplay in the Hebrew text of Genesis 2-3 that indicates an intimate relationship between man (*adham*) and the ground (*adhamah*). God formed man of dust from the ground (Genesis 2:7; 3:23), made him to till the ground (2:5; 3:23; cf. 2:15), cursed the ground because he sinned (3:17), and decreed that he should return to the ground from whence he came (3:19). The emphasis throughout Genesis 2-3 seems to be on the frailty and transitoriness of all God's creation, whether vegetable, animal, or man" [John T. Willis, *The Living Word Commentary: Genesis*, p. 102-103]. "Our study of the meaning and use of 'flesh--bashar' in the Old Testament shows that the word generally is used to describe the concrete reality of human existence from the perspective of its frailty and feebleness" [Dr. Samuel Bacchiocchi, *Immortality or Resurrection? -- A Biblical Study on Human Nature and Destiny*, p. 62].

I imagine there would be little debate between most traditionalists and me over the *physical body* of man (and by "man" I refer to both male and female -- Genesis 1:27). Our bodies are *mortal*, and thus subject to death. At some point, unless we are privileged to be alive at the *Parousia*, we shall die (Hebrews 9:27). Thus, our bodies will return to the ground ... dust returning to dust.

The promise of our Lord, however, is that He will awaken us from our "sleep in the dust of the ground" (Daniel 12:2) and we shall be changed, this mortal shall *put on* immortality (1 Cor. 15:50f), and we shall thus be enabled to forever dwell in the presence of our Lord. The hope of the child of God, therefore, is inextricably linked with the *resurrection of the body* from the dust of the ground. *Without* resurrection, either Christ's or our own, *we have perished* (1 Corinthians 15:12-18).

THE SPIRIT

The physical body is not inherently immortal. Indeed, after the fall, man was barred from the garden and the tree of life (Genesis 3:24) lest he "take also from the tree of life, and eat, *and live forever*" (Genesis 3:22). Thus, the body itself is destined to die (suffer the loss of life; return to the ground). For some (the redeemed) the hope exists of one day awaking and *putting on* "everlasting life" (Daniel 12:2), but that is yet future. At the present time there is nothing inherently immortal about our physical bodies.

Thus, the traditionalists (those who believe in man's *inherent* immortality) must search elsewhere for that special "immortal something" that they believe is part of man's makeup. Some assume it is the "spirit" of man that is immortal. Genesis 2:7 declares, "Then the Lord God formed man of dust from the ground, and breathed into his nostrils the breath of life; and man became a living being." It is this "*breath* of life," this "*spirit* of life," that is proclaimed by some to be immortal, and which consciously survives the death of the physical body.

"In the Hebrew there are two words for breath: *neshamah*, and more commonly *ruach*. In general, they are used interchangeably for 'breath' and 'spirit'" [Leroy Edwin Froom, *The Conditionalist Faith of Our Fathers: The Conflict of the Ages Over the Nature and Destiny of Man*, vol. 1, p. 36]. The Greek word employed is "*pneuma*."

"In the OT Hebrew '*ruah*' means first of all wind and breath, but also the human spirit in the sense of life force and even personal energy. ... It is explicit that God is the source of human breath. ... In the NT Greek '*pneuma*' can mean wind. It can also have the meaning breath. ... Both 'spirit' and 'mind' are used of the whole person and not simply of component parts" [*Eerdmans Dictionary of the Bible*, p. 1248].

The body of man is animated and sustains life as long as the "breath" dwells within it. In other words, a *breathing* body is a *living* body; a body where the breathing has *ceased* for an extended period is a *dead* body. God animated the physical body by placing within it the "breath of life." Life is a *gift* of the Life-Giver. He can also withdraw it. Psalm 104:29, speaking of animals, declares, "Thou dost take away their spirit/breath, they expire, and return to their dust." When the breath departs from the body, the body returns to the dust. Solomon points out that men and beasts "all have the *same* breath/spirit" (Ecclesiastes 3:19).

This is an interesting fact, and a troubling one, for those who would suggest the "immortal part of man" is the "spirit." Animals have the *same* spirit! Thus, if this is the immortal part of man, why not also of the other living creatures? The simple fact of the matter is, when the breath is withdrawn, men and animals die. God is the Giver of this gift of the breath of life, and thus this life-force returns to Him who gave it. "The dust will return to the earth as it was, and the spirit/breath will return to God who gave it" (Ecclesiastes 12:7). This passage does not suggest some "immortal spirit" (which is the "*real*" *us*) flies off to heaven to dwell with God. It merely declares the *life-force* has departed the body (thus rendering it a *dead* body). Since God is the Giver of this life-force, it is depicted as returning to Him who bestowed it.

Notice Ezekiel 37 (the vision of the valley of dry bones). The prophet was asked, "Can these bones live?" (vs. 3). Ezekiel didn't really commit himself, so the Lord said of the bones, "Behold, I will cause *breath* to enter you that you may *come to life*. And I will put sinews on you, make flesh grow back on you, cover you with skin, and put *breath* in you that you may *come alive*" (vs. 5-6). The prophet watched as the bodies were recreated and reformed. "But there was no breath in them" (vs. 8). Then he was told to prophesy, "Come from the four winds, O breath, and breathe on these slain, that they come to life" (vs. 9). He did so, and "breath came into them, and they came to life, and stood on their feet" (vs. 10). This is almost reminiscent of Gen. 2:7, isn't it? God formed man, and breathed into him the breath of life, and man became a living being. The breath is the life-force of the body. Without it the body is dead. And this gift of the breath of life comes from God. "In Him we live and move and exist (have our being)" (Acts 17:28). "He Himself gives to all *life* and *breath* and all things" (Acts 17:25).

It should also be pointed out that "spirit" is not infrequently used in Scripture to represent the less physical aspects of man's being: personality, emotions, attitude, and the like. Thus, one might be "mean-spirited" or have a broken or contrite spirit (Psalm 51). These terms do not suggest an immortal being trapped inside the body, but merely reflect the mental and emotional aspects of man's nature. "In both the Old and New Testaments, spirit is used of humans and of other beings. When used of humans, spirit is associated with a wide range of functions including thinking and understanding, emotions, attitudes, and intentions. ... spirit is used extensively with human emotions. ... A variety of attitudes and intentions are associated with spirit" [*Holman Bible Dictionary*, p. 1300].

Some suggest that Psalm 31:5 ("Into Thy hand I commit my spirit"), which was voiced by Christ on the cross, proves that the "spirit/breath" is the immortal something which survives death, and is that immortal, conscious, personal part of us that lives on with God. However, the "spirit" of both men (good and wicked) *and* animals is withdrawn unto God. This seems to preclude such dualistic notions (unless you want heaven infested with the "immortal spirits" of rodents and roaches). All that is suggested by this expression is that the one expiring is entrusting back to God the gift of the breath of life. The confident hope and expectation of such a statement, of course, is that He will raise us back up and bestow the gift of life once again. Paul, as he contemplated his impending death, wrote confidently: "I know whom I have believed and I am convinced that He is able to guard what I have entrusted to Him *until/for that day*" (2 Timothy 1:12). I think Paul also knew that his *breath of life* was in good hands, and would one day be bestowed again when his body was raised from the dust of the ground and reconstituted.

"There is no indication in the Bible that the spirit of life given to man at creation was a conscious entity before it was given. This gives us reason to believe that the spirit of life has no conscious personality when it returns to God. The spirit that returns to God is simply the animating life principle imparted by God to both human beings and animals for the duration of their earthly existence" [Dr. Samuele Bacchiocchi, *Immortality or Resurrection? -- A Biblical Study on Human Nature and Destiny*, p. 74]. "Do not trust in princes, in mortal man, in whom there is no salvation. His breath/spirit departs, he returns to the earth; in that very day his thoughts perish" (Psalm 146:3-4).

THE SOUL

Well, if it isn't the spirit/breath which is that "immortal something" within us that survives the death of the body, these traditionalists theorize, then it *must* be the "soul." This is the one that most traditionalists choose as being the immortal part of man. In fact, the expression "immortal *soul*" has become very common in Christendom. The readers might be surprised to discover, however, that the phrase "immortal soul" never appears in the Bible ... not even one time.

"Then the Lord God formed man of dust from the ground, and breathed into his nostrils the breath of life; and man became a living soul/being" (Genesis 2:7). Some traditionalists virtually equate this last phrase ("living soul") with "immortal soul." But, that is not what the passage says. God put breath within this body and the body became a living being. The exact same words are used of animals in Scripture. Further, the text doesn't say man was *given* a soul -- it says man *became* a soul. That is a significant difference.

A fellow minister once told me: "The one thing which distinguishes man from monkey is his 'living soul.' To my knowledge this expression is used only of man; I don't find it used of bugs or bulls." Thus, according to this minister, that which makes man unique among the living creation of God is: man has a "living soul," and those other life forms do not. Again, we see this phrase "*living* soul" *incorrectly* being equated with "*immortal* soul."

It would probably shock a great many to know that the phrase "living soul" is actually used *more often* in Genesis with reference *to animals* than with reference to *man*! Notice some of these other passages where "living soul" *is* used of bugs, bulls, birds and beasts.

GENESIS 1:20 ~ "Then God said, 'Let the waters teem with swarms of *living souls,* and let birds fly above the earth in the open expanse of the heavens.'"

GENESIS 1:21 ~ "And God created the great sea monsters, and every *living soul* that moves, with which the waters swarmed after their kind, and every winged bird after its kind; and God saw that it was good."

GENESIS 1:24 ~ "Then God said, 'Let the earth bring forth *living souls* after their kind: cattle and creeping things (here are the "bugs and bulls") and beasts of the earth after their kind;' and it was so."

GENESIS 2:19 ~ "And out of the ground the Lord God formed every beast of the field and every bird of the sky, and brought them to the man to see what he would call them; and whatever the man called each *living soul,* that was its name."

GENESIS 9:15-16 ~ "...and I will remember My covenant, which is between Me and you and every *living soul* of all flesh; and never again shall the water become a flood to destroy all flesh. When the bow is in the cloud, then I will look upon it, to remember the everlasting covenant between God and every *living soul* of all flesh that is on the earth."

To help validate this particular view, let me quote from an article by a well-known and respected scholar in the *Churches of Christ*: Dr. Jack P. Lewis (who was formerly a professor at *Harding*

Graduate School of Religion). In an article titled "Living Soul," which appeared in the March 16, 1976 issue of *Firm Foundation magazine*, he began by quoting Gen. 2:7. Then, he wrote the following (I am only quoting a small portion of that article): **"It is in particular the line of reasoning premised upon this verse which argues that man has a living soul and that animals do not have souls that I wish us to look. For many people this verse in Genesis describes the one distinctive thing that makes man different from animals.** The phrase at issue in this passage is 'nephesh hayyah' which occurs in several Old Testament passages and is translated into Greek as 'psuche zosa.' That which has been obscured to us because of variety in our English translation is that the creatures are also 'nephesh hayyah.' Only in one out of the several passages where 'nephesh hayyah' occurs is man the exclusive object of discussion. It would seem that arguments which try to present the distinctiveness of man from the term 'living soul' are actually based on the phenomena of variety in translation of the *King James Version* and have no validity in fact. Had the translators rendered all these occurrences by the same term, we would have been aware of the fact that both men and animals are described by it."

As Dr. Lewis has pointed out, many of the translations (perhaps following the lead of the *KJV* and its self-proclaimed desire to provide "variety" in translation) have rendered this term "living *creature*" when it is used of animals, but "living *soul*" when speaking of man. Yet the term is exactly the same for both in the original.

The word itself simply conveys the concept of "being," or "life." When God took this body He had created from the dust of the ground and breathed into it the breath of life, that body then *became* a living, breathing *being*, and *this is said of both man and animal*. And that is *all* the original text says! Nothing is ever said in these passages about either man or beast (or bug or bird) being anything other than "living *beings*."

"Soul" is not what a living, animate physical body *has*, rather "soul" is what a living, animate physical body *is*. They cannot be separated. "Body and soul cannot be observed separate from one another. Body and soul do not form two separate substances. Instead, they comprise the one individual human in inseparable union. ... Also in the New Testament body and soul are two inseparable aspects of the one human being ~ Matthew 6:25" [*Holman Bible Dictionary*, p. 202].

"The Hebrew word *nephesh* is a key Old Testament term (755 times) referring to human beings. ... A person does not *have* a soul. A person *is* a living soul (Genesis 2:7). That means a living being that owes *life itself* to the Creator just as the animal does (Genesis 2:19). ... The soul does *not* represent a divine, immortal, undying part of the human being after death as the Greeks often thought" [*ibid*, p. 1295].

John T. Willis, in his commentary on Genesis [*Sweet Publishing Company*], writes, "The Hebrew expression *nephesh chayyah*, which some insist on translating 'a living soul,' is used of fish and marine life in Genesis 1:20,21; land animals in 1:24; beasts, birds and reptiles in 1:30; and beasts and birds in 2:19. If 'soul' means the eternal part of man ... in Genesis 2:7, it must mean the eternal part of a fish ... in Genesis 1:20, 21; etc." [p. 103-104]. "The word translated 'being' in the Revised Standard Version (*nephesh*) means the whole person" [*ibid*, p. 104].

"While man became a living soul, he did not thereby automatically become an immortal soul, or being. The same Hebrew term, 'living soul,' is applied to the lower animals. In fact, *nephesh* (soul) is four times applied to the lower animals before it is used of man ~ in Genesis 1:20, 21, 24, 30. And out of the first thirteen usages in Genesis, *nephesh* is nine times used of the lower animals. ... Man *became* a living soul ~ a single entity, an inseparable unit, a unique individual. ... The soul is the living person or being himself, not a separate, independent 'something'" [Leroy Edwin Froom, *The

Conditionalist Faith of Our Fathers: The Conflict of the Ages Over the Nature and Destiny of Man, vol. 1, p. 34-35, 39].

"Far from referring simply to one aspect of a person, 'soul' refers to the whole person" [*Eerdmans Dictionary of the Bible*, p. 1245]. This word, like "spirit," can also be used figuratively to refer to the seat of emotions in place of personal pronouns, or to refer to one's entire self/being. It also can refer to life itself. When Jesus spoke of the destruction of both "soul and body" in Gehenna, He was referring to the fact that only God has the power to destroy not only the body, but also the very *being* of a person. Men can only kill the body, but God can always raise it right back up. Only God can so destroy a person's *being* that nothing exists! Thus, "soul" conveys the idea of not just a physical body, but the very *beingness* of the person. Man can end another man's "being" *temporarily*; God can end a man's "being" *forever*.

The "soul" is even said to reside in the blood. "For the soul of the flesh is in the blood" (Leviticus 17:11). In Genesis 9:4 we are told the "soul" *is* the blood. This simply means the *life* of the body. It in no way speaks of some "immortal something" actually living *in* the blood, or *being* the blood. Just as life is connected to breath/breathing, so also is life connected to the coursing of blood through one's veins. Without either the body is dead (a *dead* soul, not a *living* soul).

"The word translated 'soul' contains no idea of a spiritual existence. ... Really the word refers to the natural life of animals and men, maintained by breathing, or in some way extracting oxygen from the atmospheric air" [*Ellicott's Commentary on the Whole Bible*, vol. 1, p. 19]. T. Pierce Brown, in an article titled "Soul and Spirit" [*Gospel Advocate magazine*, June 14, 1979], wrote, "A consideration of EVERY (emphasis *his*) passage in which these terms are used leads us to the conclusion that the term 'soul' is a term that was applied in the Bible to every being that normally has sensory capacities (life), whether or not they have that capacity when the term is applied to them. For example, one might see a body of a dead person and say, 'That poor soul is dead.' The Bible uses the term that way, even as we do, and it has nothing at all to do with the immortality or mortality of the soul. It simply means that the PERSON (the one who HAD life -- soul -- sensory capacity) is dead."

"A doctrine of the immortality of the soul is not stated in the Bible and is not clearly defined in early rabbinical literature" [*Encyclopedia of Jewish Religion*]. "Summing up, we can say that the expression 'man became a living soul -- *nephesh hayyah*' -- does not mean that at creation his body was endowed with an immortal soul, a separate entity, distinct from the body. Rather, it means that as a result of the divine inbreathing of the 'breath of life' into the lifeless body, man became a living, breathing being, no more, no less. The heart began to beat, the blood to circulate, the brain to think, and all the vital signs of life were activated. Simply stated, 'a living soul' means 'a living being'" [Dr. Samuele Bacchiocchi, *Immortality or Resurrection? -- A Biblical Study on Human Nature and Destiny*, p. 46].

Although the Bible does not teach this doctrine, in 1513 A.D. at the *Fifth Lateran Ecumenical Council*, the Pope issued a decree (aimed primarily at Luther and his associates) that condemned "all who assert that the intellectual soul is mortal." It was declared that the soul was immortal, and "we declare every assertion contrary to the truth of illumined faith to be altogether false; and, that it may not be permitted to dogmatize otherwise, we strictly forbid it, and we decree that all who adhere to affirmations of this kind of error are to be shunned and punished as detestable and abominable heretics and infidels who disseminate everywhere most damnable heresies and who weaken the Catholic faith."

Curtis Dickinson, a longtime acquaintance, wrote, "The Pope's decree turned many from hope in a resurrection to belief in an immortal soul" [*The Witness*, vol. 35, #11, November, 1995].

Needless to say, this decree brought forth strong opposition from those who sought to teach the truth of the Scriptures. Luther declared it was the Pope, not the Bible, who taught, "the soul is immortal." In his *Table Talk* Luther declared, "Now if one should say that Abraham's soul lives with God but his body is dead, this distinction is rubbish. I will attack it. That would be a silly soul if it were in heaven and desired its body!" William Tyndale (1484-1536), an English Bible translator and martyr, wrote, "And ye, in putting them (the departed souls) in heaven, hell and purgatory, destroy the arguments wherewith Christ and Paul prove the resurrection." Tyndale argued that if souls were already in either bliss or misery, "then what cause is there of the resurrection?" And what cause is there even of judgment? In another part of this same writing, Tyndale said, "The true faith putteth forth the resurrection, which we be warned to look for every hour. The heathen philosophers, denying that, did put that the soul did ever live. And the Pope joineth the spiritual doctrine of Christ and the fleshly doctrine of philosophers together; things so contrary that they cannot agree. And because the fleshly-minded Pope consenteth unto heathen doctrine, therefore he corrupteth the Scripture to stablish it. If the soul be in heaven, tell me what cause is there for the resurrection?"

In summation, the nature of man is: Body + Breath = Being. Man is a unified whole, not a conglomeration of distinct, disparate entities. Man *is* a living being; man does not *possess* a living being. Man is entirely mortal in nature; no part of him is inherently immortal, although through God's grace man has the *potential* and the *promise* of a conferred immortality *in Christ Jesus* at the resurrection. The Lord "*alone* possesses immortality" (1 Timothy 6:16), but if we "*seek for* immortality" (Romans 2:7) we shall "*put on*" immortality (1 Corinthians 15:54) after our resurrection from the dust of the ground. For the redeemed of God there is this promise: "God has *given* us eternal life, and this *life is in His Son.* He who has the Son *has the life*; he who does *not* have the Son of God *does not have the life*" (1 John 5:11-12). Our great Savior Jesus

Christ has "brought *life* and *immortality* to light through the gospel, for which I was appointed a preacher and an apostle and a teacher" (2 Timothy 1:10-11). May we each be teachers and preachers of the *true* nature of man, and the *true* nature of our hope of immortality, which is in Him ... *not* in *ourselves*.

Chapter 2
Imago Dei
Created in the Image of God

Imago Dei is a Latin theological term signifying a unique, though somewhat mysterious, relationship between deity and humanity. "Then God said, 'Let Us make man in Our image, according to Our likeness; and let them rule over the fish of the sea and over the birds of the sky and over the cattle and over all the earth, and over every creeping thing that creeps on the earth.' And God created man in His own image, in the image of God He created him; male and female He created them" (Genesis 1:26-27).

The Hebrew word for "image" in this passage is "*tzelem,*" which refers to the nature or essence of a thing and not necessarily the physical form. Similarly, the word for "likeness" in this passage is "*demut,*" which is used to indicate a simile, not an exact replication of actual form. Thus, the verse is not suggesting that man resembles God in physical appearance (head, arms, legs, feet, etc.), but that the resemblance is with regard to aspects of God's essential nature.

Even then, it is only a "likeness," *not* total equality. For example, the passage seems to imply that part of the "likeness" and "image" is with regard to rulership over creation, and yet man's authority, though greater than the rest of creation, is lesser than God's. It is only in the *image* or *likeness* of, not equal to. "Neither of the words imply that persons are divine. They were endowed with some of the characteristics of God. There is a *likeness* but not a *sameness*" [*Holman Bible Dictionary*, p. 688].

"This is the book of the generations of Adam. In the day when God created man, He made him in the *likeness* of God. He created them male and female, and He blessed them and named them Man in the day when they were created" (Genesis 5:1-2). "Whoever sheds man's blood, by man his blood shall be shed, for in the *image* of God He made man" (Genesis 9:6). "For a man ought not to have his head covered, since he is the *image* and glory of God" (1 Corinthians 11:7). "With it (the tongue) we bless our Lord and Father; and with it we curse men, who have been made in the *likeness* of God" (James 3:9). See also Psalm 8, in which there is at least an implication of such.

Some have assumed, and actively proclaim, that these passages declare man is immortal *by nature* .... that he is *inherently* immortal (since he is created in the "image" and "likeness" of the immortal God). This is merely an assumption, however, since the Scriptures make no such claim for the terms "image" or "likeness." Indeed, 1 Timothy 6:16 clearly declares that He "*alone* possesses immortality." It is also an illogical claim, for why would this single attribute of divine nature be the only one given to man? Why not the others? Why not eternal pre-existence, omniscience, omnipotence, omnipresence, or any other strictly divine attribute? "There is no valid reason, then, why immortality alone should be singled out as the one unique characteristic intended by the phrase 'image of God.' We must therefore conclude that creation in the divine 'image,' or 'likeness,' no more proves man's immortality than it proves his eternal pre-existence, omniscience, omnipotence, or possession of any other exclusively divine attribute" [Leroy Edwin Froom, *The Conditionalist Faith of Our Fathers: The Conflict of the Ages Over the Nature and Destiny of Man*, vol. 1, p. 32]. "Early theologians were greatly influenced by Greek philosophy in their interpretation of the 'image of God.' They saw an individual as a spirit being living in a physical body. This Greek dualism was the background out of which the early Christian theologians drew their understanding" [*Holman Bible Dictionary*, p. 688].

Many feel the ultimate testimony as to the "image of God" is seen in Jesus, "who is the image of God" (2 Corinthians 4:4). "And He is the image of the invisible God, the first-born of all creation" (Colossians 1:15). Thus, it is suggested by some that the best way to determine the true "image of God" is to discern the nature of Jesus Himself. What were the *qualities of His life* which made Him God-like, so that when one saw *Him* one saw the *Father*? It is also suggested that we today may truly realize this special quality within ourselves by being "conformed to the image of His Son" (Romans 8:29).

As one can imagine, there are many theories as to the significance of being created in the "image" and "likeness" of God. Thomas Aquinas (1225-1274) regarded this as the human ability to think and reason, to use language and art, far surpassing the abilities of any animal. Thus, being in the image of God, for some, refers to intellectual and relational abilities not found in lesser life forms -- the ability to think and reason, specifically to make moral decisions.

Others feel it refers to the powers of self-transcendence and self-awareness. Thus, we are creatures capable of being introspective, retrospective or prospective. We may reflect upon the past and anticipate the future, and even discern the workings of God in nature, history and our own lives. It is awareness far superior to that of the rest of creation. Still others regard "image of God" as a reference to man being gifted with mind and intelligence, or the power of choice, or the capacity to love and express emotion, the existence of will, conscience, imagination and moral responsibility. Some see it as the capacity for worship.

The noted rabbi Moses Maimonides (1135-1204) suggested that by using one's intellect, one is able to perceive things without the use of the physical senses, an ability that makes man "like" God. The PBS television show *Faith and Reason* stated "Humans differ from all other creatures because of their rational structure ~ their capacity for deliberation and free decision-making."

Ron Rose, in *Heartlight Magazine*, wrote, "Mankind was designed to reason independent of instinct, to dream and sing and express emotion, to create and build and invent, to feel love and compassion and hope, to ask why and why not." The *Holman Bible Dictionary* declares, "More accurate is the suggestion that the image consists in humankind's lordship over and stewardship of creation, for this is the theme of the following verses ~ Gen. 1:28-31" [p. 675].

In my view, perhaps the best explanation is the one given by Dr. Samuele Bacchiocchi in his excellent book *Immortality or Resurrection? -- A Biblical Study on Human Nature and Destiny* [p. 44]. He writes:

"The image of God is associated not with man as male and female, or with an immortal soul given to our species, but rather with humankind's capacity to be and to do on a finite level what God is and does on an infinite level. The creation account seems to be saying that while the sun rules the day, the moon the night, and the fishes the sea, mankind images God by having dominion over all these realms (Genesis 1:28-30).

"In the New Testament, the image of God in humanity is never associated with male-female fellowship, or physical resemblance, or a nonmaterial, spiritual soul, but rather with moral and rational capacities: 'Put on the new nature, which is being renewed in knowledge after the image of its Creator' (Colossians 3:10; cf. Ephesians 4:24). Similarly, conformity to the image of Christ (Romans 8:29; 1 Corinthians 15:49) is generally understood in terms of righteousness and holiness. None of these qualities is possessed by animals. What distinguishes people from animals is the fact that human nature inherently has godlike possibilities. *By virtue of being created in the image of God, human beings are capable of reflecting His character in their own life.*

"Being created in the image of God means that we must view ourselves as intrinsically valuable and richly invested with meaning, potential, and responsibilities. *It means that we have been created to reflect God in our thinking and actions.* We are to be and to do on a finite scale what God is and does on an infinite scale."

Chapter 3
Qoheleth's Depiction of Man

Perhaps the renowned actress Betty Davis (1908-1989) summed it up best when she reflected, in that husky, sultry voice of hers, "Getting old ain't for sissies!" It is surely no secret to any of us that as we grow older we are typically faced with increased infirmities and decreased abilities. In short, we begin wearing out. There are some genuine blessings to old age, but on the other hand there are some serious challenges as well. Jonathan Swift (1667-1745) once observed, "Every man desires to live long, but no man would be old." Nevertheless, the latter *is* the reality that one must confront if he/she would achieve the former. The longer we live, the older we become. Although there is some truth in the adage that one is only as old as one *thinks* himself to be ... or *chooses* to be ("mind over matter," if you will) ... yet there is still no denying, even among those with a positive mental outlook, that the human body *wears down* and *wears out*. We are *mortal*, thus we each have a rendezvous with the dust of the ground from which we came.

"The Lord God formed man of dust from the ground" (Genesis 2:7). "By the sweat of your face you shall eat bread, till you return to the ground, because from it you were taken; for you are dust, and to dust you shall return" (Genesis 3:19). Moses wrote, "Thou dost turn man back into dust" (Psalm 90:3), and Abraham, "the father of the faithful," observed, "I am but dust and ashes" (Genesis 18:27). Job, as he considered his great affliction, wondered, "Thy hands fashioned and made me; wouldst Thou destroy me? Wouldst Thou turn me into dust again?" (Job 10:8-9). Later, Job displayed his understanding that our Creator God does indeed have the power and authority to withdraw the breath of life from any man, and, by so doing, to return him to the elements from which he was created. "If He should determine to do so, if He should gather to Himself His spirit and His breath, all flesh would perish together, and man would return to dust" (Job 34:14-15). David wondered what possible profit there would be in his own shed blood and his return to the ground ~ "Will the dust praise Thee? Will it declare Thy faithfulness?" (Psalm 30:9). The *living* give praise to God and declare His faithfulness, but the *dead* are incapable of such (Ecclesiastes 9:5-6). As this mortal body wears out, "the dust will return to the earth as it was, and the breath/spirit will return to God who gave it" (Ecclesiastes 12:7). This is the fate of all living beings/souls, both man and beast, "For the fate of the sons of men and the fate of beasts is the same. As one dies so dies the other; indeed, they all have the same breath/spirit and there is no advantage for man over beast. ... They all go to the same place. All *came* from the dust and all *return* to the dust" (Ecclesiastes 3:19-20). Of the animals the psalmist writes, "Thou dost take away their breath/spirit, they expire, and return to their dust" (Psalm 104:29).

Admittedly, this all seems like a rather grim prospect. Man is but "animated dust" who, when that divinely given breath of life is withdrawn, simply returns to the dust of the ground from which he was formed, as do the other living beings/souls formed by God. However, the *hope* given by our Creator is that a day of resurrection is coming! "Those who sleep in the dust of the ground will awake" (Daniel 12:2), some to experience everlasting life, others to experience the sentence of the *second* death. Due to the influence of Hellenism, primarily, as well as the philosophical speculations of Plato, much of Christendom has taken a sad detour from the biblical teaching concerning the holistic nature of man, and has instead postulated and promoted the doctrine of inherent immortality. This is entirely contrary to the teaching of Scripture, although far too many Christians are unaware of this fact. Such teaching truly detracts from, and diminishes, the fact of a coming resurrection to immortality. What need is there to raise this body from the dust of the ground if we are already experiencing the joys of being in the presence of our Lord and all our departed loved ones? Such teaching reduces the resurrection to an *irrelevancy* at best. The New Covenant writings, however, make it the central aspect of the gospel of our Lord Jesus Christ. Paul says that if there is no resurrection, then we who have died *have perished* (1 Corinthians 15:18). Some today might counter, "No, Paul, we have *not*; we're singing around the throne, more alive *now* than ever before." Although some might not take kindly to me saying this, it is nevertheless my strong conviction that this is false doctrine.

As noted, the greatest frustration of life is the fact of death. God's original intent for mankind was that they would live forever in His presence in a perfect paradise created here upon earth. As a result of the fall of man, however, that divine design was temporarily thwarted. With sin came death. All things began the process of deterioration. Ultimately, our breath leaves our body and we return to the dust of the ground, there to sleep the sleep of death until that day when our Lord comes to awaken us. At that point there shall be a transformation of all things, and God's original intent for His creation shall be realized: we shall be *changed*, this mortal shall *put on* immortality (1 Corinthians 15:52-54), and we shall dwell forever in His presence in the new heavens and earth. This hope of immortality was felt during the time prior to the incarnation, but it was not fully made known until the coming of the One who made that hope a reality. Deity "*alone* possesses immortality" (1 Timothy 6:16), but Jesus Christ "has brought life and immortality to light through the gospel" (2 Timothy 1:10). Therefore, the prize of "eternal life" shall be *given* to "those who *seek for* glory and honor and immortality" (Romans 2:7). It is not ours *inherently*, but is a gift to those who trust in Him, who is the giver of life. "For the wages of sin is death, but the free gift of God is eternal life in Christ Jesus our Lord" (Romans 6:23). Immortality is a *gift*, and it is to be acquired *only* in Him. If we were all *already* immortal *by nature* (i.e., inherently possessing "immortal souls" incapable of having their life force extinguished), there would be no need of this *gift*. Indeed, as Plato said, death would simply free us from this bodily prison to an even greater *life*. The reality taught in Scripture, however, is that we are *mortal*, and *immortality* is a gift from God to those deemed worthy of this eternal life. "The witness is this, that God has *given* us eternal life, and this life is in His Son. He who has the Son has the life; he who does not have the Son of God does not have the life" (1 John 5:11-12). It doesn't get much plainer than that.

It is also very plain, to even the most casual observer of life, that the difficulties of advancing age can be quite daunting. Some handle this inevitable physical decline rather well; others clearly do not. Regardless of how one faces this stark reality, there is no denying the fact that "it is appointed unto men once to die" (Hebrews 9:27). This is a divinely ordained appointment we shall *all* keep (unless we are privileged to be alive at the Lord's *Parousia*), and for those who are destined to live well into that period known as "old age" there will be various degrees of debilitation that must be endured. These are listed quite poetically in God's Word in the book known to us as *Ecclesiastes*. Indeed, scholars declare that this passage "ranks among the finest of the world's literature, especially when it is read aloud by a good reader" [*The Expositor's Bible Commentary*, vol. 5, p. 1192]. Dr. Paul Kretzmann observes, "This paragraph is one of the most beautiful poetical passages in the entire Bible and deserves to be studied for its form as well as for its content" [*Popular Commentary of the Bible*: The OT, vol. 2, p. 276]. The passage to which these scholars refer, of course, is Ecclesiastes 12:1-8.

Background ~ The word "Ecclesiastes" is merely the *transliteration* of a Greek word referring to "one who addresses an assembly." The Hebrew word is *Qoheleth*, which means essentially the same thing, and can also be rendered "preacher." The "preacher" responsible for this "address" is, in the view of most biblical scholars, Solomon, although this was seriously questioned in the 19th century, with some scholars suggesting the writing may be the work of as many as nine authors. Solomon, the second son of David and Bathsheba, reigned over Israel for forty years (971-931 B.C.). He was a very *wise* man, as well as a very *poetic* one, and people traveled from far and wide to listen to his words of wisdom (1 Kings 4:29-34). The primary *purpose* of this phenomenal book, according to Dr. Gleason Archer, is "to convince men of the uselessness of any world view which does not rise above the horizon of man himself" [*A Survey of Old Testament Introduction*, p. 475]. Everything in life is "vanity" (empty, meaningless) when embraced apart from a God-centered world view. In short, it is a refutation of a purely materialistic, humanistic, hedonistic perception of and approach to life. "The conclusion, when all has been heard, is: fear God and keep His commandments" (Ecclesiastes 12:13).

The advice of "The Preacher" is that those who are genuinely *wise* will seek out a relationship with the Lord God *early in life*. "Remember your Creator in the days of your youth" (Ecclesiastes 12:1). Why? There are obviously any number of reasons for this sound advice, but Solomon focuses on the fact that "childhood and the prime of life are *fleeting*" (Ecclesiastes 11:10). All too soon we find ourselves at the winter months of life, and if we have neglected a relationship with the Lord during our *prime*, it is unlikely that very many of us will seek it out during the days of our physical *decline*. There are "evil days" coming, Solomon writes, during which a majority will say, "I have no delight in them" (Ecclesiastes 12:1). Figuratively speaking, the bright, warm days of spring and summer will be replaced with the cold, dark days of winter. The celestial lights become darkened and one storm follows another (Ecclesiastes

12:2). It is a season in which, for many, the days of *discomfort* will far outnumber those of *delight*. "When the light of youthful life is darkened by the shadows of advancing old age, one misfortune or calamity follows another" [Dr. Paul E. Kretzmann, p. 276]. "The phrase refers to the grievances, infirmities and inconveniences of old age" [*The Pulpit Commentary*, vol. 9 ~ Ecclesiastes, p. 296]. Ecclesiastes 12:2 speaks *figuratively* of "the infirmities of old age of which *winter* is a proper emblem, as *spring* is of youth" [Adam Clarke, *Clarke's Commentary*, vol. 3, p. 836]. "The rhythm of life is like the rhythm of the year. Spring and summer give place to the clouds of autumn and winter. It becomes progressively harder to throw off troubles and anxieties" [*The Expositor's Bible Commentary*, vol. 5, p. 1192]. "The point is that as we grow older, we all have some traces of these marks of age, even if they do not develop to the extremes that this chapter describes. So the Teacher is justified in reminding young people that they cannot afford to put off faith in God their Creator until they are older. God wants the best of their lives" ... not the leftovers [*ibid*].

The Metaphors Employed

The wise King Solomon has declared his case in a *general* manner in Ecclesiastes 12:1-2. He then develops his argument with a series of magnificent metaphors, which, as already noted, many scholars feel constitute some of the finest poetic literature ever penned. Thus, his initial statement "conveys a general impression, and this is then elaborated into particulars," which terms clearly refer, in dramatic form and fashion, to "the gradual decay of old age, with the various members and powers that are affected being represented under tropes and images" [*The Pulpit Commentary*, vol. 9, p. 297]. Let us briefly notice each of these fabulous figurative statements.

The keepers of the house tremble [vs. 3] ~ Some translations refer to these as the *watchmen* or *guardians* of the house. Most scholars concur that the reality in view is the aged person's arms and/or hands. I remember my own paternal grandfather's hands, and how they shook so terribly in his latter years. It was so bad that he could barely feed himself or lift a cup to take a drink without spilling most of what he sought to consume. "The hands and arms are appropriately called the keepers of the house, for with them man guards his body in various ways. The shaking and palsy of old men's limbs are thus graphically described" [*The Pulpit Commentary*, vol. 9, p. 297]. "The arms and hands that minister to the body begin to tremble" [*The Expositor's Bible Commentary*, vol. 5, p. 1193].

The strong men stoop [vs. 3] ~ Other versions of the passage speak of these mighty ones being bowed or bent. "Bent over with the weight of age, the legs no longer standing upright, but crooked and misshapen with the various ailments of age" [*Kretzmann*, p. 276]. The legs of the young are as "pillars of marble" (Song of Solomon 5:15), but in those of advanced age that strength diminishes. "The legs become feeble, and unable to support the weight of the body" [*Clarke*, p. 836]. "The legs that once carried the body so strongly weaken and sag at the knee" [*Expositor's*, p. 1193].

The grinding ones stand idle because they are few [vs. 3] ~ This is clearly a reference to the teeth (more specifically, to the molars). Problems with the gums, accompanied by ensuing loss of teeth, is one of the great difficulties many experience in old age. As the ability to grind one's food diminishes, the diet of the aged changes. Much *softer* foods are required since "the few teeth that remain are incapable of properly masticating hard substances" [*Clarke*, p. 836].

Those looking through the windows grow dim [vs. 3] ~ The eyes, which admit light to the body, become increasingly darkened, thus the view from the "windows" grows dim, as in the fading light of day. This is such a common occurrence among those of advanced age that when the eyes do *not* begin to fail it is worthy of note. "Although Moses was one hundred and twenty years old when he died, *his eye was not dim*, nor his vigor abated"

(Deuteronomy 34:7). "The eyes, called by Cicero (106-43 B.C.) 'the windows of the mind,' become dim" [*Pulpit*, p. 308].

The doors to the street are closed and the sound of grinding fades [vs. 4] -- Most interpreters, focusing on the word "grinding," feel this may still be a reference to the teeth. Therefore, they tend to believe the "closed doors" refer to the lips. With the increased loss of teeth, the mouth becomes more and more compressed and sunken, giving the appearance of being clamped tightly shut. Thus, the sound of grinding (with few teeth and a mouth clamped shut) would indeed be diminished. Several places within the poetic literature of the Bible refer to the mouth/lips as a "door" (Psalm 141:3, for example). Other scholars disagree, however; feeling that the teeth have already been discussed in the previous verse. Some, therefore, key in on the word "sound" and believe the "doors" are the ears. "The organs of hearing gradually close, marooning the owner within the cramped house of his own body" [*Expositor's*, p. 1193]. "Jewish expositors understood these doors to be the *excretive apertures* of the body, which lose their activity in old age -- which seems an *unseemly* allusion" [*Pulpit*, p. 298]. This "grinding," then, would be explained as the *straining* to excrete waste products from the body (a straining which gradually *fades* as the body increasingly loses control over these processes). Certainly, not a pleasant image to contemplate, and yet this too is one of the unpleasantries often experienced during physical decline. Obviously, there is quite a diversity of understanding with respect to this particular phrase. "Hitherto the symbolism has been comparatively easy to interpret. With this verse inextricable difficulties seem to arise" [*ibid*].

Men rise up at the sound of birds [vs. 4] -- Some scholars believe that this image depicts the voice of the aged man becoming increasingly high-pitched. "The old man's voice becomes a 'childish treble,' like the piping of a little bird" [*Pulpit*, p. 299]. "The voice rises in pitch and grows thin and squeaky like the twitter of a bird" [*Expositor's*, p. 1193]. The much more likely interpretation is simply that "the old person sleeps badly and wakes at the first bird call" [*ibid*]. "It is usually taken to mean that the old man sleeps lightly and awakes at the chirrup of a bird" [*Pulpit*, p. 299]. Adam Clarke writes, "His sleep is not sound as it used to be; he *slumbers* rather than *sleeps*, and the crowing of the cock awakes him. And so much difficulty does he find to respire while in bed, that he is glad of the dawn to rise up and get some relief. The chirping of the sparrow is sufficient to awake him" [p. 837]. With regard to the first interpretation, some refer to a well-known line from Shakespeare's work "As You Like It" (act 2, scene 7) ~ "His big manly voice, turning again toward childish treble, pipes and whistles in his sound. Last scene of all, that ends this strange eventful history, is second childishness and mere oblivion; sans teeth, sans eyes, sans taste, sans everything."

All the daughters of music shall be brought low [vs. 4] ~ It is felt by some interpreters that this is a reference to the ears ~ i.e., diminished hearing. "The ears, growing deaf, no longer enjoy the singing as in former days" [*Kretzmann*, p. 276]. "The sounds of singing women or song-birds are dulled and lowered, heard only as faint, unmeaning murmur" [*Pulpit*, p. 299]. This sounds very similar to a statement made by Barzillai the Gileadite. "I am now eighty years old. Can I hear anymore the voice of singing men and women?" (2 Samuel 19:35). A few scholars see the possibility of sexual undertones in this statement, the suggestion being that the sound of singing women no longer arouses him sexually. "It may be a straightforward statement that singing women no longer *move* him, since their voices do not come to him with any clearness" [*Expositor's*, p. 1193].

They are afraid of heights and of dangers in the streets [vs. 5] ~ Have you ever watched an aged person driving down the road? Some of them are so overly cautious on the roadways that they actually pose a danger to themselves and to others. In the ancient world, however, the danger may well have been due to their inability to get out of the way of animal drawn carts, fast moving crowds, and other dangers on the streets. Thus, they were more easily trampled or run down. "Verse 5 mentions two very concrete experiences that frighten old people. They have a fear of heights and are afraid of the traffic in the streets. The latter is specially applicable today in our big cities; but the narrow streets of an Eastern town, with camels, donkeys and bustling traders, were doubtless almost as terrifying to a slow-moving pedestrian" [*Expositor's*, p. 1193]. Clearly, *these* two depictions are not metaphors, but actual fears of many aged persons. However, "we need not treat *all* the descriptions as metaphorical" [*ibid*].

The almond tree blossoms [vs. 5] ~ "In Palestine, the almond tree begins to blossom in midwinter; and although the petals are pink at their base, they are white towards the tip. The general impression of the tree in flower is of a white mass" [*Expositor's*, p. 1193]. "The tree thus becomes a fit type of the old man with his white hair" [*Pulpit*, p. 300], who produces that white covering in the *winter* of his life.

The grasshopper drags himself along [vs. 5] ~ The *King James Version* reads, "the grasshopper shall be a burden." The significance of this translation "would be that even a small thing like a grasshopper seems unduly heavy" upon the frame of the aged, "although it is difficult to see why a grasshopper should be singled out in this way" [*Expositor's* p. 1193]. Much more likely is the idea that as winter comes, and the grasshopper faces death, it loses its ability to hop about with great energy, now just dragging itself along as it grows ever closer to death. "We think Delitzsch and some others are right in taking the verb in the sense of 'to move heavily,' 'to crawl along'" [*Pulpit*, p. 300].

The caperberry is ineffective [vs. 5] ~ This is the rendering of such translations as the *New American Standard Bible*. Others, like the *King James Version* and the *New International Version*, read, "desire shall fail" and "desire no longer is stirred." The Hebrew word that is rendered "desire" in some translations "is found nowhere else in the Old Testament, and its meaning is disputed" [*Pulpit*, p. 301]. Both the *Septuagint* and Jerome's *Latin Vulgate* understood this rather rare Hebrew word to be a reference to the berry of the caper tree, "which is found throughout the East, and was extensively used as a provocative of appetite, a stimulant and restorative. Accordingly, the writer is thought here to be intimating that even stimulants, such as the caper, affect the old man no longer, and cannot give zest to or make him enjoy his food" [*ibid*]. Others agree that the caperberry is indeed intended, but believe that the reference is to the fact that when this berry becomes ripe, it bursts and falls to the ground. They see this as a figure of man reaching the end of his days and falling to the dust of the ground in death. Still others perceive the "desire" to be *sexual* in nature, and point to the fact that the caperberry was at times used as an aphrodisiac. Therefore, it is their view that Solomon is referring to the fact that in many aged persons there is diminished sexual desire.

Dust Returns to Dust

"The Teacher has exhausted his description of the failing faculties, omitting little. It only remains to speak of the inevitable end, the long home of Sheol" [*Expositor's*, p. 1194]. "For man goes to his eternal home, and the mourners go about the streets" (Ecclesiastes 12:5). The passage literally says, "unto his forever house." This is simply a reference to "the grave or Hades" [*Pulpit*, p. 301]. Psalm 49:11, in many versions, reads, "Their graves are their houses forever." Job referred to the grave as "the land of darkness and deep shadow" (Job 10:21); "the house appointed for all living" (Job 30:23). The *dwelling* of the deceased is the *grave* (Hades, Sheol). Some have a problem with the grave being referred to as the "forever" (Greek: *aionios*) home of the dead. They believe this negates a resurrection. This only demonstrates their lack of understanding of this term, however. "Much of the difficulty about *aionios* would be obviated if critics would remember that the meaning of such words is conditioned by the context ~ e.g., 'everlasting' applied to a mountain and to God cannot be understood in the same sense" [*Pulpit*, p. 301]. This Greek term will be examined in some depth in a later chapter of this book. Many disciples also have difficulty with the concepts of *death* and *Hades*. So many misconceptions about these biblical truths have surfaced over the centuries that there are more *fallacies* than *facts* associated with them in the minds of many Christians. Both of these will also be dealt with in great depth in this present work.

The *Book of Tobit* also demonstrates a Jewish awareness of the nature of man and the perception that at the withdrawal of the spirit/breath of man (as well as beast) the physical body returns to the dust of the ground from which it came, thus going to its "eternal home." In Tobit 3:6 we read, "Now therefore deal with me as seemeth best unto Thee, and command my spirit (breath) to be taken from me, that I may be dissolved, and become earth: for it is profitable for me to *die* rather than to *live*, because I have heard false reproaches, and have much sorrow. Command, therefore, so that I may ... go into the *everlasting place*." This, of course, is "everlasting" (Greek: *aionios*, Hebrew: *olam*) only in the sense of "an indeterminate duration of which the maximum is fixed by the intrinsic nature of the persons or things themselves" [*Emmanuel Petavel*]. In other words, the nature of "forever" is often directly determined by the nature of the object described. The grave (Hades, Sheol) is *aionios* or *olam* in the sense that no natural process will reverse the condition of those who sleep therein. However, God Himself has promised to step in at some point and awaken those who sleep in the dust of the ground, and "death and Hades" will be "thrown into the lake of fire" where they will be utterly obliterated and cease to exist (Revelation 20:14). At that point the "forever abode" is brought to a forever end. Thus, if there was no promise of *resurrection* all of life would indeed be "vanity of vanities." If there is no *resurrection* then "your faith is worthless ... and those who have fallen asleep in Christ *have perished*" (1 Corinthians 15:17-18). Our "forever house" in the ground *would indeed be without end*, if not for the fact of our Lord's own resurrection and His promise to come one day to raise *us* up as well. Therefore, *in Christ Jesus*, life's ultimate *frustration* is overcome and we, along with Him, gain the *victory* over death and the grave.

In Ecclesiastes 12:6, Solomon gives the reader two final pairs of metaphors. These describe the actual *death* of the aged person. "Remember Him before the silver cord is broken and the golden bowl is crushed; the pitcher by the well is shattered and the wheel at the cistern is crushed." Again, there is some diversity of opinion among biblical scholars as to the interpretation of these figures. In the first set we have depicted, most believe, the *light of life*, whereas in the second set of figures we have depicted the *water of life*. When the cord that attaches the light to the ceiling is severed, and the bowl comes crashing down to the floor below, breaking apart, *the light goes out*. This is a figure of death. When the pitcher at the well is shattered, thus being unable to hold water, and the wheel which lowers it into the well and then raises it again, is broken, there is no access to the life-giving water within the well. Again, this is a figure of death. Some feel this latter figure may have reference to the human circulatory system, with the former referring to the central nervous system. "Whatever the interpretation of the details, the fixed fact is that of death" [*Expositor's*, p. 1194]. "The pictures in this verse have met with a variety of interpretations, but they certainly describe total collapse" [*ibid*].

The great and inevitable reality being specified by *The Preacher* in the passage we have reviewed is that we are mortal, and that all too soon the days of youth have passed and we are into the winter of life, and that the *end of our days* comes much too quickly. One of the most common sayings of the aged is, "Where have the years gone? It seems just yesterday that I was young." Given the certainty of this physical decline and our return to the dust of the ground,

Solomon's advice is to make the most of the time in which you still have the energy and vitality of youth, and spend it wisely in serving the Lord. It will certainly yield an everlasting reward. "Remember your Creator in the days of your youth, *before* the evil days come and the years draw near when you will say, 'I have no delight in them'" (Ecclesiastes 12:1). "The conclusion, when all has been heard, is: fear God and keep His commandments" (Ecclesiastes 12:13). Sound advice for us all.

Chapter 4
Defining Death
Physical, Relational, Eternal

A fellow minister of the gospel recently wrote me the following: "When people misunderstand or incorrectly define words, they usually reach false conclusions. This is a fundamental problem of those who teach error." I would agree completely with this observation. Frankly, it is sometimes even a serious problem among those who teach *Truth*. Therefore, when dealing with difficult doctrines, one needs to carefully define the various terms involved which are integral to that doctrine. In this chapter we will examine in some depth the biblical perception of the concept of *death*. In the religious world speculation abounds with regard to this reality. We know that it is appointed unto man once to *die*, and then comes judgment (Hebrews 9:27), but what *is* this thing called *death*? What does it involve? How does it affect us?

Some believers have traditionally characterized death as a *separation*. What is essential for us to determine in each context, however, is: (1) What is being separated from what/whom, and (2) what is the ultimate *effect* of that separation? The full impact of death cannot truly be perceived without this larger perspective. In other words, merely acknowledging that a *separation* occurs does not truly define death. One must further seek to determine what happens to that which has experienced this separation. What is the *result*, or resultant state? Only then will one truly grasp the *biblical* concept of death.

Let me just plainly state the problem at the beginning of this analysis. There is a perception among many within the religious world that *death* does not really exist. No one ever *truly* dies, it is asserted. Instead, a person's "inner being" is just released from one state of existence to live more fully than before in another state of existence. Thus, even though a funeral is held, the traditional teaching is that the "real person" is not actually dead, but just alive somewhere else. *Death*, therefore, is not viewed as a *loss* of life, but rather a *transferal* of life to another realm. It is the *separation* of some distinct, undying spirit-being, which is said to indwell our fleshly bodies, from this "physical prison house" that had previously restricted it to this temporal realm. Thus, "death" is viewed as a *release* from that which had restrained the "real us" so that we might be even more alive than ever before. Thus, grandma isn't really dead, she's just set free from her worn out physical body, and is now happier than she's ever been! How strange, therefore, in light of such teaching, that death is referred to in the Bible as an "enemy" (1 Corinthians 15:26). Would not such theology make death a "friend"? Why then is this "friend" cast into the lake of fire (Revelation 20:14) where it will be "abolished" (1 Corinthians 15:26)? And what need is there of a resurrection of the dead unto judgment and sentencing, righteous *or* wicked, if the former are already "home" and "singing with the angels" and the latter are already being tortured mercilessly in the flames?

In his *Table Talk*, Martin Luther (1483-1546) declared, "Now if one should say that Abraham's *soul* lives with God but his *body* is dead, this distinction is rubbish. I will attack it. That would be a silly soul if it were in heaven and desired its body!" William Tyndale (1484-1536), an English Bible translator and martyr, wrote, "And ye, in putting them (departed *souls*) in heaven, hell and purgatory, destroy the arguments wherewith Christ and Paul prove the resurrection." Tyndale argued that if *souls* were already in either bliss or misery, "then what cause is there of the resurrection?" Indeed, what cause is there of a *Judgment* on the final day when the sentence has *already* been passed and carried out? Tyndale continued, "The true faith putteth forth the *resurrection*, which we be warned to look for every hour. The heathen philosophers, denying that, did put that the soul did ever live. And the Pope joineth the spiritual doctrine of Christ and the fleshly doctrine of philosophers together; things so contrary that they cannot agree. And because the fleshly-minded Pope consenteth unto heathen doctrine, therefore he corrupteth the Scripture to stablish it. If the soul be in heaven, tell me what cause is there for the resurrection?"

This view of "death" was dramatically displayed in the December, 2001 issue of *The Banner of Truth* (a publication of some within the group known as *Churches of Christ*) in a lengthy poem entitled "There Is No Death" by J. L. McCreery. The title really says it all. In this poem the author states (and this is just a small snippet):

> We bear their senseless dust to rest,
> And say that they are "dead."
> They are not dead! They have but passed
> Beyond the mists that blind us here
> Into the new and larger life
> Of that serener sphere.

> And ever near us, though unseen
> The dear, immortal spirits tread ~
> For all the boundless universe
> Is Life ~ there are no dead!

Throughout the poem the author speaks of these "dead" ones being "transplanted into Paradise," and he declares, "they still are here and love us yet." Thus, "death" has merely *separated* these persons from us; they are not really dead (deprived of life), but actually more alive than ever before. Death is thus not cessation or extinction of life, according to this traditional view, but an *enhancement* of it ... at least for the *righteous* "dead." For the *wicked* "dead," this separation would be perceived more as a "life of loss" than a "loss of life." For the record, *I disagree completely with this view.*

Yes, the concept of "death" appears many times in Scripture, and it is used several different ways. In each a *separation* does take place of one thing from another, and the dramatic *effect* in each is a *loss* of life, not an *enhancement* of life. The three types of "death" that are of primary concern to humans are often characterized as: physical, spiritual (though I believe "relational" is far more accurate and appropriate), and eternal. "Theological distinctions are usually made between physical death, spiritual death, and eternal death and in general these are vital; but ... it appears that death in its totality is the result of sin. One must remember also that in the *biblical* view, man is a psychosomatic *unity*. The *whole* man is the subject of death" [*The Zondervan Pictorial Encyclopedia of the Bible*, vol. 2, p. 70]. This latter is an important distinction. Many disciples embrace a *dualistic* view of the nature of man ~ man being made up of distinct, separate living parts, one of which is subject to death, the other of which is not (and which *survives* the death of the other ... indeed is freed to *fuller life* by the death of the other). I do not believe the Scriptures teach this view of the nature of man. Man's nature is not *dualistic*, but *holistic*, according to the Bible.

PHYSICAL DEATH

This is perhaps the best-known type of death. In Genesis 2:7 we are taught that God formed man from the dust of the ground (the common elements of the physical universe around us), and He "breathed into his nostrils the breath of life; and man became a living being/soul." The important point to note here in this passage is that an animated physical body is a *living* body. The person is a living *being*. "Living soul" is what a person *is*, not what a person *has*. When the breath of life is withdrawn from man, what is left is no longer a *living* body, but a *dead* body. That body then returns to the elements from which it was drawn. "By the sweat of your face you shall eat bread, till you return to the ground, because from it you were taken; for you are dust, and to dust you shall return" (Genesis 3:19). "Thou dost turn man back into dust" (Psalm 90:3). Solomon describes this withdrawal of "breath/spirit" this way: "Then the dust will return to the earth as it was, and the breath/spirit will return to God who gave it" (Ecclesiastes 12:7). In Psalm 104:29 (which is actually speaking of animals) we read, "Thou dost take away their breath/spirit, they expire, and return to their dust."

Physical death is a loss of the breath of life, and the *effect* is the return of the body to the earth. A *separation* takes place. The *body* is separated from the *breath*, and a *loss of life* results. I don't think anyone would suggest that this separation should be perceived as a physical *enhancement* of life. When body and breath are separated, the result is a *dead* body, not a living, breathing one. Life is not *enriched* physically, but rather *terminated*. Life for this person is *extinguished*. This is a somber appointment each of us must keep (unless privileged to be alive at the *Parousia*) -- "It is appointed unto men once to die, and after this the judgment" (Hebrews 9:27). "Although variously interpreted throughout the OT and NT, death is basically understood as the termination of life on earth. Most frequently it indicates the end of an individual's existence" [*International Standard Bible Encyclopedia*, vol. 1, p. 898].

"In the NT, as in the OT, humans are *mortals* (only God is immortal) whose lives end in biological death" [*Eerdmans Dictionary of the Bible*, p. 330]. "Unlike the Greeks, who largely understood a person as a soul entrapped in a body, the ancient Hebrews depicted the person as a psychosomatic (body-soul) unity. When this body-soul union failed in death, the Hebrews did not visualize the escape of the soul from the body, but the actual death of the *self*" [*Holman Bible Dictionary*, p. 347]. "Unlike Greek philosophers who downplayed the significance of death by emphasizing the immortality of the soul, the biblical writers affirmed that death is real" [*ibid*, p. 349].

RELATIONAL DEATH

The Bible often refers to that condition of being separated from one's God (during this present life on earth) as a type of "death." This is commonly characterized among men as a "spiritual" death so as to distinguish it from *physical* loss of life, although, once again, I believe the phrase "*relational* death" more aptly characterizes and conveys the biblical reality. In many ways this "death" constitutes a loss of the "abundant life" one has in an intimate *relationship* with one's God. "Your iniquities have made a *separation* between you and your God, and your sins have hidden His face from you, so that He does not hear" (Isaiah 59:2). This "separation" is viewed as a type of "death," although the person continues to remain alive *physically*. It is a "death" in the sense that it is a loss of life: that "abundant life" that comes from intimacy with deity. That blessed union is severed with the life Giver, and the result is: one is cut off (with regard to intimate relationship) from the very source of that abundant life Himself. That is indeed a separation best characterized as a "death" .... a loss of life.

Jesus likens Himself to a vine on one occasion, and He declares that we who are "in Him" are all branches. However, if we should be "separated" from this vine (severed from Christ), the result is "death" ~ we wither and die (John 15:1-6). This is a separation resulting in loss of life. Jesus declares that He is the life (John 14:6), thus to be separated from Him is to be separated from the abundant life He came to bring.

This "relational death" is alluded to in 1 Timothy 5:6 ~ "But she who gives herself to wanton pleasure is dead even while she lives." Although physically still a living, breathing body, nevertheless in relationship to the life-Giver Himself she is *separated* by her sins. And to be separated from *Him*, and that abundant life in Him, is truly a *loss of life*; a "death." Living in sin is not an "enhancement" of that abundant life, but truly a repudiation and negation of it. The ultimate result of such a willful severing of one's being/soul from Him during this physical existence will be a judgment one day of unfitness for everlasting existence and relationship with Him in the new heavens and earth. To willfully separate from Him *here* will result in an everlasting separation from Him *hereafter*.

All of us, at some point in our physical lives, are "dead in our sins" and thus "separate" from our God. This is the concept of "relational death," and it is seen often in Scripture. Yes, it is a "loss of life" in the sense we are not in a relationship with the life-Giver, and if we hope to put on immortality at the resurrection, then we must come to Him who is the way, the truth, and the LIFE. "He who has the Son has the life; he who does not have the Son of God does not have the life" (1 John 5:12). Thus, being separate from Him is truly a loss of life; a "relational death." We are dead in our trespasses and sins, and as such are fit only for ultimate destruction in the lake of fire, which is the second death.

"All men are by nature spiritually dead, that is, alienated from God the Source of life by sin, insensible to divine things, unresponsive to His laws" [*The Zondervan Pictorial Encyclopedia of the Bible*, vol. 2, p. 71]. "... and therefore, although they still live in this world, their attitude to sin, the law and the world is to be that of dead men" [*ibid*, p. 72]. Jesus told the church in Sardis, "You have a name that you are alive, but you are dead" (Revelation 3:1). They had separated themselves from relationship with and service to their Lord, and that is truly a "death" experience; a loss of life. Notice carefully the following passages:

"And you were dead in your trespasses and sins, in which you formerly walked according to the course of this world" (Ephesians 2:1-2).

"And when you were dead in your transgressions ... He made you alive together with Him, having forgiven us all our transgressions" (Colossians 2:13).

"For this son of mine was dead, and has come to life again; he was lost, and has been found" (Luke 15:24 ... the words of the father in the *Parable of the Prodigal Son*).

"But Jesus said to him, 'Follow Me; and allow the dead to bury their own dead'" (Matthew 8:22). Here we see both the physical and relational (literal and figurative) uses of this concept of death.

Matthew Henry, in his commentary on the wanton widow in 1 Timothy 5:6, refers to such persons as being "dead in trespasses and sins; they are in the world to no purpose, buried alive as to the great ends of living." To become separated from one's purpose in life, and from one's God, is truly to be "dead" even though still *physically* animated. Thayer, in his Greek lexicon, describes this "death" as "the loss of a life consecrated to God and blessed in Him on earth" [p. 283]. It is a loss of life's purpose and focus; indeed, it is a loss of *relationship* with the life-Giver Himself. It is truly a "death,;" a cessation of union with Him. Such carries only one ultimate prospect: *eternal* death.

ETERNAL DEATH

"Those who remain in spiritual death throughout their lives and do not believe on the Son of God, die in their sins (John 8:21, 24), and in the Day of Judgment will be consigned to a state of eternal separation from God, called in Scripture the second death (Revelation 21:8)" [*The Zondervan Pictorial Encyclopedia of the Bible*, vol. 2, p. 71]. There is obviously a vital connection between relational death and eternal death. These two "cannot always be clearly distinguished ... since spiritual death merges into eternal death" [Arndt, Gingrich, Bauer, *A Greek-English Lexicon of the NT and Other Early Christian Literature*, p. 351].

It is this "eternal" death, the "*second* death," to be experienced in the lake of fire, that is the ultimate destiny of the wicked. What is the nature of this second death? Is it just a continuation of life? Is it a life of loss as opposed to a loss of life? Is it the *cessation* of life or the *preservation* of life? Is it *termination* of life or *perpetuation* of life? For the record, I will declare that, based on years of extensive, intensive study of the Scriptures on this matter, my firm conviction is that the biblical view is: the second death is a *termination of life itself*. It is not only an everlasting separation from the G*iver* of life; it is also, and thereby, an everlasting separation from the *gift* of life. In the lake of fire the raised unredeemed will be ultimately and completely destroyed, deprived of life, and will cease to be. This will not be a pleasant experience; no death is. It will be agonizing. It will be torment. It will be "hellish." But the *process* of dying will *result* in a death, and that death (that separation from life and the life-Giver) will be forever! From the *second* death there will be no resurrection to life. It is a *forever* death .... an *eternal* death, both qualitatively and quantitatively (as will be noted in the next chapter).

Yes, I believe "death" *is* a separation. But the *result* -- the ultimate *effect* -- of such a separation is not an *enhanced* life, it is a *forfeited* life. Whether it is physical, relational or eternal, the Bible portrays "death" as a severing of one from *life itself*, not a preservation or continuation of life. It is a *loss* of life, and in the final reckoning it is a *forever* loss.

Conclusion

In each of the above aspects of death a "separation" *has* occurred, and in each that separation *results* in a *loss of life* in some sense, either literally or figuratively. Thus, it is the *resultant state* of such a separation in each of these three views of death that truly defines "death," rather than the mere fact of separation itself.

Another exegetical factor, leading to theological confusion in the minds of some, is that many fail to perceive the distinction between literal and figurative language in one's analysis of the biblical concept of death. *Both* are employed, and a failure to perceive this fact can indeed lead to a confused theology. For example, *relational* death is often depicted in highly figurative terms; *physical* death is typically very literal and stark in its presentation in Scripture (although figurative language is also used at times). One can be *relationally* "dead," yet *physically* "alive" ... and both at the same time. One can be physically animate, yet completely severed (with regard to relationship) from one's God ... and at the same time. "Remember that you were at that time *separate* from Christ, excluded from the commonwealth of Israel, and strangers to the covenants of promise, having no hope and *without God* in the world" (Ephesians 2:12). There was a "separation between you and your God" (Isaiah 59:2), and that separation constituted a "death." Such persons were cut off from life. Not *physical* life, but the abundant *relational* life in Him.

There is a literal bodily "life," just as there is a literal bodily "death" (when the body becomes inanimate and returns to the dust from which it came). There is also a figurative "life" in relationship with deity, just as there is a figurative "death" (when one is *separate* from such a relationship with deity). This latter is typically characterized as "spiritual/relational death," the former as "physical death." Thus, there is no conflict whatsoever in declaring the wanton widow "dead even while she lives," for two completely different applications of "death" are in view: one literal, one figurative; one physical, one relational.

With regard to "relational death" something *has* ceased to exist. What no longer exists, because of the widow's willful, wanton sin against her God, is a saving *relationship* with God. She has been severed from the very Source of Life Himself. She is dead with regard to relationship with deity; that relationship no longer exists! It was *this* that the father similarly spoke of in the *Parable of the Prodigal Son* (Luke 15). Because of the son's willful severing of himself from the home of the father, he was, during that time, considered "dead," but came back to "life" when the relationship was restored (Luke 15:24, 32). Thus, this "death" is indeed an *extinction* of something precious beyond compare, both now and potentially later (i.e., the hope of immortality, an *everlasting* relationship with the Father in His eternal home).

Yes, physical death is indeed a *separation* of the *entire person* from life (i.e., the *animation* of the physical body). Man is a unified whole, not a separate eternal spirit-being trapped temporarily within a mortal body. Deity "*alone* possesses immortality" (1 Timothy 6:16). Thus, when man dies, according to the biblical view, man is dead ... ALL of him, not just a *part*. Relational death, however, is more figurative, and indicates that sin has brought about a *separation* of a man from his God with respect to intimate relationship and fellowship. This is a death that does not necessarily render one's *physical body* dead, but which renders one's *relationship* with God as dead. The body can still continue to function while a person lives in open rebellion against his or her God. The consequence of such continued relational separation from God in this present existence, however, is a literal forever separation of the person himself from God after resurrection and judgment. At the Great Separation of sheep and goats, Jesus will tell the lost, "I never *knew* you; depart from Me" (Matthew 7:23) ~ there had been no *relationship*; they did not *know* each other. Those who remain relationally "dead to God" in sin throughout their lives here on earth will one day, after the resurrection, stand before God in judgment. They will be sentenced to the "*second* death," and will be cast into the lake of fire. There they will be *destroyed* "both body and soul/being" (Matthew 10:28). It will be a cessation of life not only for the body but also for the very *being* (soul, personhood) of the man. In other words, he will, when the destruction is complete, *cease to be*. In the *destruction* of one's being, there is *cessation* of being: as independent persons/souls/*beings*, they cease to *be*/exist.

F. LaGard Smith, in his book *After Life*, writes that man's "eternal destiny is not a matter of better or worse. It's nothing less than a matter of *life* and *death*" [p. 189]. Smith, in this excellent 334 page in-depth study, has taken his stand with an ever-increasing number of leaders within Christendom, who, after much study and reflection, have come to realize that the traditional teaching on the nature of man, death, and final punishment is completely false. F. LaGard stated at the outset of his study that many of our "fundamental assumptions" in this area have been mistaken. He also understands the personal *danger* in seeking to expose this: "One challenges orthodox understandings at one's peril, and never without the full backing of God's own word on the matter" [p. 10]. Therefore, he, as do I, seek to base this challenge of the traditional teaching on *in-depth* examination of the Word. Nothing less will do.

It is personally reassuring to see more and more Christian leaders coming to this perception, and being courageous enough to speak out. Homer Hailey, in the last days of his 97-year-long life, wrote a book on this subject entitled *God's Judgments and Punishments*. He too declared that the "second death" actually means that, for the wicked, "their existence comes to an end in the lake of fire" [p. 178]. Such leaders in my own faith-heritage as Edward Fudge and Curtis Dickinson have also written much in support of this position, and many of their insights will be shared throughout this work. Dillard Thurman, the late editor of *Gospel Minutes*, also did much to challenge the traditional error on the nature of man and his eternal destiny. In fact, he devoted the entire Feb. 1, 1985 issue [vol. 34, no. 5] to debunking the teaching that the dead go off to conscious bliss or misery at the moment of death. He wrote, "The hope and aspiration of many has been shifted from His coming again to receive His own, to an immediate immortality and heavenly bliss immediately at death! Jesus DID NOT promise that!" [emphasis *his*]. Dr. Leroy Garrett, the editor of *Restoration Review*, wrote an excellent study of this in the November, 1990 issue entitled *Is Hell Fire Endless?* And this only scratches the surface of the list of scholars who have embraced the biblical concept of conditionalism (that immortality is conditional, not inherent).

In a letter to me, dated October 16, 1990, a well-known and highly respected Christian scientist, lecturer and author, John Clayton, wrote, "Dear Al, I was recently in a lectureship in Athens, Georgia, and spent a great deal of time talking with the preacher and one of the elders about Edward Fudge's book [*The Fire That Consumes*]. I think the *thinking* part of the Church is really being stimulated by this book and is really coming to a recognition that a lot of the traditional teaching on heaven and hell really doesn't stand up in an examination of the facts." He closed the letter by saying, "I hope all of us who are willing to *think* will continue to examine this concept. It is a much more logical approach than some of the traditional concepts of hell." Again, I am greatly encouraged to see more and more Christians coming to a clearer understanding of God's Word on this matter ... and taking a bold public stand.

Our God has placed before mankind a solemn choice: life or death. We must choose. "I call heaven and earth to witness against you today, that I have set before you LIFE and DEATH, the blessing and the curse. So choose life in order that you may live!" (Deuteronomy 30:19). "For the wages of sin is death, but the free gift of God is eternal life in Christ Jesus our Lord" (Romans 6:23).

"And this is the testimony: God has *given* us eternal life, *and this life is in His Son*. He who has the Son *has life*; he who does not have the Son of God *does not have life*" (1 John 5:11-12). Jesus Christ is the way, the truth, and the LIFE (John 14:6). If we turn to Him we shall find everlasting life; if we reject Him we shall *perish* (John 3:16). It is my prayer that each of us will *choose life* and thus come to know the joys of being forever in His presence. "For what is a man profited if he gains the whole world, and loses or forfeits *himself?*" (Luke 9:25)

Chapter 5
How Long is Forever?
Analyzing the Attributes of Aionios

Walt Whitman (1819-1892) once observed, "The clock indicates the moment ~ but what does eternity indicate?" Men have pondered the concept and scope of *eternity* since the earliest days of our existence upon this earth. In some ways, it is truly beyond our comprehension, since we are finite beings seeking to fathom the infinite; the temporal seeking to comprehend the eternal. On the other hand, our Creator *has* endowed us with an *awareness* of the eternal realm and its realities (Ecclesiastes 3:11). Thus, there is that innate yearning within our hearts and minds to more perfectly grasp that which is above and beyond ourselves. *Eternity* truly transcends the space/time continuum, yet we, who inhabit the latter, may indeed, through honest spiritual inquiry, gain a glimpse into the former.

A long-time missionary to Thailand, who lives and works in Khon Kaen, recently wrote, "Al, A preacher spoke on this same subject (the nature of final punishment) a couple of weeks ago on TV, and hinged all of his talk on the word *'forever.'* He said there are fifty-four places in Scripture where *'forever'* actually *ended.* I did not get the name of this preacher, however I would be very much interested to hear *your* thoughts on *'forever'* and its meaning."

Essentially, the question is -- *How long* is forever? Does this biblical term signify "time without end," or are we somewhat misled by even associating the element of *time* with the concept of *forever?* Are there other possible meanings and applications of *forever* in God's Word? I have had people boldly declare to me that the word "eternal" *only,* and *always,* means "unending continuity." Indeed, some have become somewhat agitated when this position is challenged. Are they correct in their assertion? Or, have they presented too narrow a view of this biblical concept? These are legitimate questions that require a reasoned response, for some of our theological tenets will be determined by our conclusions.

The Greek word in question here is: *Aionios,* an adjective usually translated "eternal," "forever," or "everlasting." Biblical Hebrew offers several combinations of the word *olam* (usually translated "forever, lifelong"). The Greek *aionios* comes from the root word: *Aion,* which means "age" or "era," and from which we acquire the word "eon." The adjective *aionios* appears 70 times in the New Testament writings (with well over 100 additional occurrences in the *Septuagint*), and although the word *does* denote that which is *unending* in some passages, it just as often *does not.* "The force attaching to the word is *not* so much that of the *actual length* of a period, but that of a period marked by spiritual or moral characteristics" [W. E. Vine, *An Expository Dictionary of NT Words*]. The reality, which some seem reluctant to acknowledge (because it affects their theology), is that *aionios* is used in two very distinct and separate ways in Scripture -- *qualitatively* and *quantitatively*. One must examine the *context*, as well as that which these words describe, in order to determine *which* meaning applies, or if *both* meanings are perhaps applicable. The *Holman Bible Dictionary* stresses that although "some aspects of both quality and duration appear in every context," nevertheless in some passages "the emphasis is on the *quality* ... rather than on *unending duration*" [p. 440]. The tendency of some to view *aion* and *aionios* as only signifying "time without end" can be exegetically misleading, for these terms may also describe the *quality* of something, with no reference to time whatsoever. Failure to perceive this fact has led to some misguided theology.

Simply stated, "forever" isn't always *forever*. In other words, about half the time *aionios* is used in Scripture it denotes the *quality* of that which is described (as being of the "eternal," rather than the "temporal," realm), rather than a reference to *quantity* of time. Thus, in a great many biblical examples, "forever" actually *ends*. A noted theologian by the name of Emmanuel Petavel correctly observes, "There are at least 70 occurrences in the Bible where these words qualify objects of a temporary and limited nature ... signifying only an indeterminate duration of which the maximum is fixed by the intrinsic nature of the persons or things themselves." In other words, the nature of "forever" is often directly determined by the nature of the object described. Thus, "eternal" or "forever" may well simply denote something will endure for as long as that object has the ability or capacity to endure. Although Plato had a huge impact upon the thinking of the Hellenistic Jews and the early Christians in this area (moving their thinking *away from* the biblical concept), nevertheless "Aristotle *returns* to the concept of *aion* as the relative period of time allotted to each specific thing" [Gerhard Kittel, *Theological Dictionary of the New Testament*, vol. 1, p. 198].

Notice just a few examples of that which Scripture describes as being "eternal," but which clearly are not intended to be "everlasting" (in the sense of unending):

1. The sprinkling of blood on the doorpost ~ "You shall observe this event as an ordinance for you and your children *forever*" (Exodus 12:24).

2. Aaron and his sons "shall have the priesthood by a *perpetual* statute" (Exodus 29:9). "Their anointing shall qualify them for a *perpetual* priesthood throughout their generations" (Exodus 40:15).

3. Caleb's inheritance ~ "Surely the land on which your foot has trodden shall be an inheritance to you and to your children *forever*" (Joshua 14:9).

4. Solomon's Temple ~ "I have surely built Thee a lofty house, a place for Thy dwelling *forever*" (1 Kings 8:13).

5. A "forever" servant ~ "You shall take an awl and pierce it through his ear into the door, and he shall be your servant *forever*. And you shall do likewise to your maidservant" (Deuteronomy 15:17). Obviously, the word "forever" in this passage is *limited* to the length of the servant's life. If the man or woman lived only ten more years, then "forever" was ten years in duration. This verse in no way suggests (as some have contended) that such a person would be the servant of another throughout endless ages, both in the temporal realm and in the eternal. "Forever" endured for only so long as the servant lived; thus, "forever" was limited; there *would be* a point of termination.

6. Unto Gehazi, the servant of Elisha, it was said, "The leprosy of Naaman shall cleave to you and to your descendants *forever*" (2 Kings 5:27).

These are just a *very few* of the many biblical examples, but they demonstrate the truth that the concept of *aionios* does not always refer to "time without end," but may actually mean "time of a *limited* duration" (the limits determined by the nature of the object described, and by the context). An excellent New Testament example, by the way, would be the fig tree which Jesus cursed in Matthew 21:19 and Mark 11:14 ~ "Let no fruit grow on thee henceforward *forever*." Again, "forever" would simply be the length of the life of this particular tree. If the tree lived another 25 years, it would never again produce fruit during that time. Thus, "forever" would be 25 years in duration. When the tree ceased to exist, so would "forever" with regard to fruit bearing capabilities.

One should also not overlook the fact that the Bible (and this is especially true in the NT writings) uses *aion* and *aionios* in a *qualitative* sense about half the time these words occur. The Scriptures speak of the distinction, for example, between this "present *age*" and the "*age* to come." This has primary reference to the various *qualities* of both ages or eras or realms, and not so much to the concept of *time*. The famous Greek scholar B. F. Westcott stated it this way: "The word speaks of *being*, of which time is not a measure." This present age may be spoken of as "temporal," for example, whereas the age to come may be characterized as "eternal." Again, this is not a statement with reference to *time*, for the latter is truly outside the parameters of space and time. Rather, the terms "temporal" and "eternal" qualify the various aspects of the *nature* of these realms ~ one being earthly, one heavenly; one physical, one spiritual; one corrupt, one pure.

A good example of the *qualitative* aspect of *aionios* is seen in Jude 7 ~ "Sodom and Gomorrah and the cities around them ... are exhibited as an example, in undergoing the punishment of *eternal* fire." A scholar by the name of Joseph A. Baird observes, "'Eternal fire,' for example, does not necessarily mean a fire that burns endlessly (quantitative meaning), but may also mean a fire 'peculiar to the realm and the nature of God' (qualitative meaning)." On this same passage from Jude, Dr. Alan Richardson writes, "The real point is the *character* of the punishment. It is that of the order of the *Age to Come* as contrasted with any *earthly* penalties" [*An Introduction to the Theology of the NT*]. This was not a volcanic eruption, nor lightning (both of which have been suggested), rather this was a fire "from the Lord" which "rained down out of heaven" (Genesis 19:24). It was not a "temporal fire" (of the earth), but an "eternal fire" (from the presence of the Almighty). "Eternal," therefore, does not suggest that judicial fire is still burning those cities to this day, but rather that its source was not of this temporal realm.

Similarly, when the inspired New Testament writers speak of "*eternal* life," the adjective *aionios* refers to "the *quality* more than to the length of life" [Dr. Donald G. Bloesch, *Essentials of Evangelical Theology*]. It is life lived in an entirely new realm; life experienced in the *eternal*, rather than *temporal*, realm. This certainly does not detract in any way from the *endlessness* of this future life, however, for Scripture clearly declares (using other terms) that it will not be terminated. One such passage is found in 1 Thessalonians 4:17 ~ "We shall *always* (Greek: *pantote*) be with the Lord."

This view of the Greek adjective *aionios* is clearly "shown to be a legitimate interpretation, and cannot (so far as the texts containing the word 'eternal' are concerned) be called a forcing of Scripture to suit a theory" [Dr. Guillebaud, *The Righteous Judge*]. Too many have limited their definition of "forever" and "eternal" for the sake of their tradition and theology, and this is unfortunate. Dr. Clark Pinnock, in his work *Prospects For Systematic Theology*, has stated the case quite well ~ "We cannot rest content with mere reiteration of earlier insights. A theology which seeks only to restate the system of some honored theological forerunner is less than fully biblical." J. I. Packer, in *Fundamentalism and the Word of God*, wrote, "We must never become enslaved to human tradition, and assume the complete rightness of our own established ways of thought and practice, and in so doing excuse ourselves from the duty of testing and reforming them by Scripture." Here is Charles Hodge's conclusion on the matter: "If we believe the Bible to be the Word of God, all we have to do is to ascertain what it teaches on this subject, *and humbly submit.*"

The reality is: "Forever" does not always mean *forever* ... at least, not in the sense that we normally take it. This may impact our traditional theology in some areas, a fact which greatly troubles some disciples .... although it *shouldn't*, if their quest is truly for ultimate *Truth*. For example, some believe the *punishing* (suffering, torture) of the wicked in the lake of fire will be *without end* ("eternal"), and they vehemently deny any *qualitative* aspect to *aionios* in this specific phrase. To suggest that "eternal punishment" (Matthew 25:46) could be anything other or less than *endless torture* is tantamount to heresy, to their way of thinking. However, is it just possible we have failed to fully perceive the significance of the concept of "eternal" when used with the reality of the final "punishment" of the wicked? Is it possible we have overlooked the *qualitative* aspect of this term? Is it also possible we have failed to distinguish between two key concepts with regard to the disposition of the unredeemed: *process* and *result*? I believe we have.

Notice Matthew 25:46 ~ "These will go away into *eternal punishment*, but the righteous into *eternal life.*" The fates of both the unrighteous and the righteous are said to be "eternal." What *are* the fates of both? The promise to the righteous is *life*. The promise to the unrighteous is *death*. "For the wages of sin is *death*, but the free gift of God is eternal *life* in Christ Jesus our Lord" (Romans 6:23). "For God so loved the world that He gave His one and only Son, that whoever believes in Him shall not *perish* but have eternal *life*" (John 3:16). God has always placed before men two great destinies: life and death; the blessing and the curse (see: Deuteronomy 30:15-20). The punishment for sin and rebellion against God has always been death. Both the reward and the punishment are said to be "eternal." But, eternal in what sense? Qualitative or quantitative? Or both?

I believe the overall context of God's Word on this matter indicates the answer is both. Both the reward and the punishment will be of that other realm, not of this temporal one. In quality, it will far surpass anything we might imagine. However, quantitatively, both reward and punishment will endure without end. Scripture also clearly portrays *that* reality. As Matthew 25:46 (quoted above) declares, the punishment and the reward are both "forever" -- for as long as the righteous are alive, the unrighteous will be dead.

Here is where those who embrace the traditional teaching on final punishment (endless conscious torture) commit a grave error in their interpretation. Scripture makes it very clear that it is the punish*MENT*, not the punish*ING*, that is forever or everlasting (if one is looking at the quantitative application of the term). Punish*ment* is a result, punish*ing* is a process which leads *to* a result (or *should*, otherwise it is more *abuse* than legitimate *punishment*). Our God never declared the *process* to be endless (i.e., a never-ending process never actually achieving the result promised), rather, God promised the process would lead to a *result* which would endure. At an execution, for example, when a person is placed within the gas chamber, the *dying process* will be most unpleasant; it will be *torment*. This punish*ing*, however, *does* ultimately bring about the desired result: a punish*ment*, which is *death!* The sentence passed upon the convicted criminal was a death sentence (not a life sentence); the punishment prescribed, therefore, is *death*, not never-ending *dying* accompanied by endless suffering. *Dying* is merely the *process*, torturous though it often may be, that brings about the *result* preordained. Although the suffering of the dying process is not to be discounted as an *aspect* of the punishment, the actual punishment itself is death: the forfeiture of life. Result, not process!

God has declared that the wages of sin is death. This punish*ment* (result) will be brought about by a horrendous punish*ing* (process), which is the dying experience. That will be torturous. It will truly be torment. But the wages of sin is death, not dying. The "eternal punish*ment*" is death. Punish*ment* is a result, not a process (that would be punish*ing*). Failure to differentiate between process and result has led some to a theology of an eternal punish*ing* (process) rather than an eternal punish*ment* (result). Thus, they actually teach that the wages of sin is never realized; the goal never achieved. Death never happens! The wicked are continually in the process of dying, they assert, but death *never occurs*. Indeed, the wicked are said to live forever; they *never* die; they just continue to exist forever in misery. Thus, it is declared "death" really means "life" (a life lived endlessly in agony). Frankly, such a doctrine is the exact *opposite* of what Scripture teaches. This view teaches there *is no death*; it has been removed as the "wages of sin." In its place one now finds "everlasting *life* in misery." The death sentence, pronounced by God, has now been commuted by man to a life sentence "at hard labor."

The punishment for sin, *according to the Lord*, is death (loss of life, not life of loss), a death that will be dispensed from His throne of justice, and which, when accomplished, will endure endlessly. From this "second death" there will be no resurrection to life, as there was with the first. Once the wicked have been destroyed, they are gone forever, never to return. Those who teach it is the process that is everlasting, rather than the result (and who teach the result is *never actually achieved in reality*), teach contrary to biblical Truth. Admittedly, most do this out of innocent ignorance, rather than mindful maliciousness. It was what most of us were taught growing up, and we simply never bothered to question it (although the thought of the traditional position may well have seemed rather extreme to us, as many have later admitted). It is time for discerning disciples to begin challenging such doctrines, and carefully examining them anew from God's holy Word. Remember: *Truth* has nothing to fear from honest, in-depth investigation!

To further illustrate the above principle of interpretation (forever *result* vs. forever *process*), notice yet another example. In Hebrews 9:12 we read that Jesus Christ, "not through the blood of goats and calves, but through His own blood, entered the holy place once for all, having obtained *eternal redemption*." Here we find a similar phrase to "eternal punishment." This time, however, it is *redemption* that is said to be "forever." We must now ask the same questions. Is it the process (redeem*ing*) that is endless, or is it the result (redemp*tion*)? Is the author of Hebrews seeking to convey the idea of a never-ending process of redeeming; one that never actually ever results in a final redemption? Is that the message here? Of course not! Redemption is a result, and it is both quantitatively and qualitatively *eternal*. It would be of no comfort to us whatsoever if our Lord was continually and forever in the process of seeking to redeem us through the continual offering of His blood, a process that never actually produced the resultant goal: redemption. If redemption itself was unobtainable, and the only thing truly enduring was the process, then redemption would never truly be *obtained*, because it is the process, not the result, that endures. *If a process is never ending, then a result is never obtained*. That is unthinkable with regard to redemption. It is equally unthinkable with regard to final punishment. Both are results, and it is the result that is said to endure. When we teach the traditional view on this matter, we in effect teach just the opposite of biblical Truth.

Consider these other "eternal" realities mentioned in the New Covenant writings: (1) **"Eternal destruction"** ~ 2 Thessalonians 1:9. What endures without end? A destroy*ing* process which never brings about the desired result? Or, is it the *result* (destruc*tion*) which is forever? Will God forever seek to destroy the wicked and evil, but never be able to achieve the desired destruction? (2)

"**Eternal consolation**" ~ 2 Thessalonians 2:16. Will the Lord be forever in the process of seeking to consol and comfort us, but never actually achieving that result? Or, will we be consoled, and will that consola*tion* be enduring? (3) "**Eternal salvation**" ~ Hebrews 5:9. Is our Lord Jesus Christ forever seeking to bring about salvation, but never actually achieving it? Or, has He secured salva*tion* for mankind through His once for all sacrifice? What endures? The process of bringing about salvation, or the resultant salvation itself? (4) "**Eternal judgment**" ~ Hebrews 6:2. Will the judg*ing* process go on forever and ever? Or, is it the judg*ment* that endures?

We could go on, but hopefully you see the interpretive principle here. A failure to differentiate between *process* and *result* can completely alter one's theology. Thus, when it comes to questions like "How long is forever?" we must exercise a tremendous amount of care. Many factors must be taken into consideration, and a failure in any of these areas of contemplation can lead to a theology totally at odds with biblical Truth. Of utmost importance in any such effort at interpretation of a passage in which the word *aionios* is connected is to determine (1) is this term being used *qualitatively* or *quantitatively*, or perhaps both?, and (2) is the focus of the teaching in the passage on *process* or *result*? Correct answers here are critical to our theological constructs.

Chapter 6
Reflecting on Hades
Truth or Tradition?

There are eleven occurrences of the Greek word *Hades* in the New Covenant documents, although one of them (1 Corinthians 15:55) is contested. "The word *Hades* is used only ten times in the NT ~ eleven times if one includes 1 Cor. 15:55, which had the word *Hades* in the *Textus Receptus* but which probably should be '*thanate*' (death), as in the more reliable manuscripts" [*The Zondervan Pictorial Encyclopedia of the Bible*, vol. 3, p. 7]. It is interesting to note, however, that the *King James Version*, which accepts the less reliable use of *Hades* in the Corinthian passage (although this word is never used elsewhere by Paul), translates it "grave" in that passage. Unfortunately, the *KJV* translates this word "hell" in the other ten references (a most regrettable rendering, and one that has contributed much to subsequent theological confusion. For example, one is left wondering how "hell" can be cast into the "lake of fire" ~ Revelation 20:14, *KJV*). It should also be noted that the *KJV* further confuses the issue by using the word "hell" to translate *other* key biblical words (*Sheol, Gehenna, Tartarus*), each of which have significantly different meanings and applications.

As to the etymology of *Hades*, most scholars recognize that it is at best uncertain. It is thought to perhaps come from the negation of a word meaning, "to see, perceive" (Greek: *a + idein*), thus implying "that which is unseen or beyond human perception." It has its popular roots in paganism, and, according to Homer, was the name both of the "underworld" and the god of that realm (also known as Pluto). "Hades is the Greek equivalent of the Hebrew Sheol, it being the translation for Sheol in the LXX sixty-one times (in every instance except in 2 Samuel 22:6)" [*The Zondervan Pictorial Encyclopedia of the Bible*, vol. 3, p. 7].

"The Greek word 'hades' came into biblical use when the translators of the Septuagint (LXX) chose it to render the Hebrew 'sheol.' The problem is that hades was used in the Greek world in a vastly different way than sheol. ... Hades in Greek mythology is the underworld, where the conscious souls of the dead are divided in two major regions, one a place of torment and the other of blessedness. ... This Greek conception of hades influenced Hellenistic Jews, during the intertestamental period, to adopt the belief in the immortality of the soul and the idea of a spatial separation in the underworld between the righteous and the godless" [Dr. Bacchiocchi, *Immortality or Resurrection? -- A Biblical Study on Human Nature and Destiny*, p. 170].

"The literature of the intertestamental period reflects the growth of the idea of the division of Hades into separate compartments for the godly and the ungodly. This aspect of eschatology was a popular subject in the apocalyptic literature that flourished in this period. Notable is the pseudepigraphical *Enoch* (written c. 200 B.C.), which includes the description of a tour supposedly taken by Enoch into the center of the earth. ... In another passage in *Enoch*, he sees at the center of the earth two places ~ Paradise, the place of bliss, and the valley of Gehinnom, the place of punishment. The above illustrates that there was a general notion of compartments in Hades that developed in the intertestamental period" [*The Zondervan Pictorial Encyclopedia of the Bible*, vol. 3, p. 7].

"In the intertestamental period the idea of the afterlife underwent some development. In Jewish apocalyptic literature Hades was an intermediate place (1 Enoch 51:1) where all the souls of the dead awaited judgment (22:3f). The dead were separated into compartments, the righteous staying in an apparently pleasant place (vs. 9) and various classes of sinners undergoing punishments in other compartments (vs. 10-13)" [*The International Standard Bible Encyclopedia*, vol. 2, p. 591].

"Under the influence of Persian and Hellenistic ideas concerning retribution after death the belief arose that the righteous and the godless would have very different fates, and we thus have the development of the idea of spatial separation in the underworld, the first instance being found in *Enoch*" [Gerhard Kittel, *Theological Dictionary of the New Testament*, vol. 1, p. 147]. "Nowhere in the Old Testament is the abode of the dead regarded as a place of punishment or torment. The concept of an infernal 'hell' developed in Israel only during the Hellenistic period" [*The Interpreter's Dictionary of the Bible*, p. 788].

Most scholars freely admit that the compartmental concept of *Hades* popular during the time of Christ was a development of the so-called "intertestamental period," and was largely influenced by pagan notions. The basic OT concept promoted in the word *Sheol* was simply "the grave." In fact, the *KJV* translates *Sheol* with the word "grave" in 31 of its 65 occurrences in the OT writings (it renders it "pit" 3 times, and unfortunately calls it "hell" in the remaining 31).

"These interpretations of 'sheol' as the dwelling place of souls (rather than the resting place of the body in the grave) or the place of punishment for the wicked, known as hell, do not stand up under the light of the Biblical usage of 'sheol'" [Dr. Bacchiocchi, p. 158]. In his classic study, Johannes Pedersen writes, "Sheol is the entirety into which all graves are merged; ... where there is grave, there is sheol, and where there is sheol, there is grave" [*Israel: Its Life and Culture*, vol. 1, p. 462]. "Any attempt to turn sheol into the place of torment of the wicked or into the abode of spirits/souls clearly contradicts the Biblical characterization of sheol as the underground depository of the dead" [Dr. Bacchiocchi, p. 161].

The late editor of *Gospel Minutes*, Dillard Thurman, devoted an entire issue of his publication [vol. 34, no. 5, Feb. 1, 1985] to the false notion of the "Intermediate State of the Dead." A person had asked him to set forth the views of his own denomination (the *Churches of Christ*) with respect to what occurs after death. Dillard wrote, "I can only state what I have found in over half a century of studying God's Word, *and that may not be what he expected to receive!*" Thurman stated, "I have heard funeral orations extol the happiness and bliss the departed has instantly with death: but on checking the New Testament assiduously, I have yet to find a single promise where the dead go into heaven on an instant pass, or have immediate conscious happiness!" He pointed out that man "is mortal," and thus is simply going to die and return to the dust. The hope of the Christian is the *resurrection*, not some false doctrine of "immortal soulism." Dillard reflected, "The hope and aspiration of many has been shifted from His coming again to receive His own, to an immediate immortality and heavenly bliss immediately at death! Jesus DID NOT (emphasis *his*) promise that!"

William Tyndale (1484-1536), an English Bible translator and martyr, wrote, "And ye, in putting them (the departed souls) in heaven, hell and purgatory, destroy the arguments wherewith Christ and Paul prove the resurrection." Tyndale argued that if souls were already in either bliss or misery, "then what cause is there of the resurrection?" And what cause is there even of judgment? In another part of this same writing, Tyndale said ~ "The true faith putteth forth the resurrection, which we be warned to look for every hour. The *heathen* philosophers, denying that, did put that the soul did ever live. And the Pope joineth the spiritual doctrine of Christ and the fleshly doctrine of philosophers together; things so contrary that they cannot agree. And because the fleshly-minded Pope consenteth unto *heathen* doctrine, therefore he corrupteth the Scripture to stablish it. If the soul be in heaven, tell me what cause is there for the resurrection?"

Justyn Martyr, who wrote around 150 AD, stated ~ "If you meet some who say that their souls go to Heaven when they die, do not believe that they are Christians!" [*Dialogue With Trypho*]. Martin Luther wrote in his *Table Talk* ~ "Now if one should say that Abraham's soul lives with God but his body is dead, this distinction is rubbish. I will attack it. That would be a silly soul if it were in heaven and desired its body!" In his *Defense*, Luther declared that it was the Pope, not the Bible, who taught "the soul is immortal." In his exposition of Ecclesiastes he wrote, "Solomon judgeth that the dead are asleep and feel nothing at all. For the dead lie there counting neither days nor years, but when they are awaked they shall seem to have slept scarce one minute."

John Milton (1608-1674), once called the "greatest of the sacred poets," declared, "Inasmuch as the whole man is uniformly said to consist of body and soul ... I will show that in death, first, the whole man, and secondly each component part, suffers privation of life ... *the grave* is the common guardian of all till the day of judgment."

In short, I must simply reject, as countless giants of faith before me have rejected, the traditional teaching that *Hades* is some intermediate holding place for disembodied immortal spirit beings previously trapped in our bodies and longing for release from their imprisonment by the physical death of the body. Such a notion is simply not the teaching of Scripture. The terms *Hades* and *Sheol* merely denote the *grave*. The dead "descend into the earth" (the grave), dust returning to dust. "For there is no activity or planning or wisdom in Sheol where you are going" (Ecclesiastes 9:10). "There is one fate for the righteous and for the wicked ... There is one fate for all men ... They go to the dead ... The dead do not know anything, nor have they any longer a reward" (Ecclesiastes 9:2-5). When we die we are dead. The *whole* man, not just the so-called "physical part" of him while some immortal spirit being trapped within him flies off to even greater life than before. Our hope and promise of life is *Jesus* and the *resurrection*.

Chapter 7
The Rich Man and Lazarus

Luke 16:19-31 contains a story told by Jesus to a group of scribes and Pharisees who were grumbling and scoffing at Him (Luke 15:1-3; 16:14-15a) because He dared to show concern for tax-gatherers and sinners who were "coming near Him to listen to Him." These religious elitists regarded themselves as superior to other men, and had little to no concern for those less fortunate, nor for those they considered beneath contempt (which was most people, even many of their own fellow religionists who were not of their particular faction or sect).

The story Jesus conveyed to these rigid religionists and sectarian separatists has come to be known as *The Rich Man and Lazarus*. It was obviously given that day to impress an eternal truth upon the hearts and minds of these troubled scribes and Pharisees. The basic message, in my view, is that our eternal destiny is determined this side of physical death, and once we breathe our last and return to the dust of the ground our fate is forever fixed. Thus, if we expect to receive mercy and compassion at the judgment, we had better display it to others during our sojourn here on earth. "For judgment will be merciless to one who has shown no mercy" (James 2:13). This was a moral Truth the scribes and Pharisees desperately needed to hear, and Jesus conveyed it to them that day in the form of this story. After all, it was His common practice to convey eternal Truths in the form of common stories (Matthew 13:34 ~ "...and He did not speak to them without a parable").

Most people have little problem with the major message of this passage of Scripture. The problem arises when seeking to determine the *nature* of the account itself. Is this a literal, historical account, or is this a parable? This has been hotly debated for many centuries, with reputable scholars and devoted disciples taking stands on both sides of the issue. My personal belief is that *this is a parable*, and therefore the figures employed should not be pressed into service to formulate a literal picture of disembodied souls or spirits in some Hadean holding place prior to the resurrection and judgment of the Last Day. Jesus simply told a parable to convey a spiritual truth to those still living, not to give us a peek into "the afterlife" to satisfy mankind's morbid curiosity. "Many have supposed that our Lord here refers to a 'real history,' and gives an account of some man who had lived in this manner; but of this there is no evidence. The probability is that this narrative is to be considered as a parable" [Albert Barnes, *Barnes' Notes on the New Testament*].

Dillard Thurman, the late editor of *Gospel Minutes*, wrote, "After having studied this matter for over fifty years, I still firmly believe this is a parable. It begins with the identical introduction as that in Luke 16:1 ~ 'There was a certain rich man...'" [*Gospel Minutes*, August 13, 1982]. The parable just before the one in Luke 16:1 begins "A certain man..." (Luke 15:11). Thus, there seems to be a string of parables here each beginning similarly: "A certain man" (Luke 15:11) .... "A certain rich man" (Luke 16:1) .... "A certain rich man" (Luke 16:19). The context also clearly reveals that each of these stories was told to the same group of people: the grumbling, scoffing scribes and Pharisees. "This parable is addressed to the

Pharisees, to whom Christ would scarcely have communicated details about the other world, on which He was so reticent in His teaching to the disciples" [Dr. Alfred Edersheim, *The Life and Times of Jesus the Messiah*, Book IV, p. 278].

The problem we are faced with in Christendom is that most of those in the traditional camp appeal to Luke 16:19-31 as a literal, historical account of the current disposition of disembodied spirit-beings. It has become the "crown jewel" in the apologetics of those who advocate an immortal soul and the perpetual torture of the unredeemed. "Many times over the years, I have observed that when all else fails, believers in the immortality of the soul will turn to the story of the rich man and Lazarus. This scripture, they apparently believe, is indisputable evidence that men, at death, go to a spirit world" [Sidney Hatch, *Daring To Differ: Adventures in Conditional Immortality*, p. 88].

"The parable of the rich man and Lazarus is often cited as the chief cornerstone in support of the postulate of man's inherent immortality and the endless duration of the incorrigibly wicked in sin and misery. It is frequently invoked to silence all dissent or question as to Immortal-Soulism. It is persistently set forth as proving beyond all peradventure that the souls of both the godly and the ungodly continue to live on uninterruptedly after death, *separate from the body* ~ but which is simply Plato's contention that death is identical with life, only in another sphere" [Leroy Edwin Froom, *The Conditionalist Faith of Our Fathers: The Conflict of the Ages Over the Nature and Destiny of Man*, vol. 1, p. 234].

When dealing with a parable, as most reputable scholars believe this account to be, one must be very cautious *not* to assume literal meaning and application for the figures employed. The figures of a parable convey a message or truth, or embellish that message or truth in some way, but they themselves do not *constitute* that message or truth itself. Thus, one must *never* seek to base doctrine upon mere figures and symbols employed in figurative language.

Dr. Edersheim stressed, "it will be necessary in the interpretation of this parable to keep in mind that its parabolic details must not be exploited, nor doctrines of any kind derived from them, either as to the character of the other world, the question of the duration of future punishments, or possible moral improvement of those in Gehinnom. All such things are foreign to the parable" [*The Life and Times of Jesus the Messiah*, Book IV, p. 277]. "We must not look in this parabolic language for Christ's teaching about the 'after death'" [*ibid*, p. 279]. "Doctrinal statements should not be drawn from parabolic illustrations" [*ibid*, p. 282].

Professor D. R. Dungan, in his classic book *Hermeneutics: The Science of Interpreting the Scriptures*, observed, "The parable in Luke 16:19-31, of the rich man and the poor man, has been made to mean almost everything within the range of theological speculation" [p. 234]. Parables were not intended to be interpreted literally (as is, for example, historical narrative), something legitimate biblical hermeneutists clearly recognize. Parables are a distinct literary form. "The very reason we do not feel compelled to interpret the parables historically is that they are presented in a somewhat stylized fashion -- the reader or hearer is immediately aware that they belong to a different genre (literary type)" [Walter Kaiser and Moises Silva, *An Introduction to Biblical Hermeneutics: The Search for Meaning*, p. 106].

"Strictly speaking, the parable belongs to a style of figurative speech which constitutes a class of its own" [Dr. Milton S. Terry, *Biblical Hermeneutics: A Treatise on the Interpretation of the Old and New Testaments*, p. 276]. "The general design of parables, as of all other kinds of figurative language, is to embellish and set forth ideas and moral truths in attractive and impressive forms" [*ibid*, p. 277].

The ancient Jews (as well as the pagans) were very fond of such stories, and there is a body of evidence, and thus some legitimate, scholarly speculation, that Jesus may well have employed a rather well-known contemporary story as He spoke to these scribes and Pharisees, a story with which these religious leaders would have been very familiar. This has led to much documentation of such accounts, many of which predate the Lord's story and are most striking in their similarity. "It seems appropriate to reopen this question and ask: Where should the origin of this parable be placed?" [*The Anchor Bible Dictionary*, vol. 4, p. 267]. *Eerdmans Dictionary of the Bible* informs us that "much of the study of the parable of Lazarus and Dives (Latin: 'rich man') in the 20th century has focused on possible literary antecedents" [p. 796-797].

"This parable is not theology. It is a vivid story, not a *Baedeker's* guide to the next world. Such stories as this were current in Jesus' day. They are found in rabbinical sources, and even in Egyptian papyri" [*The Interpreter's Bible*, vol. 8, p. 290]. "Similar stories existed in Egypt and among the rabbis; Jesus could easily have adapted this tradition to his own purpose" [*The Jerome Biblical Commentary*]. "This parable follows a story common in Egyptian and Jewish thought. .... This parable does not intend to give a topographical study of the abode of the dead, it is built upon and thus confirms common Jewish thought" [*International Standard Bible Encyclopedia*, vol. 3, p. 94]. *The Catholic Encyclopedia*, vol. 1 (online version) states that the imagery of this parable "is plainly drawn from the popular representations of the unseen world of the dead which were current in our Lord's time." "Jesus told this story to reinforce the fact that the riches of the Pharisees were not necessarily a sign of God's approval. Some interpreters suggest that the kernel of the story was a popular story of those times and possibly derived from an Egyptian source" [*New Commentary on the Whole Bible*, based on the classic commentary of *Jamieson, Fausset, and Brown*].

Josephus (a Jewish historian, c. 37-100 A.D.), in his work *Discourse to the Greeks Concerning Hades* (in which he notes that the concept of a soul being created immortal by God is "according to the doctrine of Plato"), presents a very similar story to that of our Lord's, including many of the same figures Jesus employed. Yes, he may have borrowed from the Lord's parable, but it is equally possible both were aware of such stories current in their culture. Several good reference works document and describe in some detail a good number of these stories that our Lord may have adapted to His own needs [*Eerdmans Dictionary of the Bible*, p. 797 .... Dr. James Hastings, *Dictionary of Christ and the Gospels*, vol. 2, p. 18 .... *The Interpreter's Bible*, vol. 8, p. 289 .... *The Anchor Bible Dictionary*, vol. 4, p. 267 .... Edersheim's *The Life and Times of Jesus the Messiah*, Book IV, p. 280-281 .... Dr. Samuele Bacchiocchi, *Immortality or Resurrection? -- A Biblical Study on Human Nature and Destiny*, p. 174-176].

My own personal conviction is that Jesus used or adapted a popular folktale well-known to His hearers for the purpose of conveying, by a means they would best comprehend and most easily remember, an eternal truth. "Jesus was accustomed to speak the language of His hearers in order to reach their understandings and hearts. And it is noteworthy how, when He employed Jewish imagery, He was wont to invest it with new significance" [Hastings, *Dictionary of Christ and the Gospels*, vol. 2, p. 18].

"In the story, then, of the rich man and Lazarus, Jesus has put them down with one of their own superstitions. ... He used their own ideas to condemn them. ... It is simply a case of taking what others believe, practice, or say, and using it to condemn them" [Sidney Hatch, *Daring To Differ: Adventures in Conditional Immortality*, p. 91]. "Since the elements of the story are taken from the Pharisees' own traditions, they are judged out of their own mouths" [*ibid*, p. 92].

It should be noted that the apostle Paul employed a similar device when he sought to impress upon certain Corinthian brethren the truth regarding the resurrection, and spoke of their practice of baptism for the dead. By speaking of this practice in his own teaching, and by *not condemning it*, Paul was certainly *not* thereby *endorsing it*. Rather, he merely used a practice *then current* among certain readers, to whom he was addressing his remarks, to drive home an eternal truth to their hearts and minds (1 Corinthians 15:29).

Another similar situation occurs in John 9:1-3. With regard to a man born blind, the disciples asked Jesus, "Rabbi, who sinned, *this man* or his parents, that he should be *born* blind?" Some of the Jews (thanks to Hellenistic influence on Jewish theology with regard to the pagan doctrines of the preexistence and immortality of souls) believed souls existed *prior* to their being placed in a physical body at birth. Thus, these preexistent souls could sin during this *prior* life, for which they would be punished during the *present* life (possibly by being born with some infirmity or deformity). Oddly enough, Jesus did not speak out against this pagan notion, but merely instructed His disciples that neither this man nor his parents had sinned so as to cause Him to be born blind. Contrary to what some might think, Jesus did not go around debunking every Jewish or pagan myth that had arisen in their theology due to pagan influence. Indeed, He at times seems to have *used them* in His dialogue with such persons to convey deeper eternal realities. This is exactly what I believe is being done with the parable of the rich man and the poor beggar.

A far more important reason for regarding the story of the rich man and Lazarus as figurative rather than literal/historical, however, is the obvious conflict with the inspired Scriptures that occurs when it is regarded as an actual account of real people and real events. These, in my estimation, are extremely serious contradictions with revealed Truth. Notice the following problems associated with a literal, historical interpretation of Luke 16:19-31.

ONE -- It would teach that judgment and punishment of the dead has occurred *prior* to the resurrection and judgment on that great and final day. The Scriptures clearly and repeatedly teach that judgment and punishment (as well as reward) occur *following* the resurrection, not *prior to it*. The "blessed" Theophylact (perhaps the most learned exegete of the Greek Church during the 11th-12th century A.D.) observed, "This is a parable and not, as some have foolishly imagined, something which actually occurred. For good things have not yet been allotted to the righteous, nor punishments to the sinners" [*The Explanation of the New Testament*].

Until a decision has been rendered in judgment before the Great Throne, is it really reasonable and biblical to proclaim that men are cast into torment or carried off to a state of bliss? This would constitute judgment, sentencing and execution *prior* to the judgment, sentencing and execution on that Great Day following resurrection. "Behold, I am coming quickly, and My reward is with Me, to render to every man according to what he has done" (Revelation 22:12). See also Matthew 25:31-46.

Judgment will occur "when the Son of Man comes in His glory, and all the angels with Him" (Matthew 25:31). *Then* the dead, who have been raised from the dust of the ground, will undergo judgment, and a great separation will occur, and some will "go away into eternal punishment, but the righteous into eternal life" (Matthew 25:46). This judging and punishing does *not* occur *prior* to the resurrection on that last day. Yet, if this parable is taken literally, it clearly contradicts the remainder of biblical teaching on this matter.

William Tyndale (1484 - 1536), in responding to Sir Thomas More, wrote, "And ye, in putting them (the departed souls) in heaven, hell and purgatory, destroy the arguments wherewith Christ and Paul prove the resurrection." Tyndale argued that if souls were already in either bliss or misery, "then what cause is there of the resurrection?" And what cause is there even of judgment? In another part of this same writing, Tyndale said, "The true faith putteth forth the resurrection, which we be warned to look for every hour. The heathen philosophers, denying that, did put that the soul did ever live. And the Pope joineth the spiritual doctrine of Christ and the fleshly doctrine of philosophers together; things so contrary that they cannot agree. And because the fleshly-minded Pope consenteth unto heathen doctrine, therefore he corrupteth the Scripture to stablish it. If the soul be in heaven, tell me what cause is there for the resurrection?"

With regard to such *prior* rewards or punishments, Dillard Thurman wrote, "There is never a hint in God's Word that this takes place before the general resurrection at the coming of Christ, our Savior!" [*Gospel Minutes*, Feb. 1, 1985]. "You will enter into *rest and rise again* for your allotted portion *at the end of the age*" (Daniel 12:13). "The day is coming ... the day which I am preparing," says the Lord of hosts; a day "burning like a furnace; and all the arrogant and every evildoer will be chaff; and the day that is coming will set them ablaze ... and they shall be ashes under the soles of your feet" (Malachi 4:1-3). This is *not* the day of one's death, but that Final Day when "those who *sleep* in the dust of the ground will *awake*" to judgment and punishment (Daniel 12:2). This parable of the rich man and Lazarus, however, *if taken literally*, stands in direct and dramatic opposition to these divine truths conveyed repeatedly in both OT and NT writings.

"A literal interpretation of the parable contradicts some fundamental biblical truths. If the narrative is literal, then Lazarus received his reward and the rich man his punishment, immediately after death and before the judgment day. But the Bible clearly teaches that the rewards and punishments, as well as the separation between the saved and the unsaved, will take place on the day of Christ's coming" [Dr. Samuele Bacchiocchi, *Immortality or Resurrection? -- A Biblical Study on Human Nature and Destiny*, p. 174].

"To use this parable as proof that men receive their rewards at death is squarely to contradict Christ Himself, who explicitly states that the righteous and the wicked receive their reward 'when the Son of man shall come in his glory.' He definitely placed the recompense at the resurrection, the time of harvest, and end of the world" [Leroy Edwin Froom, *The Conditionalist Faith of Our Fathers: The Conflict of the Ages Over the Nature and Destiny of Man*, vol. 1, p. 261]. "Furthermore, if the narrative is literal, then the beggar received his reward and the rich man his punishment immediately upon death, in the interim *before* the judgment day and the consequent separation of the good and evil. But such a procedure is repugnant to all justice. Paul said that God 'hath appointed a day, in the which he will judge the world in righteousness' (Acts 17:31). That was still future in apostolic times" [*ibid*, p. 262].

"The Pharisees had made God's Word void, as concerns the condition of the dead, by their 'traditions' derived from pagan Platonic philosophy, which in turn had been borrowed from Egypt, Babylon, and Persia. So it was that Dives is here pictured as in a place of torment, living in insufferable flames. It was simply Hebraized Platonism, and was in no way condoned or endorsed by Christ" [*ibid*, p. 262-263]. Thus, on this one point alone we must completely reject the notion that this account is either literal or historical. To accept it as such places it in direct conflict with the remainder of Scripture on the subject of final punishment. For this reason alone the particulars of the parable must be regarded as *figurative*.

TWO ~ To embrace this parable as literal, historical narrative would also make one guilty of promoting the view of a mortal man inherently possessing an immortal soul or spirit. Such is simply *not* taught in Scripture, and constitutes pagan dualism. The Lord "*alone* possesses immortality" (1 Timothy 6:16), and immortality for man (the *whole* man) is entirely derived, and will not be "put on" until *after* the resurrection, "at the last trumpet," and only then by the redeemed (1 Corinthians 15:50f).

In point of fact, this parable doesn't even mention "souls" or disembodied "spirits." That is an assumption of biased interpreters. If this account is of disembodied *spirits* (ethereal beings devoid of bodies and bodily organs), then is it not strange that the account speaks of eyes, a tongue and a finger? -- real physical body parts. And what relief would a drop of water on a tongue serve to a spirit? Would it provide *any* relief? Would it not vaporize in the flame? Or is all of this figurative also, just like the rest of the parable? I believe that is exactly the case.

"Contenders for literalism suppose that the rich man and Lazarus were disembodied spirits, destitute of bodies," yet "they are portrayed as existing physically, despite the fact that the rich man's body was duly buried in the grave. Was his body carried away into Hades together with his soul by mistake?" [Dr. Samuele Bacchiocchi, *Immortality or Resurrection? -- A Biblical Study on Human Nature and Destiny*, p. 173]. Dillard Thurman declared that this "fanciful notion" of some bodily presence in a Hadean holding area "won't hold any more water than the rich man could dip his finger in! If fingers and tongues were still in the grave, or if they were figurative, then this must be accepted as a parable, and treated as such!" [*Gospel Minutes*, June 22, 1984]. "The passage says nothing about souls or spirit-beings. Furthermore, this would contradict the entire teaching of Scripture, from Genesis 2:7 on, regarding the nature of man. A soul is a living breathing creature, not a ghost" [Sidney Hatch, *Daring To Differ: Adventures in Conditional Immortality*, p. 90].

Again, nothing is said whatsoever in this parable about either "souls" or "spirits." There is absolutely no indication at all that Jesus is talking about some "immortal something" trapped in our physical bodies that flies off to some Hadean holding area at the moment of physical death. To promote such a view is contrary to the teaching of Scripture on the nature of man. Jesus simply made use of a common story, which reflected current Jewish/pagan thinking, to convey a moral message to His hearers.

THREE ~ Scripture also makes it abundantly clear that the grave (*Hades, Sheol*) is not a place of conscious activity for the dead. The dead "sleep" in the dust of the ground, they are not holding conversations with other departed, disembodied spirits across vast chasms. "The Scriptures teach that the death state is one of quiet, silent, unconscious sleep. How much more evidence is necessary to convince any reasonable person that this is simply a story which Jesus told in order to make a point with His adversaries?" [*ibid*]. "The *resurrection from the grave* will be the time for happiness and bliss for God's saints. It is *not* when they are yet *asleep in Jesus*" [Dillard Thurman, *Gospel Minutes*, Feb. 1, 1985].

"A literal interpretation of the parable also contradicts the uniform testimony of the Old and New Testaments that the dead, both righteous and ungodly, lie silent and unconscious in death until the resurrection day" [Dr. Samuele Bacchiocchi, *Immortality or Resurrection? -- A Biblical Study on Human Nature and Destiny*, p. 174].

FOUR ~ "Jesus was also not teaching that lost souls have the privilege of praying to patriarchs long dead, who will answer from another realm!" [Dillard Thurman, *Gospel Minutes*, Aug. 13, 1982]. If this parable is to be taken literally, however, we have lost souls praying to people like Abraham, and Abraham answering. There is apparently (if taken literally) a "vast gulf" between the two "compartments of Hades," and yet are we to suppose they can freely converse among each other?

"Since we deride the Catholics for praying to 'the Virgin Mary,' a host of saints, etc., how can we keep a straight face and advocate that folk offer their prayers to Abraham after death? But not only did the rich man pray, his prayer was answered!" [Dillard Thurman, *Gospel Minutes*, June 22, 1984]. "But there is also a flaw in Abraham! He acts as judge and jury, by-passing both God and His Son with his decree. He even accepts the term 'father,' though Jesus taught 'And call no man your father upon the earth; for one is your Father, which is in heaven' (Matthew 23:9). If this be a factual, historical report, it opens up Pandora's Box ... and raises more devils than we can cast out!" [*ibid*].

As Leroy Edwin Froom points out in his massive two volume work (over 2000 pages of extensive research), "a literal application breaks down under the weight of its own absurdities and contradictions" [*The Conditionalist Faith of Our Fathers: The Conflict of the Ages Over the Nature and Destiny of Man*, vol. 1, p. 260]. "Pagan Platonism, polluting the Jewish faith, which Jesus cited but did not endorse in this legendary fable-parable, should never be allowed to corrupt sound Christian doctrine" [*ibid*, p. 269]. "The story of Dives and Lazarus was never designed to teach conditions on the other side of death. That is an extraneous contention that has been introduced without warrant. It is fallacious as an argument and is unworthy of the name of sound exegesis" [*ibid*].

"Parables were used by the Lord to teach truths; and after the primary truths are gleaned, the parable should not be distended and distorted to cover that which the Lord did not intend!" [Dillard Thurman, *Gospel Minutes*, Aug. 13, 1982]. This is exactly what many have done with this particular parable of our Lord. They have forced literalism upon the figures of this story, and in so doing they actually perpetuate the pagan perceptions which found their way into the doctrines of ancient Judaism and Christendom. Any passage of Scripture taken out of context becomes a pretext! In this case, a pretext for the continued promotion of false teaching with regard to the nature of man and his eternal destiny.

For many reasons, therefore, I completely and unequivocally reject Luke 16:19-31 as anything other than a parable, likely based on common lore, representing the eternal truth that our eternal destinies are determined by our actions and attitudes in this life, and that one's fate is forever fixed at death. To fabricate a theology of disembodied spirits and Hadean holding cells and everlasting torture of the wicked from this passage is an unconscionable abuse of biblical interpretation and should be rejected by all disciples intent upon discerning and declaring *Truth*.

Chapter 8
The Thief on the Cross

A passage often appealed to by those who advocate the immediate conscious existence in an intermediate state of some "immortal spirit-being" that survives the death of the physical body is Luke 23:43. Here Jesus made a statement to one of two criminals as that man was dying on an adjacent cross, a man who had previously said to Him, "Jesus, remember me when You come in Your kingdom!" (vs. 42). To this dying, penitent thief Jesus replied, "Truly I say to you, today you shall be with Me in Paradise."

The argument by the traditionalists is that this verse assures us the penitent thief would be "in Paradise" with Jesus *that same day*. Since the *body* of the thief was likely placed in the *grave* that same day, and since it was not resurrected, they conclude it must be his *soul/spirit* that went to Paradise that day. This, they declare, *proves* the conscious existence of some spirit-being trapped within one's physical body that is freed to greater existence by one's physical death.

It's interesting to note (and most seem to overlook this point) that the thief asked to be remembered *when* Jesus came *in/into* His *kingdom. When* exactly would that have been? Was it on the day of His death and burial? Most scholars would argue that it was *not*. Most state the victory was not truly won until at least the third day when Jesus Christ *arose from the dead*. Others will declare it was not until the ascension several weeks after that. Still others will point to the day of Pentecost, or even to the *Parousia*, as the ultimate coming of the kingdom. But almost nobody suggests our Lord came in or into His kingdom on the day of His death. Thus, some scholars see a problem early on in the traditional interpretation of this statement by Jesus: how did it accurately address the request of the dying thief on the cross with respect to the coming of the kingdom?

On the night of His betrayal and arrest, just hours before the statement to the thief on the cross, and during the establishment of the Lord's Supper, Jesus declared to His disciples, "I shall never again drink of the fruit of the vine until that day when I drink it new in the kingdom of God" (Mark 14:25). Was Jesus expecting that kingdom to arrive in just a matter of hours? During the many days following the resurrection, our Lord was continuing to speak to the disciples about this kingdom, and the disciples even then were unclear as to *when* all of this was to occur (Acts 1:3-7). Thus, not even *they* were under the impression that this kingdom "came" on the day of Jesus' death. Indeed, how was Jesus to "come into" His kingdom that day when *He was dead?* Thus, there is much to suggest that the day of our Lord's death was *not* the day when He came into His kingdom. Some even interpret Paul's statement in 2 Timothy 4:1 about the kingdom of Christ (written decades later) to be an as yet *unrealized* (thus *future*) experience.

But the above is only a *minor* difficulty with the traditionalists' position on this passage. There are far greater problems associated with their interpretation. However, before one can truly perceive the significance of our Lord's statement to this thief, one must first come to an understanding of the biblical concept of *Paradise*.

The word *Paradise* is of Persian origin. It was incorporated into the Hebrew language during the time of Persian influence, and passed into the Greek language through its extensive use by Xenophon. The Hebrew word "*pardes*" occurs three times in the pages of the OT writings:

Nehemiah 2:8 where it is translated "forest."

Ecclesiastes 2:5 with reference to "gardens and parks."

Song of Solomon 4:13 where the author refers to his bride as "an *orchard* of pomegranates."

The word literally means "a park; a garden." In time it came to signify "a place of exquisite pleasure and delight." The *Septuagint* uses the Greek word "*paradeisos*" (transliteration: *paradise*) consistently in Genesis 2-3 for the "*Garden* of Eden." It is also used in reference to the Jordan Valley (Genesis 13:10) and again of the Garden of Eden in Joel 2:3.

In the NT writings the Greek word "*paradeisos*" appears only three times:

2 Corinthians 12:4 where Paul says he was "caught up into Paradise;" probably equivalent to the "third heaven" of vs. 2, which many biblical scholars suggest signifies being in the very presence of God in heaven (although this event may have been more *vision* than literal journey, as Paul himself acknowledges).

Revelation 2:7 where Christ promises those who overcome -- "I will grant to eat of the tree of life, which is in the Paradise of God." This tree is in the very presence of God in heaven, positioned on either side of the river of the water of life which flows from the throne of God and of the Lamb (Revelation 22:1-5). Thus, the tree is said to be right before the throne of God *in Heaven*, which is identified as being "the Paradise of God."

Luke 23:43 where we find the statement of Jesus to the thief on the cross.

"Later Jewish tradition locates 'Paradise' as an abode of the righteous dead in Hades, however the apocryphal books do not!" [*Zondervan Pictorial Encyclopedia of the Bible*, vol. 4, p. 598]. Notice that it is according to *later Jewish tradition* that Paradise is said to be located in the Hadean realm. This is *not* the teaching of inspired Scripture. Not even the *Apocrypha* locates Paradise in Hades. Nowhere in the Bible is Paradise ever associated with some so-called "intermediate state or realm" for the dead. This doctrine originated with *men*, and is *not* taught in Scripture.

The word "Paradise," as it is used in the New Testament writings, obviously refers to the eternal abode of God (what we generally term "Heaven"). "In the NT 'paradise' means heaven in 2 Corinthians 12:4 and Revelation 2:7. Accordingly, it naturally denotes heaven in the remaining instance: Luke 23:43" [*Davis Dictionary of the Bible*, p. 569]. "It is evident that Luke 23:43 speaks of a *heavenly* Paradise" [*New International Commentary on the NT*]. "There can, therefore, be no doubt that *paradise is heaven*. The Fathers made a distinction between paradise and heaven which is *not* found in the Scriptures" [Charles Hodge, *Systematic Theology*, vol. 3, p. 727]. "Paradise is not a shadowy waiting-room, but a blissful abode within the very courts of heaven itself" [*New International Commentary on the NT*].

The Jews "have a multitude of fables on the subject" [*Adam Clarke's Commentary*, vol. 5, p. 497], and their literature is "full of fancies and discrepancies" [*New International Commentary on the NT*]. The *Gospel of Nicodemus* even maintains that this thief on the cross is still alive today in the original Garden of Eden somewhere on the earth's surface. According to the *Narrative of Joseph*, the penitent thief is the *only* resident of Paradise.

"Jesus, however, did not endorse the *later Jewish tradition* that paradise was at any time a compartment of Hades" [*Zondervan*

Pictorial Encyclopedia of the Bible, vol. 4, p. 599]. Curtis Dickinson wrote, "In the days of Jesus, the Jews held many widely diverse views regarding 'Paradise,' but none of them were based upon Divine revelation, so no weight should be attached to such opinions. We will stick to what is revealed in the Bible" [*The Witness*, vol. 30, no. 8, August 1990].

Thus, the first major point that needs to be made, and *stressed*, at this juncture is that Jesus was *not* speaking of some compartment in Hades or Sheol, but was rather referring to Heaven itself -- the abode of the Father.

The biggest problem associated with Luke 23:43, however, is in connection with the word "today." What did Jesus mean when He stated that this dying thief would be with Him in Paradise "*today*"? Was this *really* what Jesus was suggesting here, or have we perhaps misunderstood and thus misapplied this entire verse?

There are several significant problems associated with the assumption that the "soul" or "spirit" of this thief left his physical body at death to enter Paradise that day. First, it assumes the inherent immortality of some "spirit-being" trapped inside the physical body which is freed by the *death* of that body. This is simply *not* taught in Scripture. The dead "sleep" in the dust of the ground awaiting the resurrection, they are not conscious spirits cavorting in some Hadean realm.

Another major problem, however, is that it seems clear from Scripture that Jesus Himself did not enter Paradise that day. Thus, how could the thief have been "with Him" *that day* if Jesus Himself was not there?! It was not until about 43 days later (He arose the 3rd day and spent 40 days more with the disciples before ascending to the Father) that Jesus returned to the abode of God. At the empty tomb, on the day of His resurrection, He told Mary, who was clinging to Him, "I have *not yet ascended* to the Father" (John 20:17). This was three days *after* His statement to the thief on the cross, and Jesus says He has *not been there yet*. Where was He? He was *dead* ... buried in the tomb. "So shall the Son of Man be three days and three nights in the heart of the earth" (Matthew 12:40). Jesus was not in Heaven, He was in the *grave*. The promise to Jesus was that He would not be *abandoned* to the grave, nor would He "undergo decay" (Acts 2:27). He would be raised. If Jesus was *not* raised, but abandoned to the grave, *all is lost* (1 Corinthians 15:12-19). No, Jesus was not in Paradise that day with the thief. They were both dead and buried.

By the way, an Islamic web site declared the Luke 23:43 and John 20:17 "discrepancy" as one of the major reasons for rejecting the Bible as authoritative for man today [*101 Clear Contradictions in the Bible*, by Shabir Ally]. Thus, we even have other religions mocking Christianity for this perceived hermeneutical dilemma. And yet, as we shall see, it is all so completely unnecessary when this passage is *correctly* rendered and interpreted.

H. Leo Boles, in his *Commentary on Luke*, correctly observed, "Evidently Jesus did not mean that this robber would go with Him to heaven that day, as it seems clear from other statements that Jesus did not go to heaven that day. His day of ascension came about forty days after that time" [p. 454]. The thief on the cross was not with Jesus "that day" in Paradise for the very simple reason that Jesus Himself was not there!

Indeed, the raising of the dead and their entrance into God's presence "in Heaven" is a *future* event, not one that occurs at the instant of death. "No one has ever gone into heaven except the one who came from heaven -- the Son of Man" (John 3:13). "Brothers, I can tell you confidently that the patriarch David died and was buried, and his tomb is here to this day. ... For David did not ascend to heaven..." (Acts 2:29, 34). Thus, it is unlikely the thief made it into the very presence of God before the throne on the day of his death. If David wasn't there, and Jesus wasn't there, and "no one" was there, then neither was the thief.

So, how do we deal with the apparent "problem" raised by the traditionalists when they quote Luke 23:43? "Truly I say to you, today you shall be with Me in Paradise." The very simple solution is to be found in an obvious *error of punctuation*. It is important to keep in mind that the early Greek manuscripts of the NT text did *not* contain punctuation, nor even spaces between the words (which was the space saving device known as "*scriptio continua*"). Even question marks were not used commonly in Greek manuscripts until the 9th century A.D. [Dr. Bruce Metzger, *The Text of the New Testament*, p. 27]. It would be many hundreds of years before punctuation would be added to the text of the New Testament, and this would be done by uninspired men with theological biases. It was not until 1205 A.D. that Stephen Langton (a professor in Paris and later the Archbishop of Canterbury) divided the Bible into chapters. Thus, it is important to note that the sectional and grammatical separations in Scripture are the devices *of men* and *not* of God.

The whole meaning of Luke 23:43 literally hinges on the placement of a single comma (a comma placed by fallible men). In the Luke 23:43 passage, the comma is traditionally placed *prior* to the word "today" ("Truly I say to you, today you shall be with Me in Paradise"). However, consider the following alternative:

"Truly I say to you today, you shall be with Me in Paradise."

By moving the comma to a position *after* the word "today" one alters the meaning of the sentence so that it is now no longer in conflict with the remainder of biblical doctrine on the nature of man and his eternal destiny. Grammatically, *either* placement of the comma is technically correct in the Greek language. Thus, there is just as much grammatical justification for the placement of the comma *after* "today" as there is for placing it *before* that word. The theological biases of the early translators (influenced as they were by the heathen doctrines of immortal soulism and subterranean realms of bliss and torment) prompted them to select a placement of the comma that seemed to substantiate their own perceptions of the nature of man and his ultimate destiny. The problem with that selection of comma placement, however, is that it contradicted the remainder of God's Word on the subject! A simple matter of *repunctuation* (as this procedure has come to be characterized) solves the problem and brings this verse back into harmony with biblical teaching.

"Translators have placed the comma before the adverb 'today,' not for grammatical reasons, but for the theological conviction that the dead receive their reward at death. One would wish that translators would limit themselves to translating the text and leave the task of interpretation to the reader" [Dr. Samuele Bacchiocchi, *Immortality or Resurrection? -- A Biblical Study on Human Nature and Destiny*, p. 176].

Actually, the phrase "I say unto you this day" (or "...today") is "a common Hebrew idiom which is constantly used for very solemn emphasis" [E. W. Bullinger, Appendix 173, from *The Companion Bible*]. Thus, it would not have been that unusual for Jesus to have said, "Truly I say to you today..." instead of applying the word "today" to the phrase which followed. His statement to the dying thief would certainly constitute a declaration with "solemn emphasis." Curtis Dickinson wrote, "The Greek adverb here rendered 'today' appears in the *Septuagint* and the New Testament 221 times. In 170 of these places the adverb *follows* the verb it modifies. For example: 'I declare to you *this day*, that ye shall surely perish' (Deuteronomy 30:18). Therefore, it would be natural to punctuate Luke 23:43 as follows: 'Truly I say to you today, you will be with me in Paradise.' Paul uses a similar turn of phrase in Acts 20:26 ~ 'I testify to you this day, that I am innocent of the blood of all men'" [*The Witness*, vol. 30, no. 8, August 1990].

"In suggesting that the words of our Lord to the thief can only be understood by re-arranging the punctuation, we are often accused of tampering with the text. This is a false accusation because *any* punctuation is an addition to the text. The correct punctuation can only be determined by comparing Scripture with Scripture" [A. W. Fowler, "Jesus' Promise to the Dying Thief," an article in *Resurrection Magazine*, Autumn 1991]. Of course, when we compare Scripture with Scripture we discover that there is no way Jesus was with this thief in Paradise *that day*, nor do the Scriptures teach immortal soulism, or Hadean holding areas for disembodied spirits, or judgment and reward prior to the resurrection on the Last Day. Thus, the placement of the comma that best harmonizes with the teaching of Scripture is to place it *after* "today." "Thus, Jesus is *not* teaching conscious existence in paradise immediately after death in an intermediate state" [*Zondervan Pictorial Encyclopedia of the Bible*, vol. 4, p. 598].

"This emphatic use of 'today' is a common idiom in both Hebrew and Aramaic which are the two Semitic languages in which the Old Testament was written. The idiom is used to introduce a solemn statement. 'I ___ to you today' when the verb is one of declaration, testification, command or oath. Some seventy occurrences of this formula are found in the Bible and forty-two are found in the Book of Deuteronomy (for example, Deuteronomy 4:26)" [A. W. Fowler, "Jesus' Promise to the Dying Thief," an article in *Resurrection Magazine*, Autumn 1991]. "The earliest translation of the Greek New Testament was into the language of Palestine's nearest neighbor, Syria. Syriac is a dialect of Aramaic. It is therefore not surprising that in one of the oldest Syriac manuscripts of the Gospels (5th century *Curetonianus*) the translator recognized the idiom and translated the passage, 'Amen say I to you today that with me you will be in the garden of Eden.' By introducing the word 'that' the translator removed the need for any punctuation to determine the sense. *We therefore have a very ancient precedent for our interpretation which ante-dates all the English versions by hundreds of years*" [*ibid*].

Is there any evidence among Bible translators, and Bible translations, for this *repunctuation*? Actually, there is more than some realize. Consider the following:

1. "And he said to him: 'Truly I tell you today, You will be with me in Paradise'" [*New World Translation of the Holy Scriptures*].

2. "And said to him the Jesus, Indeed I say to thee today, with me thou shalt be in the Paradise" [marginal reading in *The Emphatic Diaglott*, by B. F. Wilson in the 1800's].

3. German Bible translator L. Reinhardt, in a footnote to this verse, wrote, "The punctuation presently used (by most translators) in this verse is undoubtedly false and contradictory to the entire way of thinking of Christ."

4. In the NT translation by J. B. Rotherham (in the year 1878), a British clergyman and Bible translator, he translated this verse: "And Jesus said to him, Verily, to thee I say, this day, with me shalt thou be in the paradise." Admittedly, this is a rather ambiguous rendering. However, in the 1897 revision, Rotherham phrased the passage this way: "And he said unto him, Verily I say unto thee this day: With me shalt thou be in Paradise."

5. E. W. Bullinger repunctuates and comments as follows: "'And Jesus said to him, Verily, to thee I say this day, with Me shalt thou be in Paradise.' The word 'today' being made solemn and emphatic" [*A Critical Lexicon and Concordance to the English and Greek New Testament*, p. 811].

6. "The English translation by Dr. Wm. Cureton of an old Syriac Version of the gospels agrees with that and renders Luke 23:43: 'And he said to Jesus, My Lord, remember me when Thou comest in Thy kingdom. Jesus said to him, Verily I say to thee today that with Me thou shalt be in the Eden's garden'" [*This Means Everlasting Life*, p. 281-282].

7. "And Jesus said to him, 'Verily, to you am I saying today, with Me shall you be in paradise'" [*The Concordant Literal New Testament*].

8. George M. Lamsa's translation from the Aramaic of the Peshitta has this footnote to the verse: "Ancient texts were not punctuated. The comma could come before or after *today*" [*The New Testament From The Ancient Eastern Text*].

9. "Indeed today I say to you, you shall be with Me in the paradise" [James L. Tomanek, *The New Testament of Our Lord and Saviour Jesus Annointed*].

10. "Verily do I say unto thee today ~ With me, thou shalt be, in Paradise" [Charles A. L. Totten, *The Gospel of History*].

11. The two volume encyclopedia *Insight on the Scriptures* [vol. 2, p. 575] says in part (under the article "Paradise"): "Luke's account shows that an evildoer, being executed alongside Jesus Christ, spoke words in Jesus' defense and requested that Jesus remember him when He got into His kingdom. Jesus' reply was: Truly I tell you today, you will be with Me in Paradise."

Curtis Dickinson wrote, "It may be asked why translators of most modern versions do not place the comma after the 'today' so that the verse will harmonize with other scriptural teaching on death and resurrection. We might as well ask why they do not translate the Greek *baptizo* as 'immerse' or *diakonos* as 'servant' instead of merely spelling them with English letters. To do so would put the translation at odds with most denominational doctrine and almost insure its failure to be accepted. When the translators put Luke 23:43 into English, they punctuated it arbitrarily according to preconceived notions. An honest translator, when faced with more than one choice of translation, will choose the one that is in harmony with the rest of God's word" [*The Witness*, vol. 30, no. 8, August 1990].

Thus, I must conclude that the traditional teaching based on Luke 23:43 is entirely false, and that it is due to a false rendering of the passage (a misplaced comma). This passage in no way teaches the thief went to be with the Lord in Paradise *that day*. Instead, the Lord merely assured this thief that he would indeed be with Him in Paradise. When will this happen? ~ When the thief is resurrected on that last great day!

Chapter 9
Samuel, Saul and the Witch

In 1 Samuel 28 we find the story of king Saul seeking out the "Witch of Endor" and the apparent appearance of the deceased Samuel from somewhere beyond the grave. Some have appealed to this event to suggest the conscious existence of a person's "undying spirit" in some location beyond this present physical realm. However, is that truly what this account suggests? Or, are there *other* possible interpretations to this admittedly difficult passage in the Bible?

God had commanded His people: "Do not turn to mediums or spiritists; do not seek them out to be defiled by them. I am the Lord your God" (Leviticus 19:31). "As for the person who turns to mediums and to spiritists, to play the harlot after them, I will also set My face against that person and will cut him off from among his people" (Leviticus 20:6). "Now a man or a woman who is a medium or a spiritist shall surely be put to death" (Leviticus 20:27).

King Saul was not an overly righteous king, but to his credit he "had removed from the land those who were mediums and spiritists" (1 Samuel 28:3). Indeed, he had prescribed the death penalty for those who were found practicing this evil, godless craft (vs. 9-10). As one commentator astutely observed, however: "Although Saul had removed the sin of witchcraft from *the land*, he had not removed it from *his heart*." At a time of personal desperation, rather than turning to his God he turned to the forces of evil for guidance.

His fate for this folly is described in 1 Chronicles 10:13-14. "Saul died because he was unfaithful to the Lord; he did not keep the word of the Lord and even consulted a medium for guidance, and did not inquire of the Lord. So the Lord put him to death and turned the kingdom over to David son of Jesse." One interesting observation to this later summation of the events of 1 Samuel 28 is that there is *no mention whatsoever* of the "spirit" of Samuel having been called up. The text only states that Saul had consulted *with this woman* from Endor, a town on the north shoulder of the hill of Moreh, near Jezreel.

There has been tremendous debate over the centuries as to what exactly occurred that day when Saul consulted this woman who was practicing the "black arts." There is no question that this woman was *not* a servant of the Lord. If she *was* in league with any spiritual force, it was with Satan rather than God. The apostle Paul warns the brethren in Corinth that there is a very real danger associated with idolatry: it places those who embrace it in fellowship with the evil forces *behind* these godless practices. There are *real spirit beings* (demons) against which the godly struggle in this life. "For our struggle is not against flesh and blood, but against the rulers, against the powers, against the world forces of this darkness, against the spiritual forces of wickedness in the heavenly realms" (Ephesians 6:12). Thus, Paul warns his readers to stay away from such activities of darkness, because "I do not want you to become *sharers* (participants; fellowshippers) with demons" (1 Corinthians 10:20).

The woman from Endor was in fellowship with the forces of darkness; she was a participant with demons. I doubt that any person would seek to refute that. She stood in opposition to God in every way, and God's punishment for such was death.

This raises an interesting question, and, for the purpose of even *asking* this question, we must make some *assumptions*. *Assuming* that mortal man *is* in possession of an inherently immortal spirit-being which indwells him and which is incapable of ever being destroyed or dying, and which thus of necessity *must* exist consciously *somewhere* after being separated from the body at the moment of biological death ... *assuming* this, simply for the sake of argument in this present study, *is it possible* for a person who is in league with the forces of *evil* to call forth *righteous*, disembodied spirit-beings from their blissful abode? Can those serving Satan really yank a saved soul out of its spiritual repose? Do the wicked of this world have that kind of power?

It seems to me this is a very *grave* (pun intended) theological problem. Personally, I can *not* imagine how such could be the case. Dr. Lewis, in his book *Cults of the Dead*, wrote: "Was the woman actually able to raise up the righteous dead (i.e., *Satan* having power over the *saints*)?" [p. 115]. This is a very troubling question, and has bothered people for centuries. Can Satan actually reach into Paradise and drag "souls" out of there for his own devious purposes?

There are two major theories which have been put forward over the centuries to try and explain this passage of Scripture (as well as many minor, less logical, and at times almost ludicrous, theories):

THEORY ONE ~ *God Himself* intervened in this situation and by *His* power raised up Samuel to appear unto Saul. And the purpose was to deliver a message to Saul. There are some problems associated with this view, however, as one might well expect. Would God work hand-in-hand with a "witch" (as the *King James Version* describes her)? Also, keep in mind that from the text itself (1 Samuel 28) there is no indication that this appearance was at the hand of God; *nowhere* does it suggest *God* did this, but rather that the *woman* called him forth. One might perhaps *assume* God did it, but such is *not stated*; it is purely *conjecture* on the part of interpreters.

God certainly had the power to raise up Samuel and send him to Saul at this time with a message, had He chosen to do so. There is no doubt about that. But *did* God do this? Again, one may *assume* it, but one cannot *prove* it. Here's something else to consider: even if God *did* send Samuel to Saul at this time, this *in no way proves* the conscious existence of an "undying spirit-being" in some Hadean holding cell after the physical death of its "host body" and prior to the day of the resurrection of that body and final judgment. God could *just as easily* have raised Samuel's mortal remains from the dust of the ground, breathed life back into this dead body, sent him to deliver this message, and then returned Samuel to his slumber in the dust of the ground (Daniel 12:2). *That also* is a legitimate possibility, and one far more consistent with the remainder of Scripture pertaining to the nature and destiny of man. The text itself does not suggest *anything* about Samuel's state *prior* to this calling up. The *only* possible allusion is when Samuel says, "Why have you disturbed me by bringing me up?" (1 Samuel 28:15). This really does not "prove" *either* interpretation, however, as this statement could just as easily refer to being disturbed from his "sleep in the dust of the ground" as to his conscious bliss in some intermediate "holding area" which was interrupted by this summons.

Yes, it is certainly *possible* that God *could* have raised Samuel and sent him to Saul, but it is odd, is it not, that the character said to be Samuel (in 1 Samuel 28:15) *attributes* the raising up of himself to *Saul* and *this woman* from Endor. Why didn't this apparition acknowledge that it was *God* who raised him up? This is more than a little puzzling. Thus, at best, the Traditionalists seek to build their doctrine upon sweeping *assumptions* with *no* textual or contextual substantiation. That is poor hermeneutics, and additionally a mighty unstable foundation upon which to build a theology.

THEORY TWO -- The other major theory proposed is that this "being" who was "raised up" was *not Samuel at all -- if indeed there was even a being present* (remember: only the woman saw him; Saul never actually *saw* this being -- go back and check this out). It is possible this was a demon pretending to be Samuel. The woman, after all, was in league with demons, *not* with God or the righteous dead. If *she herself* saw something, what she saw *may* have been one of the very beings with whom she was in fellowship. The text actually seems to indicate she was *shocked* by what she saw, which has led some to speculate she was more of a "fake" (to earn money), and thus it surprised *even her* when something actually appeared, which apparently, from the text, only she could see.

The early church Fathers typically took one of two views: (1) Either God Himself raised Samuel from the dead and sent him to Saul (they simply could not abide the view that a "witch" could raise the *righteous* from the dead), or (2) this was "just demonic deceit, and what appeared was not really Samuel, but a demon in his guise" [*Origen and the Witch of Endor: Toward an Iconoclastic Typology*]. Some have even suggested that *God* Himself sent a *demon* to deliver this message, and perhaps even to frighten this woman into repentance, or to allow her, and Saul, to suffer the consequences of their delusion resulting from their association with the forces of evil. "And for this reason God will send upon them a deluding influence so that they might believe what is false" (2 Thessalonians 2:11). "And just as they did not see fit to acknowledge God any longer, *God gave them over*" to that which they had chosen in His place (Romans 1:24-32). The fact that the *biblical summary* of Saul's sin on this occasion (found in 1 Chronicles 10:13-14) *never mentions* Samuel being present at all, but *only* that Saul consulted with this *woman*, has led many to believe that this narrative was simply an example of "demonic deceit."

But what does one do about the *message* given that day by "Samuel"? Could this message have come from a demon? Would demons speak words of truth? And for what purpose? Let's not forget that Paul warns us to be aware of the fact that "deceitful workers disguise themselves as apostles of Christ" and "even Satan disguises himself as an angel of light. Therefore it is not surprising if his servants also disguise themselves as servants of righteousness" (2 Corinthians 11:13-15). Satan even quoted Scripture on occasion.

And don't forget the "spirit of divination" that possessed the slave girl (Acts 16), which kept crying out this message after Paul, "These men are bond-servants of the Most High God, who are proclaiming to you the way of salvation" (vs. 17). Paul cast out this evil spirit in the name of Jesus Christ, even though what was being proclaimed by that demon was *true*. We should never discount the possibility, indeed the *likelihood*, that the forces of evil will at times *speak words of truth* if in so doing it serves to further their ultimate deception and continue their undermining of God's purposes.

It is at least a *possibility* that a message of truth was indeed conveyed to Saul; one which was credible enough to make him believe he *was* hearing from Samuel, and perhaps even from God. Would this not, therefore, lend a sense of validity and credibility to the *testimony*, indeed the *work*, of this medium and spiritist? Would not Saul, the king, now perhaps be led to believe that these mediums and spiritists *were indeed* in contact with God Himself and the departed "spirits" of the righteous? Would this not perhaps lead Saul to rethink his ban on their activities, and thus give them a free hand throughout the land? Would Saul now be led to perhaps believe these mediums actually had the *approval* of God, since God had spoken to him through their mediation? Yes, Satan is a cunning and devious foe. It is at least *possible* this could have been the explanation for this "appearance" of "Samuel" to Saul, and it is certainly not beyond the power of Satan to perform such a feat of deception, nor is it outside the parameters of biblical teaching that God would *allow* such a delusion to come upon those who had persisted in rejecting His counsel. The forces of evil, Jesus warns, "will show great signs and wonders, so as to mislead, if possible, even the elect" (Matthew 24:24). This very likely is exactly what Saul encountered that day.

Dr. Kretzmann writes, "That this apparition could *not* have been the real Samuel is evident ... the devil has no jurisdiction over those who have fallen asleep in the Lord." He goes on to warn, "What the diviners or clairvoyants state is not all falsehood and deception; for the devil is able, with God's permission, to perform works which, to all appearances, are identical with miracles, and to uncover the future. Christians, therefore, will take the greatest care in fleeing from the temptation of consulting such soothsayers" [*Popular Commentary of the Bible*, vol. 1, p. 505].

As a side note: there is an interesting passage in the *Babylonian Talmud* which shows how some of the ancient Jews perceived this event: "A Sadducee once said to Rabbi Abhu, 'Ye say that the souls of the righteous are treasured up under the throne of glory; how then had the witch of Endor power to bring up the prophet Samuel by necromancy?' The Rabbi replied, 'Because that occurred within twelve months after his death; for we are taught that during twelve months after death the body is preserved, and the soul soars up and down, but that after twelve months the body is destroyed, and the soul goes up, never to return'" [*Treatise Shabbath*, fol. 88, col. 2]. So I guess there is a twelve month grace period where one can still capture a "roaming soul" before it is secure in a place of repose! Really?! This has about as much authority and believability as many of the fanciful theories of the "afterlife" promoted in more recent times in Christian circles.

Well, what can be said *with any certainty* about this event in 1 Samuel 28? Actually, very little. There is much we just don't know, and probably never will know this side of heaven. We can *speculate* a great deal, and form numerous *opinions*, and make countless *assumptions*, but we have very little in this passage with which to form definitive *doctrine* with regard to such matters as the nature of man or the nature of what occurs between death and the resurrection. Even if one takes the events of this account literally, as most Traditionalists do, and even if this "witch" (or even *God*, for that matter) *did* raise up the real Samuel, it in no way proves conscious existence of "immortal spirit-beings" in some so-called "Intermediate State," for Samuel could *just as easily*, and far more consistently with Scriptural teaching, have been raised from an *unconscious sleep* in the dust of the ground than from a conscious state in some nether realm (the same argument being true of *Moses'* appearance at the Transfiguration of Christ, by the way ~ Matt. 17:3). There is simply insufficient information in this account from which to formulate *any* doctrine one way or the other. Indeed, the whole incident raises far more questions than it provides answers, at least with regard to the nature of man and his eternal destiny.

As mentioned earlier, nothing is said of any conversation of Saul directly with Samuel himself, but rather the inquiry was *directed to*, and the guidance *came from*, the medium (1 Chronicles 10:13-14). Indeed, 1 Samuel 28:6 makes it very clear that God had chosen *not* to respond to Saul *through any means.* "When Saul inquired of the Lord, the Lord did not answer him, either by dreams or by Urim or by prophets." God *was not speaking to Saul* at this point in Saul's life. This is brought out again in vs. 15-16 where both Saul and "Samuel" make it clear that *the Lord had departed from Saul and was no longer speaking to him through any means.* Does it not seem rather odd, therefore, that God would suddenly decide to speak to Saul through a "witch," or through one supposedly raised from the dead (Samuel), when He would *not* speak through any of the normal means available to Saul?

Frankly, I seriously question whether this "being" (which Saul *never saw*, by the way) was actually Samuel. Even if the woman was not speaking herself, and Saul heard some other voice, it could easily have been the work of a demon. I think it is really important to keep in mind that this chapter in question begins with the clear statement that *God was not speaking to Saul by any means*. That is a very important point. Isn't it just possible that fact remains constant *throughout* the passage? It just may be that this whole event was *not* from God at all, but a demonstration of the power of evil over one who has given himself over to *it* instead of to God. The forces of evil can be very, very deceiving and misleading in a person's life, and will ultimately prove destructive, as it did with Saul. The Bible never declares that *any* of this event came from God. If anything, the opposite seems far more likely.

One final thought -- in 1 Samuel 28:19 this apparition, which Saul thought was Samuel, declared, "tomorrow you and your sons *will be with me*." Well, this turned out to be a true statement, for the next day Saul and his sons were *dead*, just as Samuel was. However, where exactly *was* Samuel, according to the *traditional* perspective? The traditionalists would claim his "immortal soul" was in Paradise. However, is that where *Saul* would be? Enjoying the comforts of eternal bliss? Snuggled up in peaceful rest in Abraham's bosom? The biblical text gives strong evidence that Saul most likely will *not* experience eternal salvation. His death is not portrayed in any way as a spiritual victory. Thus, in what sense would Saul and his sons be *with* Samuel? The only view truly consistent with Scripture is that they would *both* be in the dust of the ground ... *dead* ... awaiting together the resurrection to judgment. Thus, if this account is taken literally, we must ask of these Traditionalists: *Were Saul and his sons saved?* Are they and Samuel now *together* ("you and your sons *will be with me*") in Abraham's bosom, experiencing the joys of their salvation? I have been asking this question of the Traditionalists for years, and *not one* has yet ever given an answer. One is left to wonder why!

Chapter 10
Preaching to Spirits in Prison

"For Christ ... was put to death in the body but made alive by the Spirit, through whom also He went and preached to the spirits in prison who disobeyed long ago when God waited patiently in the days of Noah while the ark was being built." ~ 1 Peter 3:18-20

Just exactly *who are* these "spirits in prison," and *how* and *when* did Jesus Christ "preach" unto them, and *what* did He preach unto them? Some scholars have declared this the most difficult passage in the Bible to interpret. The great reformer Martin Luther (1483-1546) has perhaps given the best response of all time, however, when he said, "I don't know *what* Peter means here!" This passage has certainly been the cause of tremendous debate throughout the centuries, and countless theories have arisen in an attempt to explain its meaning. Following are the major interpretations proposed as to the significance of this text.

FIRST ~ Christ went to *Hell* or *Hades* (both views have been advanced) between the time of His death and resurrection and preached to the lost souls in torment there. For example, the *Symbolum Apostolorum* (the *Apostles' Creed*), which was developed between the second and ninth centuries, states, in part, "I believe in God the Father Almighty, Maker of heaven and earth. And in Jesus Christ His only Son our Lord; who was conceived by the Holy Ghost, born of the Virgin Mary, suffered under Pontius Pilate, was crucified, dead, and buried; *He descended into hell*; the third day He rose again from the dead; He ascended into heaven, and sitteth on the right hand of God the Father Almighty." That Jesus literally went to *Hell* to preach to the lost was the view of Clement of Alexandria (c. 200 A.D.), among others. Generally, it is felt by those who embrace this particular view that the *only* lost souls preached to on that occasion, however, were the ones from the time of the flood. All *other* lost souls were simply ignored.

There are obviously some major problems associated with this interpretation, not the least of which is the "doctrine of the second chance." Was Jesus really extending the opportunity of salvation to "lost souls" already in torment? And if so, why *only* to these *select few* lost souls, and not to *all* lost souls? *The Pulpit Commentary* states, "*If* this passage *does* mean that Christ preached to the dead, it only speaks of the dead in the days of Noah; it seems incredible that these comparative few should be singled out from the great mass of mankind for so great a blessing. I might remind you, too, that *if* these words mean that the impenitent dead have a second chance, they stand alone in Scripture, at least as far as I am aware" [vol. 22, p. 158].

SECOND -- The *Roman Catholic* view (which was put forward primarily by Cardinal Bellarmine, c. 1600 A.D.) is that Christ went to the place known as *Limbo* between His death and resurrection. His purpose for going there at that time was to release the souls of the righteous who had repented prior to the flood, but who could not enter heaven until after the coming of the Messiah. Thus, *Limbo* was the abode between heaven and hell where the disembodied spirits of the OT saints were kept in waiting, according to this view. I don't think we have to go into too terribly much investigation into Scripture to discover that such a view has no basis in biblical Truth.

THIRD ~ A third view is that during the time between His death and resurrection Jesus preached to the "fallen angels" who were being kept in bonds until Judgment (in a special location known as *Tartarus* ~ 2 Peter 2:4). These were also the ones (according to this view) who were known as the "sons of God," and who took wives for themselves from among the daughters of men (Gen. 6:1-4). This interpretation was promoted quite vigorously at the turn of the previous century by Friedrich Spitta.

FOURTH ~ The fourth major view, one held by some of the modern scholars, is that *after* the resurrection, when Jesus ascended into heaven, He passed through the Hadean realm, and also through the areas where fallen angels were being held, and proclaimed His *victory* to them as He returned to the Father. This was not a proclamation for the purpose of *saving* them, but rather a declaration of their ultimate eternal *defeat*.

FIFTH ~ Personally, I do not believe *any* of the above theories have a great deal of merit. The major interpretation which I am convicted best fits the context, and which best harmonizes with the remainder of Scripture, is that it was the Spirit of Christ who preached the message of salvation *through* His servant Noah unto the people of Noah's day, and that this proclamation occurred *during* those years *prior* to the flood. This was also the view of St. Augustine (c. 400 A.D.), was the view which dominated the theological scene for centuries, and is the interpretation embraced by most scholars today.

We know that Noah was "a *preacher* of righteousness" (2 Peter 2:5), so we know that these lost beings (bound and imprisoned *in sin*) were having the message of salvation *proclaimed* to them through *his efforts*. We also know that the OT proclaimers were preaching their message to the lost people about them *by means of* "the Spirit of Christ *within* them" (1 Peter 1:10-11). Therefore, Peter, in the context of the very book wherein we find our difficult passage, *confirms* for us that the "Spirit of Christ" was *proclaiming* the "good news" *through the OT spokesmen of God*. And *among* those OT proclaimers, according to Peter, was *Noah*. Thus, Christ was preaching to those people *before* their physical deaths, *prior to* the coming of the flood, *through Noah*.

John Wesley (1703-1791) wrote in his commentary on Peter's epistles, "By which Spirit He preached = *Through* the ministry of Noah. To the spirits in prison = The unholy men before the flood." Jamieson, Fausset & Brown, in their classic "*Commentary Critical and Explanatory on the Whole Bible*" (1871), wrote, "Christ, who in our times came in the flesh, *in the days of Noah* preached in Spirit *by Noah* to the spirits *then* in prison." They then point to Isaiah 61:1 to show that those who are in *bondage* to sin and its wages (death) are characterized as being "*in prison*." They continue, "So the same Spirit of Christ (who preached *through* the OT spokesmen -- 1 Pet. 1:11) enabled *Noah*, amidst reproach and trials, to preach to the disobedient spirits *fast bound* in wrath." *Disobedient*, not *disembodied*. Adam Clarke stated that it was "by the ministry of Noah" that the Spirit of Christ preached to "the inhabitants of the antediluvian world" [*Clarke's Commentary*, vol. 6, p. 861].

Clem and Dillard Thurman (editors of the *Gospel Minutes*), have long defended this interpretation vigorously in their publication. Clem, for example, in an article dated April 27, 1990, wrote that this view "is *clearly* shown" in the context of the passage. Dillard, in an article dated Nov. 23, 1979, wrote, "There is nothing in the passage that suggests that Jesus preached *while dead*. The 'spirits in prison' are very definitely placed in the days of Noah, and it is also shown that Christ (as the eternal Word) was preaching *through* Noah *by* the Holy Spirit."

Dillard, in that same article, further writes, "Notice carefully *what* is said. Jesus was put to death in the flesh, and died *like any mortal man*. But He was quickened, or made alive by the Spirit. By what Spirit? By the same Spirit by which He once preached to spirits imprisoned by sin and Satan in the days of Noah! *When* did this happen? The passage plainly states it: 'When once the long-suffering of God waited in the days of Noah.' The word 'when' is an adverb of time that tells *when* the action took place: in the days of Noah! The idea of the Son of God being off on a preaching junket for the three days and nights that His body was in the tomb is utterly foreign to any Bible teaching! *If false doctrines had not first brought forth this fanciful idea, this passage would not have been twisted to support the error.*" Albert Barnes declared, "...this whole passage refers to His preaching to the antediluvians in the time of Noah ... no argument can be based on it in proof that He went to preach to them *after* their death, and while His body was lying in the grave" [*Barnes Notes on the New Testament*].

In the final analysis, the view that best harmonizes with Scripture is the one that declares the Spirit of Christ, speaking *through* Noah, preached to those who were in bondage to sin during the time prior to the flood. I don't find anything in this view inconsistent with the remainder of God's Word, whereas I *do* find problems with the *other* interpretations. In short, I find nothing whatsoever in this passage which suggests the concept of some Hadean holding area for disembodied, eternal spirit-beings, or that Jesus went and preached to them during the time between His crucifixion and resurrection. Such teaching, in my view, is *imposed* upon this passage (*eisegesis*) rather than honestly and legitimately *drawn from it* (*exegesis*).

Chapter 11
Spirits of Just Men Made Perfect

    I am thoroughly convicted that the Scriptures teach the *holistic* view of man. One of the important truths conveyed in the OT Scriptures, as the nature of man is considered, is that man is a *unified whole*, rather than a loose fusion of separate and disparate entities. It was much later that the pagan nations began to influence the thinking of the people of God in the direction of two (dichotomy) or three (trichotomy) distinct parts to man. This dualistic manner of conceptualizing human beings has persisted throughout most of Christian history, yet such false notions only began to influence *Jewish* thinking during the so-called Intertestamental Period. Such was *never* the biblical view. The traditional teaching (to which a great many of us in Christendom have been exposed all our lives) that some "immortal being" resides within our physical bodies, and that this "eternal spirit being" is finally released from its fleshly prison to a greater spiritual existence by the death of its human host, is a *fabrication of pagan philosophy* (Plato, for example, was a bold advocate of such a view), but *never* a truth promoted in God's Word.

As we all know, however, there are a few passages that, at least on the surface, *seem* to promote the position that some "eternal, immortal spirit being" dwells within our bodies, and that this being (the "real" us) soars off to a realm of either eternal bliss or misery at the precise moment of physical death. For example, the account of an unnamed rich man and a beggar called Lazarus (Luke 16:19-31) is regarded by some as "proof positive" that such a "spirit being" travels to some "intermediate state" at the moment of physical death. I don't believe this *parable* even remotely teaches such a doctrine. Others feel our Lord's promise to the thief on the cross is yet *another* proof of immediate transport to paradise upon physical death. What about the fact that we are said to be created in the "image of God"? And we could list many other examples from Scripture.

One such passage, and this was brought to my attention by an individual who was examining his own beliefs on this topic, is Hebrews 12:23. This disciple of Christ wrote, "Would you help me understand a difficult text? I *want* to believe in *Conditional Immortality*, for which you so vigorously argue, but I am having a tough time making sense of Hebrews 12:23, specifically with reference to that part of the verse which speaks of '*spirits* of righteous men made perfect.' I have consulted many commentaries, but they all explain this in a *dualistic* fashion. I know you have surely thought about this verse. Might you be so kind as to help me understand this?" As I alluded to previously, part of the problem in properly interpreting such passages lies in our previous perspectives on the nature of man that we *bring to* the text. If one has been *indoctrinated* to perceive man as a composite of *distinct* living entities (mortal and immortal), then one's understanding of the passage will be greatly influenced by this doctrine. Before one ever takes an isolated passage, such as the one we find in Hebrews 12:23, and seeks to understand some portion of it, one must invest the time and energy to thoroughly, and *without bias*, examine the entirety of God's Word with regard to the *overall topic* in question (which will deal with the nature of man and the nature of his eternal destiny). Only when one truly comes to understand the "big picture," theologically speaking, can one hope to reconcile *single statements* in Scripture with the *whole* of biblical teaching.

Those who have embraced the pre-Christian, anti-biblical *Platonic* perception of the nature and destiny of man, for example, will clearly view the statement in Heb. 12:23 as an endorsement of the view that some "immortal spirit being" dwelling inside the physical body departs at death to live more fully in another realm, while its host body rots away within this temporal realm. For example, Robert A. Peterson, in his exchange with Edward Fudge (which has been preserved in the book: "*Two Views of Hell: A Biblical and Theological Dialogue*"), cites this passage as evidence that "the Bible teaches the continued existence of the *immaterial part* of human beings after death and before the resurrection of the body" [p. 167]. He had previously opined within the text of this written dialogue, "The expression 'the spirits of righteous men made perfect' refers to believers who have died and gone on to be with the Lord. They have not ceased to exist at death. They exist as *disembodied spirits* who experienced entire sanctification when they died" [p. 105]. This is the explanation of many within Christendom, and I am sure we have all heard it taught and preached time and again. In fact, we've likely heard it so *often* that we tend to accept it as fact *without examination*. And, as with many other such traditional dogmas, we may well have blindly, and tragically, embraced that which is *false*.

The ultimate hope of mankind is *not* that he *inherently possesses* within his physical body some "immortal spirit being" that is utterly incapable of ceasing *to be*: a spirit being *just as immortal* as God Himself. Instead, the ultimate hope of man is in the *promise of God*, demonstrated in the *resurrection* of Jesus, that he will be raised from the dust of the ground and *given* immortality. Our Lord "*alone* possesses immortality" (1 Timothy 6:16). Therefore, this is *not* a quality *inherent* to man. It *can* be *conferred*, however. Jesus

Christ "brought life and immortality to light through the gospel" (2 Timothy 1:10). Eternal life is a *great gift from God* through Jesus Christ, not an *inherent right of man* because he possesses within his fleshy body an immortal spirit being that not even God Himself can destroy. Paul declares that "eternal life" will be *given* to those who "*seek for* immortality" (Romans 2:7). So, why are men "seeking for" that which they *already possess*?! The reality is: the Lord *alone* possesses it; thus, He alone can bestow it. And that *gift* of grace is through His Son. "God has *given* us eternal life, and this life is in His Son. He who has the Son has the life; he who does *not* have the Son does *not* have the life" (1 John 5:11-12). Eternal life ~ immortality ~ is a *gift* from Him who alone possesses it, and that gift is reserved for those who have *sought it* by means of a *relationship* with Him during our sojourn in this temporal realm. At the *resurrection*, all will be raised from the dust of the ground to face the One who *alone* possesses *that which we seek*. Upon some this blessed gift will be bestowed; the rest will experience the second *death* (i.e., life and immortality will be *denied* them). Although mankind continues his journey here below (with some already sleeping in the dust of the ground, and others yet to be born), from the view of the Throne the human journey stands *completed*. He who stands outside of time and space, sees the whole as a *completed* reality. Appreciating this divine perception is important to our interpretive efforts, as it finds its way into certain expressions of His inspired revelation to man. This is especially seen in the book of *Revelation*, for example, where God sees (and *portrays* for us) the consummation of all things as a *completed* reality, although from *man's* perspective (bound within time and space) it continues to unfold.

With all of this firmly in mind, in the book of *Hebrews* we are presented with a multi-faceted overview of the critical *distinctives* between God's different covenants with mankind, with the focus being on the *supremacy* of His current covenant, "a better covenant, which has been enacted on better promises" (Hebrews 8:6), over His previous dealings with His creation. It's not that the particulars of that which came before was defective, it's simply the superiority of *substance* over *shadow*. When one's children grow and mature, one's relationship with them also undergoes *change*. This is no less true of man's relationship with his Creator as we are collectively guided by His Spirit into a more mature covenant relationship; a covenant in which we have moved from *legislation* to *liberty*. Time and again in this epistle we find the old contrasted with the new. Such is the *context* of that portion of Hebrews wherein we find our present "problem" passage. *Contextually,* Christians are being informed that when they come to the Father through the Son (when they "come to Mt. Zion"), it is a far *different* experience than when the people approached their God at Mt. Sinai. The writer of this epistle points out the fear that gripped the people of God during the latter experience, and then contrasts this with the experience of those who enter His presence through the sacrifice of His Son.

According to an in-depth study of this passage conducted by the *Biblical Research Institute* (which one may find online at their web site), "The experience at Sinai is contrasted with that of Christian believers to demonstrate that theirs is superior. By faith Christians can see themselves present on Mount Zion, within the heavenly Jerusalem, in the presence of the heavenly community. What is still future is described as a present reality apprehended by faith." As the concluding phrase suggests, "faith is the assurance of things hoped for, the conviction of things not seen" (Hebrews 11:1). I am not yet standing perfected in that new heavens and earth, yet *by faith* I am fully *assured* that what my God already perceives as *done,* I will one day *do*. Thus, in an *eternal* sense, that for which we *seek,* within our space/time sojourn, is already *secured* outside of such temporal constraints. It is *by faith* that we embrace this reality, even though it is yet *future* for us. "All these died in faith, without receiving the promises, but having seen them and having welcomed them from a distance" (Hebrews 11:13).

As the apostle Paul confidently stated just before his death, "I *know* whom I have believed and I am convinced that He is able to guard what I have entrusted to Him *until that day*" (2 Timothy 1:12). Paul placed his very life ... indeed, his *hope of life* (immortality) ... into the hands of his God, knowing that on the day of *resurrection* he would discover his trust had not been misplaced. He who promised is faithful. We, like Jesus, will not be abandoned to the *grave*, but will be raised up to receive the gift of life "at His coming" (1 Corinthians 15:23). Yes, we can *envision* ourselves, even now, within the company of those gathered on Mt. Zion within the New Jerusalem (the Bride of the Lamb) ~ the perfected of all time: past, present and future ~ and even though we may return to the dust of the ground, having *yet* to experience that glorious event, we close our eyes in the "sleep of death," knowing that we shall awake to the reality we had previously perceived *by faith*.

What a glorious *assembly* that will be when all those who love the Lord will *finally* and *forever* be together in the eternal city of our God on the holy mount (Zion). We will be gathered into the company of the angelic host: assembled with "myriads of angels" (Hebrews 12:22). We will be with our God (vs. 23) and His Son (vs. 24). All those who are enrolled in heaven (whose names appear in the book of life), all those who are complete, *mature*, perfected *in Him* (which we are even now, *by Him*, regarded as being), all those who are the called out ones of all time, will be assembled together in a holy gathering where the expressions of joy and praise will be beyond anything we can begin to imagine. What a *powerful* contrast, in both scope and spirit, to the *previous* gathering of God's people at Mt. Sinai. The latter (at Zion) will most certainly be a far superior assembly.

Many scholars believe that the reference to the "first-born" ~ those within this great assembly thusly characterized ~ are the people of Israel (i.e., the redeemed of the old covenant). In Exodus 4:22-23, God characterizes the Israelites as "My first-born." If so, then these redeemed ones would "not be made perfect (complete)" without, or separate and apart from, our own completeness (perfection) as the redeemed under the new covenant. This may well be what the Hebrew writer had in mind in Hebrews 11:39-40 ~ "All these, having gained approval through their faith, did not receive what was promised, because God provided something better for us, so that apart from us they should not be made perfect." Again, we see the contrast, and the superiority, of the new covenant over the old, and yet those under the old are incorporated into the great assembly at Mt. Zion. Thus, "by one offering He has perfected for all time those who are sanctified" (Hebrews 10:14). In *our* coming to God we join with all *others* who came to God by the same path ~ *faith*, and together we are perfected (made complete) by the one sacrifice given for all. In this way, in the sight of our God, who is the Judge of all men, we are rightly regarded as "spirits of righteous/just men made perfect."

The word "spirit" is what seems to *confuse* people in this passage. We have been conditioned to believe it refers to some "immortal spirit being" dwelling within our fleshly body. "The term 'spirit' is used several times in the book of Hebrews, but it *never* designates a disembodied spirit" [*Biblical Research Institute*]. Indeed, the Hebrew writer declares that even those saints *still living* have been "*perfected*" by our Lord's sacrificial act. Thus, to assume that this is a state achieved only *after* death is to completely miss the point of the teaching of this fine epistle. In a dissertation presented by R. Bryan Kane titled "Zion in Hebrews 12:22-23," this biblical researcher observed that the root word from which we get the term "perfect/perfected" appears 25 times in this epistle, and it refers "to the perfect accomplishing of Christ's mission ... and the Holy Spirit's sanctifying work" on the hearts and minds of believers. Kane classifies this as "a 'now and not yet' eschatological paradigm." Jesus is the "perfecter of faith" (Hebrews 12:2), and this perfection is available to all who by faith receive *His* faith.

The term "spirit" most certainly does not need to signify some *being* of a different dimension that may, in some way, be indwelling physical bodies of this dimension (such is the philosophy of Platonic dualism, not the holistic teaching of Scripture). It is more commonly used to denote the spiritual character of a man: his emotions, intellect, personality; that which tends to motivate us from within. The term "spirit" is not infrequently used in Scripture to represent the less physical aspects of man's being. Thus, one might be "mean-*spirited*" or have a broken or contrite *spirit* (Psalm 51). These terms do *not* suggest an immortal being trapped inside the body, but merely reflect the mental and emotional aspects of man's nature. "In both the Old and New Testaments, spirit is used of humans and of other beings. When used of humans, spirit is associated with a *wide range* of functions including thinking and understanding, emotions, attitudes, and intentions. ... spirit is used extensively with human emotions. ... A variety of attitudes and intentions are associated with spirit" [*Holman Bible Dictionary*, p. 1300]. Thus, we are all made of "*like spirit*" with our Lord Jesus; made complete, mature in Him (i.e., of like mind, attitude, purpose), just as Paul said Timothy was of "kindred spirit" with himself (Philippians 2:20). Our goal should always be: "Have this attitude in yourselves which was also in Christ Jesus" (Philippians 2:5).

Adam Clarke points out in his commentary on this very passage that "'the spirits of just men made perfect' are the *full-grown* Christians: those who are *justified* by the blood and *sanctified* by the Spirit of Christ" [vol. 6, p. 782]. In contrast to this, he mentions those nominal "Christians," who, consistent with a *different* "spirit," engage in conflict with one another. When James and John desired to incinerate a Samaritan village, Jesus rebuked them, declaring, "You do not know what kind of *spirit* you are of" (Luke 9:55). Jesus wasn't referring to some "immortal spirit being" dwelling inside of them, but to their attitudes and intentions and motivations. As we grow and develop *in Jesus*, and through the transforming power of *His Spirit* who indwells us, we can *mature* "in spirit," becoming "conformed to the image of His Son" (Romans 8:29).

Frankly, I find absolutely nothing either *textually* or *contextually* that even remotely suggests to me that the writer of *Hebrews* was providing "proof positive" that some immortal spirit being trapped inside our physical bodies finds it ultimate freedom and perfection at the moment we drop dead physically. On the other hand, I find great comfort and joy in the assurance conveyed that our Mt. Zion experience is one far superior in every way to the Mt. Sinai experience of our forefathers in the faith. The beauty of the supremacy of the former over the latter is that it includes all the redeemed who lived and died in faith prior to the one great sacrifice that brings us all together into the company of the heavenly host as the *One Family*, now made *complete*. Though viewed as *accomplished* from the perspective of the Throne, it is a reality we, who are *in Him*, confidently *await* during the days of our own sojourn, assured that whether we're asleep or awake, when He comes we shall know the fullness and perfection of His eternal embrace *firsthand*. Lord, hasten that day!

Chapter 12
Dead Body – Dead Faith

The glorious Good News brought to us from above is that we are saved by the grace of God through faith in the free gift of His beloved Son, who redeemed us from the curse of sin by taking that sin upon Himself and then offering Himself as the once-for-all perfect atoning sacrifice on the cross. In Him we have been redeemed; His blood covers us and continually cleanses us of all sin; we are secure in His loving embrace. We receive this gift in simple faith, and we then daily display our love and gratitude for this gift in our attitudes and actions. With the help of the indwelling Spirit, we are increasingly transformed into the image of Jesus, bearing spiritual fruit in our lives as we journey toward the promise of that eternal dwelling in the new heavens and earth. We are saved not by any meritorious act on our part ~ the dead cannot enliven and raise themselves ~ but solely by His grace. We now live because He loves us; we now serve because we love Him.

Although it is not within us to enliven ourselves (this is the work of God's Spirit), it *is* within us (again, with the help of His indwelling Spirit) to enliven our faith in evidentiary acts of love and gratitude. It is one thing to *believe* (have faith) in God, and what He freely offers by virtue of His Son's sacrifice, it is quite another to *display* the reality of that belief (faith). James informs us that even the demons believe (have faith) in God, trembling at the very thought, yet that belief does not, in and of itself, save them (James 2:19). John pointed out that many of the Jewish rulers "believed (had faith) in Him, but because of the Pharisees they would not confess their faith for fear they would be put out of the synagogue, for they loved praise from men more than praise from God" (John 12:42-43). It is one thing to *say* you have faith, it is quite another to *show* it. The former, devoid of the latter, is faith devoid of life. James declared, "Faith by itself, if it is not accompanied by action, is dead" (James 2:17). I like the way *The Message* words some of what James says in this chapter: "Does merely talking about faith indicate that a person really has it? ... Isn't it obvious that God-talk without God-acts is outrageous nonsense? ... Use your heads! Do you suppose for a minute that you can cut faith and works in two and not end up with a corpse on your hands?"

James summed up his argument in this chapter with this statement: "As the body is dead when there is no breath left in it, so faith divorced from deeds is lifeless as a corpse" (James 2:26, *New English Bible*). A body devoid of breath is inanimate; it does nothing; it lies there lifeless. In the same way, faith devoid of any evidentiary action on the part of the one professing said faith, is inanimate; it does nothing; it lies there lifeless. A body that will not breathe accomplishes nothing; neither does a faith that will not show itself. Neither is *alive*; both are *dead*. James, to illustrate his point, tells us how both Abraham and Rahab demonstrated the vitality of their faith: showing it to be alive by their actions. Although it was not their actions that justified them (they were justified by their faith, as Paul points out in Romans 4), nevertheless their actions visibly validated the genuineness of their faith, demonstrating their spiritual resolve to actively *live* by faith, rather than just giving empty *lip-service* to it.

There are some disciples, however, who have a problem with the statement in James 2:26 (as worded in several versions and translations). The problem lies in the use of the word "spirit." The *New International Version*, for example, reads, "As the body without *the spirit* is dead, so faith without deeds is dead." Other major translations also employ the word "spirit" in this passage [*KJV, NASB, RSV, ESV, HCSB, ASV*]. Although this is not necessarily an *incorrect* rendering, it can be a somewhat *misleading* one. The Greek word used by James in the text is *pneuma*, which, although it can be translated "spirit," and often is, primarily signifies "breath." The use of the word "spirit," unfortunately, conveys to the minds of many today the Platonic concept of some immaterial, immortal being trapped within a physical body that is freed to greater life at the moment of physical death. Thus, for those who have embraced this doctrine, a body without the spirit means *to them* a dead body from which the "immortal soul" has "flown off to heaven" (or hell). Needless to say, such a doctrine, in my view, is about as far from biblical truth as one can get.

Those who embrace the Platonic view of the nature of man, however, delight in the wording of James 2:26 in the above mentioned versions of the Bible, for, on the surface, it does seem to endorse their view (based upon how these people typically understand the term "spirit" -- *i.e.*, "immortal soul"). Guy N. Woods insists that the term *pneuma* "refers, in this instance, to the immortal nature of man" [*A Commentary on the Epistle of James*, p. 151]. "The body is the animal frame of man which houses the spirit: the immortal nature" [*ibid*]. "The spirit (the immortal nature) is eternal and therefore not subject to dissolution or decay" [*ibid*, p. 152]. If, on the other hand, the Greek word *pneuma* is allowed to signify "breath," which is its primary meaning, the passage conveys a much different message to our minds. Notice how the following versions render the text of James 2:26.

Contemporary English Version ~ Anyone who doesn't breathe is dead, and faith that doesn't do anything is just as dead!

New English Bible ~ As the body is dead when there is no breath left in it, so faith divorced from deeds is lifeless as a corpse.

New American Bible ~ Be assured, then, that faith without works is as dead as a body without breath.

New Living Translation ~ Just as the body is dead without breath, so also faith is dead without good works.

God's Word Translation ~ A body that doesn't breathe is dead. In the same way, faith that does nothing is dead.

Worldwide English NT ~ A body is dead if it does not breathe. In the same way, believing is dead if it does not do anything good.

It is my conviction, based upon the consistent teaching about the nature of man throughout Scripture, that this is the far better rendering, and certainly better represents the truth James sought to convey. I am certainly not alone in that belief. Dr. W. Robertson Nicoll, in *The Expositor's Greek Testament*, suggests "breath" is the preferred translation of the word *pneuma* [vol. 4, p. 29]. Another noted Greek scholar, Dr. A. T. Robertson, translates the phrase as: "apart from breath." He goes on to observe, "It is not easy to tell when one is dead, but the absence of a sign of breath on a glass before the mouth and nose is proof of death." He adds that James' illustration here is a "startling picture of dead faith in our churches and church members with only a name to live, as in Revelation 3:2" [*Word Pictures in the New Testament*]. "There is no reason for thinking that James intends to give *pneuma* the meaning 'spirit' and not 'breath'" [R. C. H. Lenski, *The Interpretation of the Epistle of James*, p. 598]. Lenski continues: "Absence proves deadness: absence of breath, deadness of the body; absence of works, deadness of the faith" [*ibid*]. Dr. John Gill (1697-1771), an English pastor and biblical scholar, and "the first Baptist to write a complete systematic theology and the first to write a verse-by-verse commentary of the entire Bible," had this to say about what James wrote: "This simile is made use of to illustrate what the apostle had asserted in James 2:17, that a body, when the breath is gone out of it, is dead, and without motion, and useless; ... the body without breath is a carcass" [*Exposition of the Entire Bible*]. Matthew Henry (1662-1714), in his classic *Commentary on the Whole Bible*, observes, "As the body without the breath is dead, so is faith without works: ... works are the companions of faith, as breathing is of life."

The obvious point of the passage is: just as breath brings animation to my body, so do godly acts bring animation to my faith. Just as the former reflects *flesh-life*, so do the latter reflect *faith-life*. "Unless our faith is of that kind which will produce holy living, it has no more of the characteristics of true religion than a dead body has of a living man" [Albert Barnes, *Notes on the Bible*]. "If faith produces no fruit of good living, that fact proves that it is dead, that it has no power, and that it is of no value" [*ibid*]. "James compares faith without works to a body without breath. ... We are to understand the body-breath relationship in terms of Jewish Christian anthropology. That is, the separation of the two does not produce a type of release for the 'spirit' (as in Orphic-philosophical thought which spoke of the body as a tomb or prison), but rather results in a dead corpse. The Greek dualistic thought would not comport well with what James has been arguing. The source behind James' analogy here may be Genesis 2:7. *Pneuma* carries with it the OT idea of 'life-giving breath.' A body without breath is dead. ... As breath enables a body to live, likewise works produce a living faith" [Ralph P. Martin, *Word Biblical Commentary*, vol. 48: James, p. 98].

James seeks to move the disciple of Christ from lifeless passivity to lively activity. To those who *say* they have faith, James simply issues the challenge: *show* it. If it is truly *vital* it will be *visible*. "I will show you my faith by what I do" (James 2:18). James comments on this further in the next chapter: "Who is wise and understanding among you? Let him *show it* by his good life, by deeds done in the humility that comes from wisdom" (James 3:13). Too many Christians appear more as corpses propped in pews inside a building than active, vibrant disciples with a functioning faith visible to their communities. Our faith must *come alive*, and that doesn't happen when it is hidden away from view. In other words, it must be active. "That faith which lies only in the cold assent of the intellect to a system of divinity is more like a lifeless corpse than a living man" [*The Pulpit Commentary*, vol. 21, James, p. 39]. "A person may boast that he possesses faith, but if the evidence of good works is lacking, such faith is spurious, hypocritical, valueless. Genuine faith is never without good works. For just as the body without breath is dead, so faith without works is dead" [Dr. Paul E. Kretzmann, *Popular Commentary of the Bible*, The NT, vol. 2, p. 506]. "James is teaching that faith without works is simply a cold orthodoxy, lacking spiritual vibrancy. James' concern is more practical than theological. The real issue for these believers is the absence or presence of a freshness, vitality and energy in their faith. When a Christian engages in practical deeds to benefit others, James says faith comes alive" [John F. Hart, *How To Energize Our Faith*].

Chapter 13
Three Dead Jewish Patriarchs

One of the central tenets of the Christian faith has always been the resurrection of the dead. Indeed, the resurrection of the body of Jesus from His borrowed tomb on the third day not only declared in a powerful way that He was the Son of God (Romans 1:4), but it also assures His disciples of their own resurrection on that last day when He comes to claim His bride. Paul tells the Corinthian brethren that if Christ Jesus has not been raised, then "your faith is futile ... and those who have fallen asleep in Christ have perished" (1 Corinthians 15:17-18). "But, Christ *has* been raised from the dead, the firstfruits of those who have fallen asleep. For as by a man came death, by a man has come also the resurrection of the dead. For as in Adam all die, so also in Christ shall all be made alive. But each in his own order: Christ the firstfruits, then at His coming those who belong to Christ. Then comes the end" (1 Corinthians 15:20-24a). Paul is clearly speaking of the death and resurrection of the physical body, a resurrection assured by the glorious resurrection of the body of Jesus following His own death and burial. To the brethren in Thessalonica, some of whom were becoming concerned about their loved ones who had died, Paul offered comfort by saying that their firm belief in the fact "that Jesus died and rose again" (1 Thessalonians 4:14) was their assurance that on the day when the Lord returns, "the dead in Christ *will rise* first" (vs. 16). Throughout his years of ministry, Paul devoted himself to "preaching the good news about Jesus and the resurrection" (Acts 17:18); not only the resurrection of Jesus, but also the promised resurrection of the deceased redeemed. Denying the resurrection of the body denies our hope of immortality. The resurrection of our mortal bodies is a vital tenet of the Christian faith.

"At the sound of the last trumpet the dead will be raised. We will all be changed, so that we will never die again. Our dead and decaying bodies will be changed into bodies that won't die or decay. The bodies we now have are weak and can die. But they will be changed into bodies that are eternal" (1 Corinthians 15:52-54, *Contemporary English Version*). The more familiar wording is: "This perishable must put on the imperishable, and this mortal must put on immortality." That which is "mortal" and "perishable" is the human body, which at the sound of the trumpet on the last day will be resurrected and transformed into a body imperishable and immortal. Thus, again, our hope of immortality (everlasting life) is directly tied to the resurrection of our bodies from the dust of the ground. Paul refers to this as the "redemption of our body" (Romans 8:23), a reality for which we eagerly wait, as does the rest of the physical creation, which anticipates a renewal to perfection along with the resurrected redeemed (Romans 8:19f). By the same power of the Spirit that raised the body of Jesus, so shall we be raised and given immortality. "If the Spirit of Him who raised Jesus from the dead dwells in you, He who raised Christ Jesus from the dead will also give life to your mortal bodies" (Romans 8:11).

There were a good many people during the time of Christ, however, who scoffed at the notion of a bodily resurrection. Many had been deeply influenced by Platonic philosophy and Hellenistic thinking with respect to the nature of man and his destiny. Resurrection had been replaced by the theology of "Immortal Soulism," the view that man was *inherently immortal* (i.e., he possessed an undying spirit trapped within his physical body). Such a theology rendered a resurrection of the body as neither necessary nor even desired. In the first century this pagan thinking had so influenced the Jews for such a long time that many had lost sight of God's promise of life at the resurrection. Thus, for many, resurrection theology was an absurdity. As Paul spoke to the people of Athens, "when they heard about the resurrection of the dead, some of them sneered" (Acts 17:32). On one occasion, as Paul stood before the Sanhedrin, he shouted, "I stand on trial because of my hope in the resurrection of the dead" (Acts 23:6). This led to a huge dispute between the Pharisees and the Sadducees, as "the Sadducees say that there is no resurrection" (vs. 8). This dispute "became so violent that the commander was afraid Paul would be torn to pieces by them" (vs. 10). Clearly, the Sadducees were not amused by this doctrine of the resurrection of the dead; they wanted nothing to do with it, and were quite aggressive against any who taught it.

According to tradition, the Sadducees derived their name from Zadok, who was High Priest during the time of King David and King Solomon of Israel. The family of Zadok held on to the high priesthood, and officiated in the Temple, until the time of the exile (a period of several hundred years). This family even formed the chief element of the post-exilic priesthood until the time of the Maccabean revolt. The Sadducees were a much smaller group than the Pharisees, but they had far more political power. They were the politicians, the social elite, and the aristocrats of their day. Although the Pharisees came to view themselves as *spiritually* superior to other Jews, the Sadducees regarded themselves as *socially* superior. While anyone could become a Pharisee, no matter his status in life (as long as he submitted to the "party line"), membership in the sect of the Sadducees was by birth only (by virtue of being born into one of the high-priestly or aristocratic families). The Sadducees were "high society."

During the "intertestamental" period of Jewish history this group embraced the Greek culture and way of life. The Saducean high priests became the chief negotiators with the various foreign governments in power over the people of Israel, and thus they began to acquire (through their pagan alliances) a considerable amount of political clout. As a result of this compromising position, they found themselves in increasing conflict with the Pharisees (who were separatists). In 1 Maccabees 1:11-15 the Sadducees are described as traitors to the Jewish people and to the Laws of God. They were not well-liked by the common people, nor did they have an abundance of vocal supporters. Religiously, the Sadducees were the "liberals," whereas the Pharisees would be considered the "conservatives," of the day. They accepted the Torah, but rejected the prophetic writings of the OT as being in any way authoritative. They also rejected the existence of angels and spirits, the Platonic concept of "immortal soulism," and even denied the hope of a resurrection from the dead (Acts 23:6-10). The Sadducees are not often discussed in the NT writings (they are only mentioned by name 13 times: 6 in Matthew, 1 in Mark, 1 in Luke, and 5 in Acts). During the early part of Jesus' ministry, the Sadducees largely ignored Him. He was a promoter of new religious ideas, but not a political threat; thus, He was not worthy of their attention. With His triumphal entry into Jerusalem shortly before His death, however, this perspective began to change. They now regarded Him as a threat to their own security, and they began to formulate plans to destroy Him (see Mark 11-12).

During His last days in the city of Jerusalem, "the Sadducees, who say there is no resurrection, came to Him with a question" (Matthew 22:23). Actually, they posed to Jesus a scenario where a woman survived seven husbands (all of whom were brothers), and then she herself died. "At the resurrection, whose wife will she be of the seven, since all of them were married to her?" (vs. 28). The account of this exchange may be found in all three Synoptic Gospels (Matthew 22:23-33; Mark 12:18-27; Luke 20:27-40).

In the course of His reply to the Sadducees that day, Jesus made the following statement: "But about the resurrection of the dead -- have you not read what God said to you: 'I am the God of Abraham, the God of Isaac, and the God of Jacob'? He is not the God of the dead, but of the living" (Matthew 22:31-32). As always, it is extremely important to note the *context* in which such a statement is made. The context of this entire exchange is *the resurrection of the dead*. That must be kept in mind as we seek to understand our Lord's remark to the Sadducees, "who say there is no resurrection" (vs. 23). Too many interpreters of this passage seek to make Jesus say something completely unrelated to the topic of man's resurrection from the dead; they suggest, instead, that He is promoting the Platonic philosophy of the inherent immortality of "the soul." Such was not even remotely the intent of Jesus. "Our problem is that we force on the text a Neo-Platonic dualism and demand a choice between immortality and resurrection. The point is simply that God will raise the dead ... this must be read against the background of biblical anthropology and eschatology" [*The Expositor's Bible Commentary*, vol. 8, p. 462]. "Greek thought sharply divided between the soul and the body, the soul's temporary prison, and saw immortality as a quality of the soul" [*ibid*, p. 1016]. This was *not* the biblical teaching, however, which regards man as *being* a "living soul," and not *having* a "living soul." Thus, immortality is tied to man himself, rather than to some "immortal spirit-being" imprisoned within his body. Jesus is *not* supporting the Hellenistic perspective on the nature of man, but is rather speaking of the certainty of a bodily resurrection of the whole man from the grave.

The quotation Jesus uses is from Exodus 3:6 (cf. vs. 16), where Moses, as he stands before the burning bush, hears the voice from the midst of the bush declare, "I am the God of your father, the God of Abraham, the God of Isaac, and the God of Jacob." At the time Moses heard this statement, these three patriarchs had been dead and buried for hundreds of years. So, what was the voice declaring? Was it suggesting that these three great patriarchs of

Judaism were still alive; that they were immortal? Some think so. John Wesley (1703-1791), in his *Explanatory Notes on the Whole Bible*, says this statement proves "the soul does not die with the body." Albert Barnes (1798-1870) states, "It proves that Abraham, Isaac, and Jacob had an existence then; that their souls were alive. They must, therefore, be still somewhere living" [*Barnes' Notes on the Bible*]. Thus, these patriarchs are not dead, but rather "they are truly alive" [Dr. Paul E. Kretzmann, *Popular Commentary of the Bible*, the NT, vol. 1, p. 125]. Some even go so far as to say *this* is the "resurrection" of which Jesus speaks ~ "The Savior teaches that the soul is *resurrected* when it leaves the body" [B. W. Johnson, *The People's New Testament with Explanatory Notes*, p. 123]. According to this view, "the resurrection" of which the Scriptures teach is the "resurrection of the soul" from its "prison house" (the physical body). Thus, Abraham, Isaac and Jacob are more alive now than they were when they walked the earth, having already been resurrected when the physical body died. This would, of course, make a later bodily resurrection an absurdity, as what need is there of a body if "the soul" is presently rejoicing in the presence of God?

Martin Luther (1483-1546), in his famous work "Table Talk," wrote, "Now if one should say that Abraham's soul lives with God but his body is dead, this distinction is rubbish. I will attack it. That would be a silly soul if it were in heaven and desired its body." William Tyndale (1484-1536), an English Bible translator and martyr, wrote, "And ye, in putting them (the departed souls) in heaven, hell and purgatory, destroy the arguments wherewith Christ and Paul prove the resurrection." Tyndale argued that if souls were already in either bliss or misery, "then what cause is there of the resurrection?" And what cause is there even of judgment? In another part of this same writing, Tyndale said, "The true faith putteth forth the resurrection, which we be warned to look for every hour. The heathen philosophers, denying that, did put that the soul did ever live. And the Pope joineth the spiritual doctrine of Christ and the fleshly doctrine of philosophers together; things so contrary that they cannot agree. And because the fleshly-minded Pope consenteth unto heathen doctrine, therefore he corrupteth the Scripture to stablish it. If the soul be in heaven, tell me what cause is there for the resurrection?"

"Such an interpretation makes Jesus' refutation of the Sadducees a farce. They denied the resurrection of *the dead bodies*, and the substitution of a statement regarding *only their souls*, would be a deception. ... It is an evasion of the real issue to say that the patriarchs were 'not absolutely dead men,' but 'living' because they were enjoying eternal life in heaven. Then the Sadducees (ancient and modern) would be right in asserting that no resurrection of *the dead bodies* will take place" [R. C. H. Lenski, *The Interpretation of St. Matthew's Gospel*, p. 876].

Again, remember the context here. The context of the whole passage is the resurrection of the dead from the grave, something the Sadducees utterly denied. "Jesus defends the fact of the resurrection, which is the issue really at stake with the Sadducees" [Dr. Craig S. Keener, *A Commentary on the Gospel of Matthew*, p. 528]. "For Jesus, the problem with the Sadducees comes down to their inadequate faith in Scripture and in God's power to accomplish the resurrection" [*ibid*, p. 529]. Abraham, Isaac and Jacob, although *heirs* of the promise of life, nevertheless, when they died, "they did not receive the things promised" (Hebrews 11:13). If, as some contend, their "souls" flew off to heaven at the moment of death, then the Hebrew writer was wrong ~ they *did* receive that promised life in the "heavenly realm." The reality is: they *will* receive it ... but at the resurrection! The parallel account in Luke's gospel makes this fact even more abundantly clear than Matthew's account. Luke writes, "But that *the dead are raised*, even Moses showed, in the passage about the bush, where he calls the Lord the God of Abraham and the God of Isaac and the God of Jacob" (Luke 20:37). Jesus says nothing about "immortal souls," but rather speaks to the truth of a bodily resurrection.

Although these three patriarchs of Judaism are dead and in the ground, yet from the perspective of the God of this universe, who is not bound by the constraints of time and space, they live. Luke also makes this clear, saying, "He is not the God of the dead, but of the living, *for to Him* all are alive" (Luke 20:38). From the view of men, who are still bound along this space-time continuum, the dead are just that: dead and buried. That which was formed from the dust of the ground has returned to the dust of the ground. From the perspective of the One who stands at both ends of the continuum, however, and thus outside the continuum, "all are alive." I don't think it is any mistake or coincidence that the voice from the bush declares, "I AM." He is the Eternal One. Thus, *to Him* the three patriarchs are perceived as *being*, even though in relation to our own temporal world they are but dust in the ground. Some are thrown off by the fact that Jesus says, "He is not the God of the dead, but of the living." They assume that this suggests no one is truly dead (thus, an endorsement of the Platonic theory). However, consider what Paul wrote in Romans 14:9 ~ "Christ died and returned to life so that He might be the Lord of *both the dead and the living*." Yes, the dead are truly dead; they have returned to the dust of the ground. But, the resurrection of Jesus from the grave secured the victory over death, and assures the dead of life ... a life that will be given *at the resurrection of the dead*. Thus, whether we live or die physically, we have a divine promise; a promise that will be realized when the trumpet sounds and Jesus returns to call us forth from the ground to be forever with Him. "His triumph included victory over death, so that even though His people may be given over to death's power temporarily, they have not ceased to be His, as the future bodily resurrection of Christians will demonstrate. He is in fact the Lord of both the dead and the living" [*The Expositor's Bible Commentary*, vol. 10, p. 146].

"'The dead' are the dead bodies in the graves. ... The whole question at issue is concerned about the dead bodies in the graves ~ shall they be raised up and live again or not?" [Lenski, p. 874]. I like the way Albert Barnes characterizes this truth: "Though the body dies and returns to its native dust, yet the Lord Jesus is still its Sovereign, and shall raise it up again. ... The tomb is under the watchful care of the Redeemer. Safe in His hands, the body may sink to its native dust with the assurance that in His own time He will again call it forth, with renovated and immortal powers. With this view, we can leave our friends with confidence in His hands when they die, and yield our own bodies cheerfully to the dust" [*Notes on the Bible*]. Paul spoke of a crown "which the Lord will award to me *on that day* ~ and not only to me, but also to all who have *longed for His appearing*" (2 Timothy 4:8). Paul did not expect to receive his reward until "that day" ... the day of "His appearing." Until that time, even though he would return to the dust of the ground, he had a blessed assurance: "I know whom I have believed, and am persuaded that He is able to guard/keep what I have entrusted to Him *for that day*" (2 Timothy 1:12). Paul was going to die; he knew that. But, he died with the understanding that Jesus had conquered death. Thus, just as Jesus arose from the grave, so would he. This is the great resurrection truth!

> God our Redeemer lives,
> And often from the skies
> Looks down and
> watches all our dust
> 'Till He shall bid it rise.

Chapter 14
Souls Under the Altar

One of the passages to which some disciples typically appeal in their effort to demonstrate the validity of the traditional view of the nature of man and the so-called "intermediate state" of the dead, is Revelation 6:9-11. In this chapter John is given a vision of six seals (the seventh is revealed in Revelation 8). In the first four we encounter what many have characterized *The Four Horsemen of the Apocalypse*. These are obviously symbols, not literal horses or horsemen, and represent vital eternal truths conveyed to John and his fellow faithful disciples during a time of great struggle and persecution. Following the vision of the four horses and their riders comes the vision of martyred "souls" crying out from underneath an altar. It is this particular vision upon which I would like for us to reflect.

"And when He broke the fifth seal, I saw underneath the altar the souls of those who had been slain because of the word of God, and because of the testimony which they had maintained; and they cried out with a loud voice, saying, 'How long, O Lord, holy and true, wilt Thou refrain from judging and avenging our blood on those who dwell on the earth?'

And there was given to each of them a white robe; and they were told that they should rest for a little while longer, until the number of their fellow servants and their brethren who were to be killed even as they had been, should be completed also." ~ *Revelation 6:9-11*

It is important to understand the nature of Jewish apocalyptic literature if we ever hope to properly interpret the passage before us. These symbols and figures were never intended to be taken literally. This is *figurative* language, and any attempt to impose literalness upon these images will inevitably lead to a theology which is both false and bizarre.

"Apocalyptic literature flourished during a time of some great national crisis when a formidable enemy threatened the life of the people ~ a time of trial and stress. This type of writing is characterized by symbols in dreams and visions, in actions and consequences, instructing and encouraging the people under such conditions. The Spirit chose this method to reveal the struggles of God's people with heathen forces and the victory of His cause and kingdom over these worldly powers" [Homer Hailey, *Revelation: An Introduction and Commentary*, p. 19].

Hailey (who preceded me by several decades as the Minister for the *Keeaumoku Street* congregation of the *Church of Christ* in Honolulu, Hawaii, where I served for six years [1992-1998] and was privileged to minister to some of the very people he led into relationship with Christ) points out that we must exercise "caution" in our interpretations of this literature, and that we should not "look for literalism in the symbols, for some are grotesque when viewed literally. Symbols, signs, and images are used to express ideas; one must look *through* John's particular vision, with its symbols and images, and strive to grasp the *idea* in the mind of God as He revealed it to John" [*ibid*, p. 36].

"As the seals are broken and the scroll unrolled, its contents are not disclosed in words but in symbols. God reveals His purpose in vivid and moving symbolism. .... Confronted with symbols and symbolic pictures, the reader faces the task of learning and interpreting their meaning and significance. .... One must ever be conscious that he is interpreting visions" [*ibid*, p. 186-187].

Professor D. R. Dungan observed, "Much of the Scriptures was written in language that was highly figurative; its poetry and prophecy, and very much of its prose, contain the loftiest of Oriental hyperbole. It becomes us, then, to acquaint ourselves with the rules governing this kind of speech. We know that if we shall interpret literal language as if it were figurative, or figurative as if it were literal, *we will certainly miss the meaning*" [*Hermeneutics: The Science of Interpreting the Scriptures*, p. 195]. Adam Clarke characterizes this whole passage as a "symbolical vision" [*Clarke's Commentary*, vol. 6, p. 994].

One of the keys to interpreting the significance of such literature (especially in the book of *Revelation*) is to keep in mind that these symbols, many of them, find their roots in, and thus derive their meaning and application from, the Old Testament writings. Dr. Milton S. Terry points out, "Constant reference should be had, in the interpretation of this book, to the analogous prophecies of the Old Testament" [*Biblical Hermeneutics: A Treatise on the Interpretation of the Old and New Testaments*, p. 468]. Therefore, when seeking to interpret Revelation 6:9-11 one should consider two things: (1) this is *figurative* language, and (2) the correct interpretation of this vision is most likely to be found within the pages of the OT writings.

As we examine the vision of the fifth seal we are presented with an image of "souls" crying out from "underneath the altar." These "souls" are obviously representative of those persons who have forfeited their lives due to their faithfulness in proclaiming the Word of God. In other words, they are *martyrs*. Now, we must be careful here in our interpretation ... these are, after all, merely symbols; this is *figurative* language, just as the horses and riders in the previous verses are not to be taken literally either. This passage does *not* depict *literal* "immortal souls" who have been consigned to a place underneath some giant altar in the "spirit world" for hundreds and thousands of years, and who cry out to God for avenging. After all, some reward *this* would be for faithfulness unto the point of death! Rather, it is a *symbol* or *figure* or *representation* of the fact that the shed blood of faithful servants is always before our God as a witness to their ultimate sacrifice, "crying out to Him" for avenging. And that shed blood *will be avenged*.

Remember what God said to Cain after he had killed his brother Abel: "The voice of your brother's blood is crying to Me from the ground" (Genesis 4:10). Was that blood, which had soaked into the dust of the ground, *literally* crying out to God? Of course not. Nobody in their right mind would suggest it was. This is clearly *figurative* language. It simply informs us, as it informed Cain, that God is cognizant of those faithful ones who have forfeited their lives in His service. Their shed blood "speaks to Him" as a continuing testimony of their faithfulness unto death, and that testimony does not go unnoticed by our Father. "O earth, do not cover my blood, and let there be no resting place for my cry" (Job 16:18). Nor will that plea emanating from the poured out blood of martyrs go unanswered. "For behold, the Lord is coming out of His dwelling to punish the people of the earth for their sins. The earth will disclose *the blood shed upon her*; she will conceal her slain no longer" (Isaiah 26:21).

Unto what does the figure in Revelation 6:9 allude? I believe we can find its OT antecedent in a couple of passages from the Pentateuch dealing with sacrifices offered unto the Lord God upon the altar, and what was then done with the blood that was shed.

Exodus 29:11-12 ~ "And you shall slaughter the bull before the Lord at the doorway of the tent of meeting. And you shall take some of the blood of the bull and put it on the horns of the altar with your finger; and you shall pour out all the blood *at the base of the altar.*"

Leviticus 4:7 ~ "And all the blood of the bull he shall pour out *at the base of the altar* of burnt offering which is at the doorway of the tent of meeting." (see also: Leviticus 4:18, 25, 30, 34; 5:9).

When a victim was sacrificed unto the Lord, *the blood* of that sacrificial victim (and martyrs are most definitely "sacrificial victims") was to be poured out at the *base* of the altar. That blood then flowed *beneath the altar* of sacrifice. Paul used similar language as he contemplated his own death, depicting his martyrdom as an "offering" which was "already being *poured out*" (2 Timothy 4:6). See also: Philippians 2:17. *The Disciples' Study Bible* comments that "the deaths of Christian martyrs are precious enough to be likened to holy sacrifices." The martyrs depicted in Revelation 6:9-11 had offered their very *lives* upon the altar of sacrifice, their *life blood* flowing *beneath* this sacred altar as a testimony to their ultimate sacrifice.

"John says that he saw the 'souls' of those slain (vs. 9). This is generally understood to mean the disembodied souls of these saints. However, the Greek word *psyche* has various meanings and probably stands here for the actual 'lives' or 'persons' who were killed rather than for their 'souls.'" [*The Expositor's Bible Commentary*, vol. 12, p. 475].

What is the significance of the pouring out of the *blood*? The *life* (soul) of the body was said to be *in the blood*. Thus, the pouring out of *blood* signified the pouring out of *life*. Leviticus 17:11 informs us that "the *life* (this is the *same word* we translate "soul") of the flesh is *in the blood*." Indeed, in Genesis 9:4 we are told that the *life* (soul) of the flesh *is* "its blood." Thus, the blood symbolizes the *life* of the body, and it should be pointed out *again* that this word which we translate "life" is the *very same word* that is elsewhere translated "soul." When an animal was offered on the altar, and its blood was shed as a sacrifice before God, its *life/soul* was *poured out* in the shedding of its blood, and this life-blood flowed *beneath the altar* of sacrifice. Does this signify that bulls and goats sacrificed upon an altar had "immortal souls" which somehow got trapped under this altar of sacrifice? Of course not. It merely signified that their *blood* was the *life/soul* of the body, and that *life/soul* was sacrificed (poured out) unto the Lord in a special offering at the *base* of the altar.

"We further cannot accept the idea of a *physical* altar of burnt offering and the *spatial* idea of these souls who have some sort of bodies lying in a mass 'under' or 'underneath' such an altar. Was there an open space under this altar of sufficient size to accommodate many martyrs? Why should the martyrs be assigned so peculiar a place in heaven?" [R. C. H. Lenski, *The Interpretation of St. John's Revelation*, p. 233]. Lenski goes on to connect this vision symbolically with the altar of sacrifice under the Law of Moses, saying these persons "who were slain for Christ's sake are connected with the altar of sacrifice because they were slain, because their blood was shed as holy blood, was poured out as a sacrifice to God and to Christ" [*ibid*].

The blood of the martyrs of all ages has been (and is being) poured out on the altar of the ultimate personal sacrifice: the offering of one's *life/soul* in faithfulness even to the point of death (Revelation 2:10). Just as the *soul* of the sacrificial animal flowed under the altar through its shed blood, so also does the *soul (life)* of a martyr flow under the great altar of personal sacrifice through his/her shed blood offered up in faithfulness to the Father, faithfulness exemplified in death. This sacrifice, declares God in this vision unto John, would *not* be forgotten, nor would it go unavenged. Just as the blood of righteous Abel "cried out" to God from the ground (*figuratively* speaking), so also does the blood of these sacrificial victims "cry out" (*figuratively* speaking) from beneath the great altar of sacrifice before our God in Heaven. It is a cry to Deity to fulfill the promise made to all faithful ones who pay the ultimate price:

"He will *avenge the blood* of His servants; He will take vengeance on His enemies" (Deuteronomy 32:43).

"There are no literal 'souls' of martyrs in heaven squeezed at the base of an altar. The whole scene is simply a symbolic representation designed to reassure those facing martyrdom and death that ultimately they would be vindicated by God. ... Apocalyptic pictures are not meant to be photographs of actual realities" [Dr. Samuele Bacchiocchi, *Immortality or Resurrection? -- A Biblical Study on Human Nature and Destiny*, p. 186].

It has become a very common tendency "to regard those who died for their witness as having a special place in heaven, with special rights of intercession. Under the influence of Neo-Platonism this led to the development of the idea of 'saints' who had the privilege of intercession for Christians upon earth. The NT, however, provides no ground for such beliefs, since it gives no place of special privilege even to those who have as 'martyrs' died for the faith" [*The Zondervan Pictorial Encyclopedia of the Bible*, vol. 4, p. 103].

To assume the traditional teaching on man's immortality from this passage in the book of *Revelation* (i.e., that our immortality is *inherent*, rather than *derived*) is merely to show total ignorance of this type of Jewish literature and of the many symbols, types and figures of the OT writings to which this literature frequently alludes. In short, these "souls" under the altar are no more literal than the locusts from the pit, the four horses and their riders, or Jesus being in actuality a lamb with seven horns and seven eyes and a slit throat. These are *symbols* which convey some truth, but which are *not the reality themselves*; the *shadows* do not constitute the *substance*. Failing to perceive this can lead to some rather bizarre, not to mention false, theology. "Souls" of slain disciples trapped under a giant altar, crying out for vengeance, *if taken literally*, is a *bizarre*, not to mention *false*, theology. It has no place in the proclamation of Gospel Truth.

Chapter 15
The Consuming Fire

As one examines the many biblical examples of God's dealings with the wicked, it will be quickly perceived that *not one single time* in all of recorded biblical teaching is the punishment for sin against God ever declared to be *torture*. The ultimate punishment, instead, is always declared to be *death*. Thus, if indeed God's final punishment for the wicked *is* endless torture, as some maintain, it is a fate *completely without biblical precedent*. Nowhere in Scripture does God ever use torture as divine punishment for man. Not even once!

"The OT and NT alike, in a multiplicity of ways, terms, figures, pictures, expressions and examples, declare time and time again that the wicked finally will pass away and be no more, that righteousness will then fill the universe, and that God will then forever be all in all. Not one time in all of Scripture does God ever say that any human being will be made immortal for the purpose of suffering conscious everlasting torment" [Edward Fudge, *The Fire That Consumes*, p. 434].

THE TYPES & SHADOWS

After examining a great many of the types and shadows of the OT writings which speak of God's dealings with the wicked, Curtis Dickinson, a well-known leader, writer and evangelist in *Churches of Christ*, observed, "It will be noted that in each case the thing that was threatened was death, *not* incessant torture. The types and shadows *in no instance* teach the idea of an immortal soul or eternal spirit being *tortured* as the punishment for sin. In all cases they show the penalty for sin to be the *death* of the person" [*What The Bible Teaches About Immortality and Future Punishment*, p. 20].

Again, there is simply *zero* biblical evidence, in all the many examples of God's dealings with the unrepentant wicked, of His punishment for sin ever constituting *incessant torture*. Such a penalty is entirely absent from the Scriptures. Thus, I repeat: If God's final punishment is indeed perpetual torture, it is a punishment without precedent. Death and destruction, on the other hand, is a divine punishment with enormous biblical precedent. It should also be noted that the language of Scripture easily lends itself to *this* ultimate destiny of the wicked. Examine the following list of NT expressions regarding the final disposition of the wicked [which is taken from Leroy Edwin Froom's monumental two volume, 2000 page study: *The Conditionalist Faith of Our Fathers*]:

Blot Out Of Existence ~ Hebrews 9:26; Revelation 3:5; 18:21

Bring To Nought ~ 1 Corinthians 1:19

Cast Away, Cast Off ~ Matthew 13:42, 48, 50; John 12:31

Consume, Devour Utterly ~ Matthew 3:12; 13:30, 40; 2 Thessalonians 2:8; Hebrews 12:29; Revelation 18:8

Crush ~ Romans 16:20

Cut Off, Cut Down ~ Matthew 3:10; 7:19; Luke 13:7, 9; John 15:2; Acts 3:23; 23:13, 31; Romans 11:20, 22, 24

Death ~ Romans 5:20; 6:21, 23; 7:5; Revelation 21:8

Destroy ~ Matthew 10:28; 27:20; Romans 6:6; 7:6; 1 Corinthians 1:19; 2:6; 5:5; 15:24, 26; Galatians 5:15; 1 Thessalonians 5:3; 2 Thessalonians 1:9; 2:8; 1 Timothy 6:9; 2 Timothy 1:10; Hebrews 2:14; 1 John 3:8

Devour ~ Hebrews 10:27; Revelation 11:5; 20:9

Die ~ John 5:24; 6:50; 8:24; Romans 7:6, 10; 8:13; 1 Corinthians 15:22, 32; Ephesians 2:1, 5; Philippians 2:27; 1 Peter 2:24

Drown ~ 1 Timothy 1:19; 6:9; 2 Peter 3:11, 12

Fall ~ Matthew 7:27; Luke 6:49

Found No More ~ Revelation 18:21

Grind To Powder ~ Matthew 21:44; Luke 20:18

Kill Outright, Put To Death ~ Matthew 10:28; 21:41; 22:7; Mark 12:9; Luke 19:27; John 10:10; Romans 7:11; 8:13; 2 Corinthians 3:6; Col. 3:15; Revelation 2:23

Lose Life ~ Matthew 7:13; Mark 4:38; John 11:42; 17:12; Acts 8:20; Romans 9:22; Philippians 3:19; 2 Thessalonians 2:3; 1 Timothy 6:9; 2 Peter 2:1, 2; 3:7, 16; Revelation 17:8, 11

Never See Life ~ John 3:36; 5:40; Acts 13:46; 1 John 3:15; 5:12

Overthrow ~ Luke 1:52

Perish ~ Acts 13:41; 1 Corinthians 3:17; Galatians 6:8; 2

Peter 1:4; 2:12; John 3:16; Revelation 11:18

Root Out ~ Jude 12

Ruin ~ Matthew 7:27; Luke 6:49; 2 Corinthians 10:8; 13:10

Swallow Up ~ 1 Corinthians 15:54; 1 Peter 5:8

Throw Down ~ Revelation 18:21

Vanish Away ~ Hebrews 8:13

"If God intended for us to understand something *other* than total death for the wicked, certainly He could have found the means in the marvelous Greek language to express such. Instead He used the plainest terms indicating destruction of the whole man" [Curtis Dickinson, *What The Bible Teaches About Immortality and Future Punishment*, p. 21]. Leroy Edwin Froom observes, "The OT uses 50 different verbs in the Hebrew language to describe the final fate of the wicked, and they *all* signify different aspects of *destruction*" [*The Conditionalist Faith of Our Fathers*, vol. 1, p. 106]. For example, the wicked will be as a vessel broken to pieces, ashes trodden underfoot, smoke that vanishes, chaff carried away by the wind, tow that is burned, thorns and stubble in fire, vine branches pruned off, wax that melts, fat of sacrifices, a dream that vanishes, and the like. Certainly *nothing* that suggests *everlasting continuation* (much less under merciless *torture*).

Dickinson continues: "The Old Testament presents four great events which portray two principal facts of Judgment Day: (1) The **deliverance** of God's own people, and (2) the certain **destruction** of His enemies. The events are:

The Flood, in which the basic punishment and sentence was the death of all except those safe in the ark.

The Destruction of Sodom and Gomorrah, in which the

punishment was total destruction by fire, which Jude plainly reveals is an example of the final fire of Judgment (Jude 7).

The Destruction of Pharaoh and his Army in the Red Sea, which was sudden and final (and in which, Moses sang, they were 'consumed' and 'swallowed up' ~ Exodus 15).

The Destruction of Jericho, from which none, not even women and children, escaped except the household of Rahab, who had become an obedient believer.

None of those prototypes of Judgment Day give the slightest support to the idea of punishment by torture" [*What The Bible Teaches About Immortality and Future Punishment*, p. 37]. In addition to the above, suggested by Dickinson, one should also not overlook:

The Destruction of the Edomites ~ Obadiah 15-21. Because of their wickedness, they "will become as if they had never existed" (vs. 16). They will be "cut off forever" (vs. 10). "Then the house of Jacob will be a fire and the house of Joseph a flame; but the house of Esau will be as stubble. And they will set them on fire and consume them, so that there will be no survivor of the house of Esau" (vs. 18). "By 100 A.D. the people of Edom had become lost to history," Homer Hailey points out [*A Commentary on the Minor Prophets*, p. 30]. A scholar by the name of D. Stuart Briscoe observed, "If you travel today in the region of Edom, you will find nothing but the most stark wilderness and the most isolated emptiness ... it is one of the most formidable, forsaken spots on earth."

The Destruction of Nineveh ~ Nahum 1. This city, because of its wickedness, will experience "His wrath poured out like fire ... and the burning of His anger" (1:6). "He will make a complete end of it" (1:8-9). "They are consumed as stubble completely withered" (1:10). "They will be cut off and pass away" (1:12). "You will be hidden" (3:11). Their place will not be known (3:17). By using these figures, the prophet is foretelling the *total destruction* of Nineveh, and that did indeed come to pass. About 200 years later, Xenophon the Athenian and "the Ten Thousand," backing out of their entanglement in Persia, passed by the site and noted that there was no evidence a city had ever stood there. In modern times the site was not discovered until 1842. Today, the site is covered by fields, a local dump, and a cemetery.

"Everywhere we find the notion of a final cessation of being, of a return to a state of unconsciousness, never that of a perpetual life in suffering" [Emmanuel Petavel, *The Problem of Immortality*].

The proponents of the traditional perspective on the nature of final punishment will often make an effort to demonstrate that our loving, compassionate, merciful God will be content with nothing less than the perpetual, never diminishing, horrific *torture* of the vast majority of mankind. Not only is this *not* what the Scriptures teach, it has the distinct disadvantage of portraying our God as a sadistic *monster* the likes of which the human mind cannot even conceive. It is to proclaim a God foreign to the inspired revelation. Thus, it is a mockery of Truth and a blasphemy against Deity.

THE CONSUMING FIRE

The Bible teaches a *different* reality for the wicked. They will be *consumed* in the fire, *NOT preserved*. There is no question but what the lake of fire will be a horrific experience. An execution is not a pleasant event, and degrees of torment are involved for the one being put to death. As one who stood with the Warden *inside* the death chamber itself, at the side of a man who was executed by the State of New Mexico on November 6, 2001, and who looked into his eyes as he took his last breath, I can assure you that weeping, gnashing of teeth, and deep torment accompany the death experience. However, the ultimate punishment is *death itself*, not the dying *process*.

Nowhere has our God prescribed *incessant torture* as the "wages of sin" or the penalty of lawlessness. Consider the following passage as representative of this perspective: "Every tree therefore that does not bear good fruit is cut down and thrown into the fire. .... And His winnowing fork is in His hand, and He will thoroughly clear His threshing floor; and He will gather His wheat into the barn, but He will *BURN UP* the chaff with unquenchable fire" ~ Matthew 3:10, 12.

Trees with bad fruit are burned (Matthew 7:19), and so are unfruitful vines (John 15:6) and useless weeds (Matthew 13:40). These figures are all employed to depict the fate of sinners at the final reckoning. They will be cast into "*unquenchable* fire." This is the Greek word *asbestos* which means "inextinguishable." It describes a fire which burns without interruption; it is an enduring fire which none can extinguish no matter how hard they might try. It is important to notice here, however, that it is the *fire* that Jesus describes as enduring, *not* that which is cast into it. To try and *transfer* the quality of endurance from the fire itself to that which is cast into it is completely unwarranted either grammatically, logically, or theologically.

That which is cast into the fire will *burn up*. This is the Greek word *katakaio* which means "to burn up; consume." It signifies to completely, utterly, totally destroy with fire. It is enlightening, in the context of this study, to note that this word is used in the LXX (*Septuagint*) in Exodus 3:2 where Moses beholds a burning bush: "The bush was burning with fire, yet the bush was NOT *consumed*." This particular bush was *preserved* in the fire (what the traditionalists proclaim will happen with the wicked), yet Jesus disagrees with this doctrine. Jesus informs us that sinners will *not* be preserved in the fire (like the burning bush was), but rather will be "burned up" ~ just the *opposite* of preservation. Thus, the view of final punishment promoted by many is actually in direct opposition to the teaching of Jesus Christ. *Jesus* says the wicked will *not* be preserved in the fire, the traditionalists say they *will*. Jesus says they will be *consumed* in the fire (unlike the burning bush), the traditionalists say just the opposite (that they will endure *without* being consumed, just as the bush). Whom will you believe? Frankly, I believe Jesus on this matter.

I'm reminded of the words of Edward White, in his classic work *Life In Christ*, in which he emphatically stated, "My mind fails to conceive a grosser misinterpretation of language than when the five or six strongest words which the Greek tongue possesses, signifying 'destroy' or 'destruction,' are explained to mean maintaining an everlasting but wretched existence. *To translate black as white is nothing to this.*"

Our God is a *consuming* fire (Hebrews 12:29; Deuteronomy 4:24), and nothing unholy will long remain when He unleashes His fiery wrath at the last day. All will be *consumed*, not *preserved*, in the outpouring of His wrath. In the apostle Peter's second recorded sermon, for example, he alludes to Deuteronomy 18 and declares to his hearers, "And it shall be that every soul that does not heed that prophet shall be *utterly destroyed* from among the people" (Acts 3:23). "That prophet," of course, is a reference to Jesus Christ. Those who do not heed *Him* will be called to account. The penalty for their rejection of Him will be "utter destruction."

This is the Greek word *exolothreuo*, which appears only here in all the New Covenant documents. It means to "exterminate; utterly destroy" [*The Analytical Greek Lexicon*]; "to destroy utterly; extirpate -- complete extermination" [*Thayer's Greek-English Lexicon*]; "to slay wholly" [*Vine's Expository Dictionary of NT Words*]. *The Expositor's Greek Testament* says that if this passage has "*any* eschatological bearing, it would support the theory of annihilation." In other words, this term is *just that emphatic* a declaration of extermination and annihilation. At the very least, it is hardly supportive of the view of those who suggest the wicked will *not* be utterly destroyed, but rather preserved alive forevermore for the purpose of perpetual torture.

At this juncture I would like to provide a rather lengthy excerpt from brother Edward Fudge's marvelous study *The Fire That Consumes*. I believe the following comments put the issue into perspective, and they reflect my own thinking quite well. Thus, I will let him express my own conviction at this point:

"The real issue between 'traditionalists' and 'conditionalists' is nothing other than this: Does Scripture teach that the wicked will be made immortal for the purpose of suffering endless pain; or does it teach that the wicked, following whatever degree and duration of pain God may justly inflict, will finally and truly die, perish, be destroyed and become extinct forever and ever?

"The evidence of Scripture indicates that extinction will be preceded (perhaps even brought about by) a period of conscious suffering which corresponds precisely to the sentence of divine justice. God is severe, but He is not a sadist. Though pagan literature abounds in description of hellish pain, the Word of God does not!

"Does the Word of God teach the eternal conscious torment of the lost? Our modest study fails to show that it does. We were reared on the traditionalist view ~ we accepted it because it was said to rest on the Bible. This closer investigation of the Scriptures indicates that we were mistaken in that assumption. A careful look discovers that both OT and NT teach instead a resurrection of the wicked for the purpose of divine judgment, the fearful anticipation of a consuming fire, irrevocable expulsion from God's presence into a place where there will be weeping and grinding of teeth, such conscious suffering as the divine justice individually requires ~ and finally, the total, everlasting extinction of the wicked with no hope of resurrection, restoration or recovery. Now we stand on that, on the authority of the Word of God. We have changed once and do not mind changing again, but we were evidently wrong once through lack of careful study and do not wish to repeat the same mistake. Mere assertions and denunciations will not refute the evidence presented in this book, nor will a recital of ecclesiastical tradition. This case rests finally on Scripture. Only Scripture can prove it wrong!"

Some have suggested this view of final punishment "endangers the faith." Henry Constable, well over a hundred years ago, answered this charge this way, "Does it imperil our faith in God? What attribute of His is attacked? His love? Is it the part of love to inflict eternal pain if it can be helped? His mercy? Is it the part of mercy never to be satisfied with the misery of others? His holiness? Is it essential to holiness to keep evil forever in existence? His justice? Can justice only be satisfied with everlasting agonies? NO; we do not endanger faith. We strengthen it, by allying it once more with the divine principles of mercy, equity, and justice. It is the Augustinian (traditionalist) theory which endangers faith, and has made shipwreck of faith in the case of multitudes, by representing God as a Being of boundless injustice, caprice and cruelty" [*Duration and Nature of Future Punishment*, p. 166]

Chapter 16
Torture or Termination?

"If anyone worships the beast and his image, and receives a mark on his forehead or upon his hand, he also will drink of the wine of the wrath of God, which is mixed in full strength in the cup of His anger; and he will be tormented with fire and brimstone in the presence of the holy angels and in the presence of the Lamb. And the smoke of their torment goes up forever and ever; and they have no rest day and night, those who worship the beast and his image, and whoever receives the mark of his name." ~ *Revelation 14:9-11*

The above passage has long been employed as "proof positive" that the lost will experience *perpetual torture* at the hands of a just and merciful God following the final judgment on that last day. Without question there are a few words and phrases in this passage that, on the surface, tend to suggest such a scenario. A deeper, more responsible exegesis, however, will demonstrate such teaching to be without foundation. "These dogmatic interpretations of

Revelation 14:9-11 as proof of a literal, eternal torment reveal a lack of sensitivity to the highly metaphorical language of the passage" [Dr. Samuele Bacchiocchi, *Immortality or Resurrection? -- A Biblical Study on Human Nature and Destiny*, p. 211].

If one fails to perceive the unique nature of the literature of Revelation, one will completely fail to perceive and correctly interpret the meaning of the above passage. Curtis Dickinson wrote, "The apostle John used language and symbols familiar to the people to whom he wrote, yet veiled to the world which was persecuting them. The Christians were familiar with Old Testament Scripture, so much of the Revelation utilized events recorded there" [*What The Bible Teaches About Immortality and Future Punishment*, p. 32]. Understanding that this is highly figurative *apocalyptic* literature, largely based on OT imagery, is critical to sound exegesis. Therefore, we must carefully examine the four primary statements made with regard to the final punishment of the lost:

Drinking unmixed the wine of God's wrath.

Torment with fire and brimstone.

The smoke of their torment rising forever.

Lack of rest day and night.

ONE ~ "...he will drink of the wine of the wrath of God, which is mixed in full strength in the cup of His anger" (vs. 10). The symbol of a cup of wine, representing the fierce anger of God, is common in OT literature. When a nation or people drink of this cup the result is *utter destruction* at the hand of God. The Lord told the prophet Jeremiah, "Take this cup of the wine of wrath from My hand, and cause all the nations, to whom I send you, to drink it. And they shall drink and stagger and go mad because of the sword that I will send among them" (Jeremiah 25:15-16). "Drink, be drunk, vomit, fall, and *rise no more* because of the sword which I will send among you" (vs. 27).

This is a destruction that would be absolute. "They will drink and swallow, *and become as if they had never existed*" (Obadiah 16). Just two verses later the prophecy changes to the figure of fire as the agent of punishment. The house of Esau is likened unto "stubble." It will be "set on fire and *consumed*," and "there will be *no survivor* of the house of Esau" (vs. 18).

"In the hand of the Lord is a cup full of foaming wine mixed with spices; He pours it out, and all the wicked of the earth drink it down to its very dregs" (Psalm 75:8). To drink this down to the dregs symbolizes a *complete, total* punishment, not just a partial one. It is a full and furious outpouring of wrath. Let not the wicked think they shall escape this fate, for "the cup in the Lord's right hand *will* come around to you" (Habakkuk 2:16). Job prays that the wicked may "drink of the wrath of the Almighty" (Job 21:20).

These are passages that speak of destruction and extinction as a result of experiencing the wrath of the Almighty. It is not *torture* but *termination* that is consistently in view. It speaks of *no survivors*, of chaff being *burned up* in fire, and of the wicked becoming "as if they had never existed." The wrath of God will be unmixed (undiluted), full and furious, and final. How could one possibly survive such an encounter? "But who can endure the day of His coming? Who can stand when He appears?" (Malachi 3:2). The answer is: *no one*.

There is nothing whatsoever in the figure of the cup of the wine of God's wrath that suggests perpetual torture of the wicked. Indeed, the OT references strongly suggest just the opposite: a fearful destruction which is total and complete and final; one from which there will never, ever be any restoration or recovery or survivor. It will be as if they had never existed.

TWO ~ "...and he will be tormented with fire and brimstone in the presence of the holy angels and in the presence of the Lamb" (vs. 10). This statement immediately brings to mind the fate of Sodom and Gomorrah. "Then the Lord rained on Sodom and Gomorrah *brimstone and fire* from the Lord out of heaven" (Genesis 19:24). The overthrow of Assyria is also depicted in similar language: "The breath of the Lord, like a torrent of brimstone, sets it afire" (Isaiah 30:33). If you read the entire context (vs. 27-33) you will see God's tongue characterized as "a consuming fire" ... God is "burning in His anger, and dense is His smoke" ... His judgment against Assyria will "be seen in fierce anger, and in the flame of a consuming fire."

God also warned Edom that "a day of vengeance" was coming in which "its streams shall be turned into pitch, and its loose earth into brimstone, and its land shall become burning pitch. *It shall not be quenched night or day; its smoke shall go up forever*" (Isaiah 34:8-10). This would also be the fate of Gog, as prophesied by the prophet Ezekiel. "And with pestilence and with blood I shall enter into judgment with him; and I shall rain on him, and on his troops, and on the many peoples who are with him, a torrential rain, with hailstones, fire, and brimstone" (Ezekiel 38:22).

It is very obvious that the passage in Revelation under consideration (14:9-11) has its roots firmly grounded in OT history and literature. Each of the four aspects of the punishment specified are taken directly from the pages of OT Scripture. *They are symbols.* Nothing more. They symbolize a fearful judgment in which God will pour out upon His enemies His full and final wrath, a wrath so *consuming* that all will vanish away before it. They will be completely consumed like stubble in an *unstoppable* fire, like chaff in a molten river. Nothing will be left but ashes (Malachi 4:1-3).

Is there "torment" involved in death by fire? Absolutely! Men recoil in horror at the thought of perishing in a fire. Few prospects instill as much terror in the hearts of men. Thus, God employed this figure repeatedly to show the seriousness and wretchedness of the fate awaiting those who oppose Him. The wicked will indeed experience "torment" (indescribable torment) when they are consumed in the fury of His wrath. "For if we go on sinning willfully after receiving the knowledge of the truth, there no longer remains a sacrifice for sins, but a certain *terrifying* expectation of judgment, and the *fury of a fire which will consume* the adversaries" (Hebrews 12:26-27).

The figure of "fire and brimstone" is used repeatedly in the OT Scriptures to represent *utter destruction*. It is *never* used to convey perpetual torture. Yes, those being destroyed utterly will experience *torment* as they are being consumed by the wrath of God. Suffering is a natural part of the process of destruction. However, there is nothing in these figures that suggests God *preserves* the wicked for the purpose of endlessly heaping upon them unimaginable tortures and torments. Yes, there is pain associated with death, but it is the latter that is the true punishment, not the former. "The wages of sin is *death*" (Romans 6:23). Paul did *not* say the wages of sin is *everlasting life* in perpetual *torture*.

In Revelation 18 we see depicted the fall of Babylon (which again is pure symbolism, and is not speaking literally of the ancient city of Babylon). The merchants and kings and others who consorted with her see "the smoke of her burning" and they stand at a distance because of the fearfulness "of her torment" (vs. 10, 15), and yet we know that "in one hour she has been laid waste" (vs. 19) and "will not be found any longer" (vs. 21). Yes, there is the presence of *torment* in the destruction of the wicked, and it will be a fearful thing to behold. But when the chaff is *burned up* it will be "found no more." The figures are *not* figures representing perpetual torture. On the contrary. The biblical figures consistently represent utter destruction. A destruction witnessed by the angels and the Lamb. "Angels who through the ages had watched the unfolding and revealing of God's eternal purpose and the conflict between good and evil, now see the consummation of that purpose and final consequence of evil" [Homer Hailey, *Revelation: An Introduction and Commentary*, p. 310]. And what is the reaction of these angelic beings when God's wrath is poured out upon the unredeemed? "They deserve it!" (Revelation 16:6).

THREE ~ "And the smoke of their torment goes up forever and ever" (vs. 11). When God poured out His fiery judgment upon Edom, the land would become desolate and "*its smoke shall go up forever*" (Isaiah 34:10). Is smoke still rising in that area? Of course not. This is figurative language. It conveys utter destruction. Nothing is left. The smoke is a *testimony* to the enduring destruction caused by the consuming fire. It is a visible *witness* of the powerful destruction that has been effected by the outpouring of God's wrath. The sword of God had descended "in judgment on Edom; the people *I have totally destroyed*" (vs. 5).

When Abraham arose the next morning and looked out over the area which had previously contained the cities of Sodom and Gomorrah, "he saw, and behold, the smoke of the land ascended like the smoke of a furnace" (Genesis 19:28). Were those cities still there? Were the inhabitants still there being *tortured* in that fire from out of heaven? No, of course not. They were gone! All that remained was the *testimony* of the smoke; a *witness* to the power of God's consuming fire. The cities and their inhabitants had been "reduced to ashes" (2 Peter 2:6) when they experienced the "punishment of eternal fire" (Jude 7). Thus, they forever serve as an example of the fate of the wicked (2 Peter 2:6) at the final judgment, who will *in like manner* be reduced to ashes by the outpouring of God's wrath in a *consuming* fire (2 Peter 3:7f; Malachi 4:1-3).

It is extremely important to notice what is *not* said in Revelation 14:11. It does *not* say the lost are tormented forever and ever. It says the *smoke* of their torment goes up forever and ever. That is a major distinction. It is not the destroying *process*, torturous though it will be, that is depicted as enduring. Rather, it is the *testimony* and *evidence* of that utter destruction that is said to be enduring. When God completely and permanently destroys the wicked, that will be a judgment forever noted in the hearts and minds of the redeemed. No more will the wicked be found to oppress them. They are gone, and gone forever, and the redeemed are *assured* of that reality by their God. This is the significance of the "forever ascending smoke" -- it is a forever testimony to the enduring judgment of God against all that opposed Him and His people. Like the rainbow, it is a visible reminder of God's judgment, as well as a reminder of His gift of life to those who escaped the punishment of the fire. Thus, the smoke is for the living, not the dead. Now, whether there will literally be smoke visible to the saints throughout eternity, or whether this is merely a symbol of the *reality* of that blessed assurance, is arguable. I personally tend to think that the smoke will not be literally present, but that God is merely suggesting *by* this symbol that the *evidence* of the utter destruction of the wicked will be *known* to us in some way, and we need never again doubt that their destruction has been forever accomplished.

Again, absolutely nothing is said in this passage about the *torment of the wicked* being "forever and ever." Rather it is the ascending smoke that is said to be an enduring testimony. One may perhaps *assume* the torment continues, but to do so flies in the face of the remainder of Scripture, and it contradicts the very OT allusions employed. Thus, it is a false assumption with no basis in biblical teaching. "The wicked will *perish*, and the enemies of the Lord will be like the flowers of the pastures; they *vanish -- like smoke they vanish away*" (Psalm 37:20).

"'Smoke' has aptly been said to be the formless relic of an object that has been consumed, or decomposed, by the action of fire. It is but a relic, a vestige, an emblem, a lingering trace of the passing, the drifting aftermath that remains from *an object that has been destroyed*. A perpetual smoke may, therefore, well stand for a *perpetual reminder* before the universe of an irreparable ruin that has taken place, a burning up that has accomplished its allotted purpose. The same inspired portrayal, it is to be ever remembered, declares that God will 'consume,' 'devour,' 'destroy,' cause to 'perish,' and 'blot out' all the wicked. That dread transaction, or operation, involves and constitutes the 'second death.' The perpetuity intended is not, therefore, of the *torment*, but of the *death* following thereafter and caused thereby" [Dr. Leroy Edwin Froom, *The Conditionalist Faith of Our Fathers: The Conflict of the Ages Over the Nature and Destiny of Man*, vol. 1, p. 409].

FOUR ~ "...and they have no rest day and night" (vs. 11). "The phrase 'they have no rest day or night' (Revelation 14:11) is interpreted by traditionalists as descriptive of the eternal torment of hell. The phrase, however, denotes the *continuity* and not the *eternal duration* of an action" [Dr. Bacchiocchi, p. 213].

This particular phrase refers to uninterrupted continuity until a desired goal is achieved. There will be no break, no reprieve, no relaxing, no respite, no "time out" until the intended purpose has been accomplished. Some people, for example, when trying to break a world record (like riding a roller coaster) will take regular *breaks* in order to go to the bathroom or to catch a quick nap. *Men* who torture other men will not infrequently *pause* during the infliction of their torments so their victims may recover sufficiently to be tortured again. There will be *no* such breaks for rest, neither by day nor by night, when destruction is poured out from God upon the wicked. It will continue until the "*wages* of sin" has been realized: *Death*. God is not the ultimate sadist, inflicting horrible torments upon creatures He keeps alive for no other reason than to torture them forever. God has promised *death* to those who choose to reject His offer of *life*. It is thus *death* that they experience, painful and torturous though it will be, rather than an eternal *life* in ceaseless miseries. The wages of sin is a *loss of life*, not a *life of loss*; it is declared to be *destruction*, not *preservation*.

Dr. Harold Guillebaud correctly explains that this phrase "certainly says that there will be no break or intermission in the suffering of the followers of the Beast, *while it continues*; but in itself it does not say that it will continue forever" [*The Righteous Judge: A Study of the Biblical Doctrine of Everlasting Punishment*, p. 24].

This can clearly be seen, and this interpretation thus substantiated, in the destruction of Edom. This nation would experience the fire and brimstone of the Lord's fierce wrath, and "it shall not be quenched *night or day*; its smoke shall *go up forever*" (Isaiah 34:10). We know for a fact that the "fire and brimstone" spoken of with reference to Edom did indeed cease when its "work of destruction" had been accomplished. Thus, the idiomatic phrase "not quenched night or day" (a *Hebraism*) clearly referred to *continuity*, not *perpetuity*. I see no exegetical reason to suggest otherwise with the passage in Revelation 14, a passage which draws from these very same OT figures.

This expression in Revelation is found repeatedly in the OT writings. "You will live in constant suspense, filled with dread *both night and day*, never sure of your life" (Deuteronomy 28:66). It would be an *unrelenting* dread; one which *never lessened*. Just as the wrath of God would be unrelenting upon those who experienced it. There would be no break, no "time out," no letting up. In Psalm 32 David described the torment he felt over his sin: "For *day and night* your hand was heavy upon me; my strength was sapped as in the heat of summer" (vs. 4). The picture here is of *unrelenting* torment of the inner man; God's hand heavy upon him. God did not relent *until* the desired result was achieved: repentance. His hand was heavy upon him *day and night*, without rest, *until* he was brought to the desired goal of repentance. The torment *ceased* when its intended purpose was *realized*. The wages of sin is not *torment*, it is *death*. The *process* by which that promised result is achieved will be *torturous* and unrelenting. An execution is never pleasant, either for the victim or the executioners. As unpleasant and tormenting as the *dying process* is, the true punishment inflicted is *death itself*, not the process by which it is realized. Although the one being executed *will suffer* as he is *dying*, his true punishment is *death* -- the loss of life. So it will be for the lost on the day of judgment.

"To sum up, the four figures present in the scene of Revelation 14:9-11 complement one another in describing the final destruction of apostates. The 'unmixed' wine of God's fury poured out in full strength suggests a judgment resulting in extinction. The burning sulphur denotes some degree of conscious punishment that precedes the extinction. The rising smoke serves as a continuous reminder of God's just judgment. The suffering will continue day and night until the ungodly are completely destroyed" [Dr. Bacchiocchi, p. 213].

Chapter 17
Salted With Fire

In Mark 9:49 Jesus made a statement that has puzzled disciples for many hundreds of years. While in the city of Capernaum, and in the privacy of a house, surrounded by the Twelve, He entered into a dialogue with them about several matters of importance. Near the end of this discourse He stated, "For everyone will be salted with fire." A small handful of versions, the *King James Version* primary among them, expands the verse to read: "For every one shall be salted with fire, and every sacrifice shall be salted with salt" (more about this expansion later). Needless to say, there has been *much* scholarly speculation as to the meaning and significance of our Lord's declaration to the Twelve. Dr. Albert Barnes, in his classic work *Notes on the Bible*, observes, "Perhaps no passage in the New Testament has given more perplexity to commentators than this, and it may be impossible now to fix its precise meaning." In his noted *Commentary on the Whole Bible*, Matthew Henry strongly concurs, stating that these "verses are somewhat difficult, and interpreters agree not in the sense of them." The scholarly team of Jamieson, Fausset and Brown, in their commentary, declare: "A difficult verse, on which much has been written ~ some of it to little purpose." Dr. Charles Ellicott has written, "The verse presents considerable difficulties, both as regards the reading and the interpretation" [*Ellicott's Commentary on the Whole Bible*, vol. 6, p. 215]. "Vs. 49 is a *crux interpretum*, and has given rise to great diversity of interpretation" [Dr. W. Robertson Nicoll, *The Expositor's Greek Testament*, vol. 1, p. 407]. "This is admittedly one of the most difficult verses in Mark. Over a dozen different interpretations are found in the various commentaries" [*The Expositor's Bible Commentary*, vol. 8, p. 709]. "These verses have been the subject of much controversy. They are obscure and difficult" [*The Pulpit Commentary*, vol. 16, Mark: part 1, p. 27]. As one can very quickly perceive, about the only thing most biblical scholars will agree upon with respect to this verse is that it is extremely difficult to interpret.

The key, however, which is true with almost all difficult passages, is to be found in properly discerning the immediate context within which the perplexing statement is contained. *Generally*, though not always, this will prove to be enlightening. Lifting a phrase, sentence or paragraph from its context, and seeking to interpret it as it stands alone, separate from its surrounding statements, is an irresponsible, though not uncommon, practice of too many readers of Scripture. It leads very quickly to what has come to be known as "proof-texting," which has been the bane of responsible biblical interpretation for centuries. This practice, sad to say, is especially popular among legalistic patternists, and the pathetic feuding among scores of factions with Christendom is the pitiful outcome of such. As is noted within the *Pulpit Commentary*, this verse is rather "obscure and difficult, but the *context* is of great assistance" [p. 27]. Thus, to aid us in our interpretation of Mark 9:49 we must seek to ascertain the doctrinal context within which this statement by our Lord is contained.

First, it is important to point out that only in the gospel of Mark is this statement of Jesus to be found. The other writers do not mention it, therefore we are unable to turn to them for any clarification. Thus, in seeking an understanding of the *context*, we are limited to what Mark writes in this particular location. However, much is revealed to us. We know, for example, that Jesus had sought some relief from the pressing multitudes so that He could provide more intimate counsel to His closest disciples. "They went out and began to go through Galilee, and Jesus did not want anyone to know where they were, because He was teaching His disciples" (Mark 9:30-31a). They came to the city of Capernaum, and then entered a house. "Sitting down, He called the Twelve to Himself" (vs. 35) and began a dialogue with them which included some dire warnings about some of the attitudes and actions they had been recently displaying. For example, we are informed that these apostles had been "discussing with one another which of them was the greatest" (vs. 34). Our Lord, therefore, had to set them straight rather quickly on what constituted genuine greatness in the sight of God, and in so doing emphasized the importance of being a *servant* to all. Such squabbling regarding who is over who also is not conducive to unity, harmony and oneness, thus for the sake of *peace* these men needed to refocus. Indeed, Jesus' final statement to them in this chapter was, "Be at peace with one another" (vs. 50). Conflict among the inner circle would have been detrimental to the mission that lay ahead of them. *Unity of the Spirit* among all of our Lord's disciples was essential, something that must be kept in mind as we seek to interpret His statement to them in vs. 49.

In addition to the debate among the Twelve over who was the greatest, we also find John saying to Jesus, "Teacher, we saw someone casting out demons in Your name, and we tried to hinder him because he was not following us" (vs. 38; cf. Luke 9:49-50). Once again the context reveals that the disciples were leaning toward an exclusionary, isolationist theology, and the Lord dispels this fallacy quickly. Not only were they individually seeking to elevate themselves over one another, but they perceived *their group* to be far above all others. "If you are not walking along *with us*, in *our* little band of disciples, then you have no part in Him." Sound familiar? We tend to do the same thing today. If you are not in *our group*, then you are not really a Christian. Not only that, but we'll do all in our power to *hinder* your service to the Lord (since, in our view, you're not really serving Him anyway, but the devil). Jesus rebukes John, though kindly, informing him that one does not have to "walk along with John" in order to be in union and sweet fellowship with Jesus. "He who is not against us is for us" (vs. 40). This is a lesson we need *today* just as much as John needed it *then*.

In their heated argument with one another over who was actually the *greatest*, and in their recent hindering of those disciples who were not "of their group," Jesus perceived the seeds of sectarianism, schism and isolationism. There were problems developing within this body of believers that needed to be addressed, and very quickly and boldly. They needed to realize that if these threats to the body were not met and defeated, the cause of Christ would be in great jeopardy from the very beginning, and that they themselves were in danger of being lost. This was a critical moment, and Jesus took them aside and issued some dire warnings. If there was anything in the body (hands, feet, eyes -- speaking figuratively -- vs. 43-48) that was a potential threat to the life of that body, it needed to be dealt with, and with great *firmness*. To cause another believer to falter or fall was no light offense (vs. 42). They were to be a *positive* influence in the world about them. However, if their light became hidden or went out; if, as the salt of the earth, they became "unsalty," then they would lose their effectiveness (vs. 50). All would be lost unless steps were taken immediately to alter their self-destructive course. *This*, then, is the immediate context within which we find our difficult statement by Jesus to these close companions who would soon play such a vital role in the establishment and expansion of His cause on earth. *Unto them* Jesus says, "Everyone will be salted with fire" (vs. 49).

The Perpetual Torture Theory

As was previously noted, there are a great many speculative theories proposed as to the possible meaning of our Lord's words in this verse. Some are so far out and ridiculous that they really do not merit much consideration, and very few scholars even give them a second glance. To quote once again the words of Jamieson, Fausset and Brown in their commentary, this is "a difficult verse, on which much has been written -- some of it to little purpose." Thus, we shall not waste any time on them. However, there are three major interpretations that really do need to be examined, as each of them has a significant number of supporters among biblical scholars. The first of these theories, and the one with which the reader may possibly be the most familiar, as it is a rather common interpretation among religious traditionalists, is the view that Jesus is speaking of the perpetual torture in fire of those who are cast into hell. Let me state at the very outset of this study that I completely and vehemently *reject* this view, as do a good many other biblical scholars.

Yes, Jesus did talk about the consequences that would befall those who caused stumbling to other believers. "It would be better for him if, with a heavy millstone hung around his neck, he had been cast into the sea" (vs. 42). Yes, there would be consequences to be faced if one did not gain control over those things that might cause harm to the cause of Christ. He spoke of "unquenchable fire" and "undying worms." It would not be pleasant. The message, then, is *purify* yourselves, present yourselves as *acceptable* sacrifices before your God, otherwise you would be cast away and destroyed. Some, therefore, see the fire in Mark 9:49 to be related in some way to the fires of hell. Since salt has a *preserving* quality, they believe the expression "salted with fire" speaks of *preserving* the body in hell so that the fire can inflict everlasting, unending suffering without that body ever being utterly consumed. Thus, the word "everyone" refers only to the lost, and the "salting with fire" suggests that God will preserve the lost alive in the fires of hell so that their torment might never end.

John Wesley (1703-1791), in his *Explanatory Notes* on this particular passage, wrote that the damned will be cast into hell, and they "shall be, as it were, salted with fire, preserved, not consumed thereby." John Gill (1697-1771), a staunch Calvinist, in his *Exposition of the Entire Bible*, declared, "as salt keeps flesh from putrefaction and corruption, so the fire of hell, as it will burn, torture, and distress rebellious sinners, it will preserve them in their beings; they shall not be consumed by it, but continued in it ... the soul in torment shall never die ... they shall be preserved in their beings in the fire, just as flesh is preserved by salt." Matthew Henry (1662-1714), in his *Commentary on the Whole Bible*, wrote, "in hell they shall be salted with fire; coals of fire shall be scattered upon them ... that by the power of God it shall be made to last always." In more recent times, commentators state: "Their being salted with fire imports and implies that as to their beings they shall be preserved even as salt preserves things from corruption so that they may be the objects of the eternal wrath of God ... kept perpetually in a state of the severest pain ... perpetually permeated by fire" [C. E. W. Dorris, *A Commentary on the Gospel according to Mark*, p. 224]. This, then, is the interpretation of those who believe God is a perpetual torturer of the lost; that He intentionally keeps them alive for the purpose of inflicting as much suffering upon them as possible, and that this unimaginable torture *never, ever ends.*

I *utterly reject* this first theory that our Lord Jesus is speaking to the twelve apostles of perpetual punishing in the lake of fire, thus declaring that the "second DEATH" (Revelation 20:14) is really a second LIFE, albeit one that is characterized by infinite misery. "The wages of sin is *death*," says the apostle Paul, "but the free gift of God is eternal *life* in Christ Jesus our Lord" (Romans 6:23). Not so, say the traditionalists. The damned have eternal life as well, just a life in torment. As John Gill stated (as previously noted), "the soul in torment shall *never die*." Well, so much for the wages of sin being *death*. So much for the lake of fire being the "second *death*." The damned will *never* die. Or, so say the traditionalists. I believe I'll stick to the Scriptures, which declare: "The soul that sins will die" (Ezekiel 18:4). It does *not* say the soul that sins will be kept alive for the purpose of perpetual torment.

I am far from being alone in my total rejection of this first interpretation of Mark 9:49. *Other* scholars find it *equally* reprehensible. Jamieson, Fausset and Brown, for example, in their commentary, describe this view as "a farfetched, as well as harsh, interpretation." They assert that this theory "is equally contrary to the symbolical sense of salt and the Scripture representations of future torment." Dr. Albert Barnes (1798-1870), in his *Notes on the Bible*, states that "this meaning is not quite satisfactory." That's putting it rather mildly. A good many other commentaries and biblical resources (such as theological dictionaries and encyclopedias) simply refuse to even *list* or *consider* this theory, not regarding it as even worthy of space in their scholarly examinations. I would concur. Dr. Paul Kretzmann asserts, "Jesus does *not* refer, in this instance, to the fire of hell" [*Popular Commentary of the Bible*, The NT: vol. 1, p. 217]. One person emailed me not long ago to inform me that his preacher had recently presented a sermon in which he used Mark 9:49 to teach that "a person in hell has fire salted down on him to *intensify* the agony." Like rubbing salt in a wound, I suppose. Thus, we find members of sects and factions portraying our loving God as some kind of Cosmic Monster who finds some strange satisfaction in raining down endless misery and suffering upon those who have religious perceptions, preferences and practices different from their own. Those who do not use musical instruments in their worship condemn those who do, suggesting God will take that "heretic" who dares to sing praises to Him with instrumental accompaniment and preserve that "apostate" alive for the sole purpose of inflicting as much misery and torment upon him or her as possible. Frankly, declaring such about our loving Father is blasphemous.

The Fiery Ordeal Theory

Some scholars believe the Lord, in this context, was preparing His closest disciples for the persecution and affliction that would soon be unleashed upon them as a result of their faith in Him. In Mark 9:31 He informed them, "The Son of Man is to be delivered into the hands of men, and they will kill Him; and when He has been killed, He will rise three days later." The next verse states, "They did not understand this statement, and they were afraid to ask Him" (vs. 32). There is nothing else in the remainder of the chapter, however, that would indicate this theme was being *further* developed by Jesus. There is no question that on *other* occasions He made it clear they would be suffering affliction for their faith. Indeed, several decades later the apostle Peter would write, "Beloved, do not be surprised at the *fiery ordeal* among you, which comes *upon you* for your testing, as though some strange thing were happening to you; but to the degree that you share the sufferings of Christ, keep on rejoicing" (1 Peter 4:12-13). This fiery ordeal coming down upon them is seen to be a *similar* thought to being "salted with fire," thus it is thought to signify the disciples would have to undergo persecution. Those who endured would be saved, those who forfeited their faith to preserve their lives would be lost. Matthew 24 is brought into the argument: "They will deliver you to tribulation" (vs. 9) ... "but the one who endures to the end, he shall be saved" (vs. 13). "In the world you have tribulation, but take courage; I have overcome the world" (John 16:33).

The *Pulpit Commentary* strongly suggests that "*This* was their 'salting with fire'" [p. 9]. Everyone who confesses the name of Jesus Christ will be salted with fire: i.e., they will experience severe tribulation in this world for their faith. Some feel that since Mark was primarily writing to the saints in Rome, it was only natural that he would mention this statement by the Lord Jesus when no other gospel author did so. Why? Because the Christians in Rome would be the victims of a great deal of *fiery persecution*, being easily accessible to the wicked governing authorities of the day. "Another interpretation sees in the fire the trials and persecutions of the disciples of Jesus. ... as salt always accompanied the temple sacrifices, so fire -- i.e., persecution, trials, and suffering -- will accompany the true disciple's sacrifice" of themselves in service to their Lord [*The Expositor's Bible Commentary*, vol. 8, p. 709]. Thus, the saints in Rome needed to "understand that the purifying fires of persecution were not to be thought of as foreign to their vocation as Christians, because 'everyone will be salted with fire'" [*ibid*].

Dr. Albert Barnes makes this observation: "The passage has no reference at all to future punishment. ... The word 'fire' here denotes self-denials, sacrifices, and trials." The *International Standard Bible Encyclopedia*, in commenting on this difficult verse, states, "perhaps the saying refers to the future persecutions in which Jesus' disciples will become sacrifices for God" [vol. 4, p. 386]. Dr. B. W. Johnson, in the *People's New Testament with Explanatory Notes*, says the statement "denotes suffering, persecution, trial and distress of any kind" [vol. 1, p. 195]. And the apostle Peter wrote, "In this you greatly rejoice, even though now for a little while, if necessary, you have been distressed by various trials, that the proof of your faith, being more precious than gold which is perishable, even though *tested by fire*, may be found to result in praise and glory and honor at the revelation of Jesus Christ" (1 Peter 1:6-7). Although this is indeed a very attractive theory in some ways, and is certainly preferable to the previous position, and although it is certainly true that disciples of Christ will undergo the "fiery ordeal" of affliction in this life, nevertheless there is really nothing within the immediate context surrounding Mark 9:49 that would suggest this was what Jesus intended in His statement. Therefore, I must also reject *this* theory as a viable interpretation for this passage.

The Holy Spirit Theory

I am personally convinced, as are the vast majority of biblical scholars, that Jesus, when He said to His close companions, "Everyone shall be salted with fire," had Leviticus 2:13 in mind: "Every grain offering of yours, moreover, you shall season with salt, so that the salt of the covenant of your God shall not be lacking from your grain offering; with *all* your offerings you shall offer salt." This was also true of blood sacrifices (bulls and rams): "And you shall present them (the bulls and rams) before the Lord, and the priests shall throw salt on them, and they shall offer them up as a burnt offering to the Lord" (Ezekiel 43:24). ALL offerings to the Lord were to be *salted*, and, in figurative language, this even applied to the offering up of ourselves unto the Lord. For example, in Isaiah 66:20 we read, "They shall bring all your brethren from all the nations as a grain offering to the Lord ... just as the sons of Israel bring their grain offering in a clean vessel to the house of the Lord." As we have already noted, the grain offering was to be salted/seasoned (sprinkled) with salt. Thus, at least symbolically and figuratively, so also would the "grain offering" of these "your brethren." The apostle Paul wrote, "I urge you therefore, brethren, by the mercies of God, to present your bodies a living and holy sacrifice, acceptable to God, which is your spiritual service of worship. And do not be conformed to this world, but be transformed by the renewing of your mind, that you may prove what the will of God is, that which is good and acceptable and perfect" (Romans 12:1-2).

Sacrifices being offered up unto God must be *purified*. Under the Old Covenant this was symbolized by the pouring out of salt upon the sacrifice. Under the New Covenant, we are *salted from above* with a different *purifying* Agent: the Holy Spirit. This "fire" falls upon us to effect a transformation from that which is old and impure to that which is new and sanctified. As we present ourselves unto Him, He pours out Himself upon us! We thus become a sweet smelling offering unto our God. Dr. Paul Kretzmann writes, "As every sacrifice of the Old Testament had to be salted, so every disciple, every believer, must be salted with fire. Jesus does *not* refer, in this instance, to the fire of hell, but to the purifying fire of His rule and leading. It is the discipline of the Word and of the Spirit of God which gradually cleanses the believers of sin, and kills the works and desires of the flesh" [vol. 1, p. 218]. "Here our Lord speaks of the spiritual sacrifice which each man offers of his body, soul and spirit (Romans 12:1), and declares that 'salt,' the purifying grace of the Eternal Spirit, is needed that it may be acceptable" [Dr. Charles Ellicott, vol. 6, p. 216]. Thus, "the idea of purification is prominent in Mark 9:49" [*The Zondervan Pictorial Encyclopedia of the Bible*, vol. 5, p. 220]. "The whole emphasis of the passage is thus in favor of Christian purification" [*The Pulpit Commentary*, p. 27].

By the way, the *King James Version* actually tends to strengthen this particular interpretation by the *textual addition* incorporated into its reading of Mark 9:49 -- "For every one shall be salted with fire, *and every sacrifice shall be salted with salt.*" That last phrase is missing from most reputable manuscripts, therefore you will not find it in more modern versions of the Bible (and you won't find it in most ancient versions either, for that matter). Dr. Bruce M. Metzger, in his fabulous, monumental work "A *Textual Commentary on the Greek New Testament*," explained this addition: "The history of the text seems to have been as follows. At a very early period a scribe, having found in Leviticus 2:13 a clue to the meaning of Jesus' enigmatic statement, wrote the Old Testament passage in the margin of his copy of Mark. In subsequent copyings the marginal gloss was added to the words of the text," thus creating the reading we find in the *KJV* [p. 103]. The scholars who produced *The Expositor's Bible Commentary* agree, stating that "a copyist finding Leviticus 2:13 a clue to the understanding of this difficult saying noted the OT passage in the margin; subsequently his marginal gloss was added" to the text [vol. 8, p. 709]. "The sacrificial salt is a symbol of the covenant relationship which the children of Israel had with God. For every disciple of Jesus, the salt of the covenant is the Divine Fire 'which purifies, preserves and consummates the sacrifice.' The fire is the Holy Spirit" [*ibid*]. Adam Clarke, in his commentary, points out that a good many scholars take this passage "as referring to the influence of the Spirit of God in the hearts of believers" [*Clarke's Commentary*, vol. 5, p. 320]. Dr. James Hastings informs the reader that Dr. Swete, in *his* study of the gospel record of Mark, "interprets the fire of the Christian life as the Holy Spirit" [*Dictionary of Christ and the Gospels*, vol. 2, p. 552].

If one looks at the overall context of this passage in Mark 9, one will again note that the primary problems that elicited our Lord's comments were (1) the apostles debating among themselves as to who was the greatest, and (2) their effort to hinder and exclude those who did not "follow along" with them. These were men who needed a lesson on *acceptance* of their fellow spiritual siblings in the *One Body* that Jesus would bring about with His sacrifice. Those things which stood in the way of such unity and harmony could prove eternally costly. Yet, there was a power that could transform them and unite them. If they were to give themselves as sweet smelling offerings to their God, they would need to be "salted" with that which would sanctify them, and in so doing serve to awaken them to the unity that should typify the Family of God. That power from on high that would transform and unite them, that with which they would be "salted," was the Holy Spirit, symbolized by the figure of "fire." As the apostle Paul, for example, went out to bring the Gentiles into this *One Body*, he stated he was called to be "a minister of Christ Jesus to the Gentiles, ministering as a priest the gospel of God, that my offering of the Gentiles might become acceptable, sanctified by the Holy Spirit" (Romans 15:16). Notice the wording here, as it clearly looks back to the Leviticus 2:13 passage. He is ministering "as a priest," his "offering" is the Gentiles, and they are "sanctified" by the Holy Spirit (i.e., the salting process) that they might "become acceptable" to God.

Rather than excluding others, and seeking to elevate themselves above others, these men within the inner circle of Christ Jesus needed to realize that He had come to offer up everyone as a sweet smelling sacrifice to the Father: "*Everyone* will be salted with fire." By virtue of the outpouring of the Spirit, both Jews and Gentiles would be brought before the Father as *One Body*. In Joel 2:28 we're told, "And it will come about after this that I will pour out My Spirit on *all flesh*." On the day of Pentecost the Spirit was poured out, just as Joel prophesied. "And there appeared to them *tongues as of fire* distributing themselves, and they rested on *each one of them*" (Acts 2:3). In the very same way, says Peter, the Gentiles (represented by Cornelius and his household; just as the 120 in the upper room were representative of the Jews ... Jew and Gentile = "all flesh" from the Jewish perspective) "have received the Holy Spirit just as we did" (Acts 10:47; cf. Acts 11:15f). The apostles that day, as Jesus spoke to them, needed to hear the same message we today need to hear, due to our tendency also to *dis*unite with one another in the *One Body*: "With all humility and gentleness, with patience, showing forbearance to one another in love, be diligent to preserve the unity of the Spirit in the bond of peace. For there is one body and one Spirit, just as you were called in one hope of your calling" (Ephesians 4:2-4). In short, *everyone* needs to be salted with fire from above; we need to be indwelt and empowered by the Holy Spirit, and thereby transformed. When this happens, barriers that divide us will come down. No longer will disciples seek to determine who is the greatest; no longer will they seek to hinder others who do not "walk along with them." Instead, sanctified by His Spirit, they will "pursue the things which make for peace and the building up of one another" (Romans 14:19). This is the "peace and joy *in the Holy Spirit*" that characterizes "the kingdom of God" (Romans 14:17).

Notice the following fabulous, astute comment by Dr. Albert Barnes in his commentary regarding this powerful statement by Jesus: "The main scope of the passage was *not* to discourse on future punishment. The chief object of the passage was to teach the apostles that 'other men,' those not 'with them,' just might *also* be true Christians," and that "they ought to be disposed to *look favorably upon*" these others, whether they are "walking about" with them or not.

It is my conviction that we in the church today desperately need this very same insight, and it is my conviction that it can and will come by the very same means: being salted with fire as we offer ourselves up to God as living sacrifices. That is: we are being filled and sanctified and transformed by the outpouring of the Holy Spirit into our innermost being. May God open our eyes that we may open our hearts to Him. Oh, the joys and blessings that will be ours when we do.

Chapter 18
Understanding the Undying Worm

In speaking of *Gehenna*, Jesus describes it as a place "where their worm does not die, and the fire is not quenched" (Mark 9:48). Some versions repeat this phrase in verses 44 and 46, although there is little textual evidence for such. Most translations, based on a superior Greek text, include it only in verse 48. What is Jesus suggesting here? Is He really describing a place where maggots are immortal? Or is this merely an allusion to *symbols* and *figures* found in the OT writings? I believe the latter is clearly the case. Or, to use the wording of the *Zondervan Pictorial Encyclopedia of the Bible*, this passage "is purely figurative" [vol. 5, p. 969].

Jesus is referring to the prophecy of Isaiah. In the final statement of this book of prophecy we find a judgment scene, and we see the joy of God's people as they behold His righteous judgment on their behalf against His (and their) enemies.

Isaiah 66:15-16
For behold, the Lord will come in fire and His chariots like the whirlwind, to render His anger with fury, and His rebuke with flames of fire. For the Lord will execute judgment by fire and by His sword on all flesh, and those *slain* by the Lord will be many.

Please note here that the text says the Lord will *slay* these ungodly ones, it does *not* declare the Lord will *torture* them. Notice also that the redeemed will be able to witness the *result* of this destruction carried out by God against the wicked:

Isaiah 66:24
Then they shall go forth and look on the *corpses of men* who have transgressed against Me. For their worm shall not die, and their fire shall not be quenched; and they shall be an abhorrence to all mankind.

Please note once again that there is absolutely *no mention* of the wicked being tortured alive forever and ever. Indeed, just the opposite. The only thing the redeemed behold are *corpses*. The wicked are dead. They have been slain by the fury of God's fire and sword. Thus, all that the redeemed see is visible evidence of death and destruction. It is one huge scene of abhorrence and shame. It is a giant garbage dump composed of the dead corpses of the wicked. They are not writhing in pain and screaming out in anguish. They are not being tortured in endless misery. *They are dead.*

What does all of this represent? Of what is this a figure? If one studies the history of armies and warfare during ancient times one will discover a very common practice of those who were the conquerors. They would lead the people they had set free (and even those they had captured) out to the scene of the battle, and there they would make them look upon the bodies of the defeated army.

In some cases this was to strike fear into the hearts of the conquered people, letting them know their army was gone and could no longer fight for them. In other cases, it was to instill disgust in the hearts of those who beheld these slain ones. It also served as an occasion of *joy* for those who had been liberated from the ravages of this now defeated and destroyed army. The liberated would behold the *lifeless corpses* of those who had oppressed them, and they would see these slain ones being consumed by maggots (the "worms") and by the fires that had been set to *burn up* (consume) the corpses so as to prevent the spread of disease. "Corruption (the worm) and burning (fire) are mentioned together as the two most common ways of disposing of dead bodies" [Kittel's *Theological Dictionary of the New Testament*, vol. 7, p. 454].

"The figure is taken from heaps of the dead slain in battle; and the prophet says that the number would be so great that their worm -- the worm feeding on the dead -- would not die, would live long -- as long as there were carcasses to be devoured; and that the fire which was used to burn the bodies of the dead would continue long to burn, and would not be extinguished until they were consumed. The figure, therefore, denotes great misery, and certain and terrible destruction" [Albert Barnes, *Barnes' Notes on the New Testament*].

Barnes is quick to point out, however, that this is *figurative* language, even though it draws from literal historical practice. He writes, "It is not to be supposed that there will be any 'real' worm in hell." It merely represented the truth that the *consumption* would continue until the *destruction* was complete. Kittel writes, "The worm does not die until it has completed its work and the bones as well as the flesh of the dead are consumed, so that all hope of restoration to life is extinguished. The expression thus denotes total destruction."

W. E. Vine, in his *Expository Dictionary of OT & NT Words*, stresses that "the statement signifies the exclusion of hope of restoration, the punishment being eternal." "Eternal," that is, in the sense that the resultant state -- death, utter destruction and consumption -- will *never, ever* be reversed. Once dead, they are dead *forever and ever*. In other words, our Lord is referring to the final punishment of the wicked, and He is indicating it will be a destruction and death so complete and total that there will never, ever be any hope of restoration to life. The wicked will be utterly consumed by actions that can't be stymied by the victims (which is the significance of the worm being "undying" and the fire being "unquenchable"); the "worm" and "fire" will *continue unabated* as/until they *consume completely* that which is committed to them.

In commenting on the passage in Isaiah 66:24, *The Expositor's Bible Commentary* states, "A comparison with Jeremiah 7:32 - 8:3 strongly suggests the prophet has the Valley of Hinnom, or *Gehenna*, in mind," and that the application is "to eternal punishment" [vol. 6, p. 354]. I agree that Jesus has this location outside the walls of Jerusalem in mind, and that He is using it figuratively to convey a message of doom for the godless.

Part of this valley was committed to use as the garbage dump of Jerusalem. It is reported by writers who lived at that time that there were always fires burning or smoldering in the dump, and that numerous maggots ("worms") could be found there consuming the waste. At times notorious criminals were cast *dead* into the garbage outside the walls of Jerusalem (sounds like a scene in *Revelation*: the wicked being cast into *Gehenna* which is outside the walls of the New Jerusalem). The bodies of these criminals were allowed to lie there (instead of receiving a proper burial, something cherished by the Jews) and to be consumed by the maggots and the fires that were always present in that foul and loathsome place. It was a scene of abhorrence and shame. Few wanted to end their days cast into the garbage to become food for maggots and fire.

This is the image Jesus is presenting to us in His statement. A day will come when the Lord will appear in judgment against His enemies. He will *slay* them with fire and sword, and their dead bodies will be cast into the garbage dump (*Gehenna*) outside the walls of the New Jerusalem. There the righteous will witness the effects of this great destruction: the dead will be piled high in testimony of the victory of God over the forces arrayed against Him, and these corpses shall be utterly consumed so that they will never pose a threat to the people of God again.

Please note that *absolutely nothing whatsoever* is said, either by Jesus or Isaiah, about the bodies of the wicked being either conscious, alive or endlessly tortured. *They are dead.* They are corpses. They have been *slain.* The *only* thing mentioned which "does not die" *is the worm.* If someone is looking for something immortal in these passages, the only thing he might find is maggots. Both the fire and the worms are said to be enduring. Such is *not* stated, however, with reference to their victims.

"Whether literally or metaphorically understood, the phrase must not be taken as the basis of a Christian doctrine of future retribution. The worm does not stand for remorse; it is simply part of a picture of complete physical corruption" [Dr. James Hastings, *Dictionary of Christ and the Gospels*, vol. 1, p. 67]. These are purely figures and symbols. They depict utter, irreversible destruction. By trying to make them literal, or by trying to transfer the qualities of the worm and fire to the objects they are said to affect, one formulates a doctrine which goes well beyond authorial intent. Such a practice is hermeneutically unsound and leads to false teaching.

Even if one allows that maggots *might* truly be immortal (which, of course, they are *not*), it says nothing about that upon which they feast. Indeed, the OT Scriptures, from which the "worm" figure is drawn, declare these maggots feast upon *corpses, not* upon the living. These are really not difficult figures to interpret if one will simply take note of the type of literature one is seeking to interpret, and if one will further recognize that the interpretation of many of these figures is to be found within the inspired writings themselves, *not* in the false fancies of paganism, and if one will employ even a small degree of common sense.

A careful exegesis of these passages in which mention is made of the "undying worm" will quickly reveal to the serious student of Scripture that they do *not* support the false doctrine of perpetual torture of the unredeemed. Indeed, sound exegesis demonstrates just the opposite reality. They portray the utter consumption and ultimate elimination of the unredeemed.

Chapter 19
Beaten With Fewer Blows

Luke 12:47-48 is a powerful passage "*peculiar* to St. Luke, and every word is full of *profoundest* interest." So wrote Dr. Charles John Ellicott (1819-1905), a man who served faithfully for many years as the *Bishop of Gloucester* (a distinguished English theologian and acclaimed academic), in his monumental commentary on the Bible [vol. 6, p. 304]. The primary reason why this passage has drawn the attention of so many Christians over the centuries is because Jesus *seems* to be *strongly suggesting* that there will be *degrees of punishment* at the time of the Final Judgment of mankind. Most men clearly understand that degrees of punishment in the *temporal* realm are quite common, but suggesting that these varying levels of punishment and/or suffering just might *also* be the norm in the *eternal* realm *troubles* some who believe the Final Judgment will be a rather *black-or-white (no shades of gray)* event: one is either lost or saved; life or death; heaven or hell, with all men fully experiencing (each to the fullest degree) one or the other. This statement by Jesus, though, seems to promote a much different perspective.

As was noted above, we are all familiar with the concept of one's punishment being *proportionate* to one's crime. Among fair-minded, *justice*-seeking peoples the world over, this is reflected in their laws. One is not executed for going five mph over the speed limit in a residential area, for example. Nor is a serial killer fined only twenty dollars for his crimes. True justice demands that the punishment inflicted *must* fit the crime committed. Among the people of Israel, for example, the Law of Moses recognized varying degrees of punishment depending upon the offense. "If the guilty man deserves to be beaten, the judge shall make him lie down and have him flogged in his presence with the number of lashes his crime deserves, but he mustn't give him more than forty lashes" (Deuteronomy 25:2-3). The Jews of Jesus' day were so careful *not* to inflict punishment *beyond* this limit (40 lashes), that they would often stop at 39, just in case they had *miscounted*. In other words, *lesser* was considered preferable to *greater* with regard to the inflicting of a painful punishment upon an offender. "For petty offences the Jews in many cases inflicted so few as four, five and six stripes" [Dr. Adam Clarke, *Clarke's Commentary*, vol. 5, p. 445].

A good *many* disciples of Jesus Christ, however, have long declared that such degrees of punishment (where the nature of the punishment is in direct proportion to the nature of the crime) will *not* apply on the day of Final Judgment. I actually had a church leader inform me some years ago that the person who ate a cookie in the church building (their sect believes eating in a church building is a mortal sin) would experience the same "*eternal torture*" as Adolf Hitler. If this is truly reflective of the nature of the "justice" of our God, then, frankly, we're *all* in trouble. It is my strong conviction, however, that such a perception of our *loving* God (and certainly the *proclamation* of such a perception) is nothing less than *blasphemous*, for it proclaims a deity that is neither just nor fair nor merciful, but rather one that is a cruel, vindictive, nit-picking ogre who would not hesitate to inflict unimaginable *torment* upon others for the least imaginable *triviality*. Little wonder that such men often reflect and project in their own dealings with others this concept of their God.

"God is *love*" (1 John 4:8, 16), and divine love does *not* present itself as some would have us believe. Yes, those who have knowingly and willfully lived in rebellion against a holy God must answer for their actions, and if God judges them unfit for eternal *life*, they must experience the wages of their sin: *death*. Execution is never pleasant, although the *suffering* experienced in said termination of life may vary from case to case (to which I can personally attest: having witnessed a number of people die, and having actually been present inside the death chamber, and at the side of, a man who was executed for murdering and raping a child). Nevertheless, an execution, no matter the amount of suffering that *precedes* that death, is still a far cry from keeping a victim alive for the *express purpose* of inflicting *endless conscious torture* upon him. Many assume it is the *latter* that the just nature of God demands. I'm convinced, however, that *Scripture* proclaims the opposite. The wages of sin is declared to be *death*, not *torture*, although the second death will most assuredly not be pleasant, and will be far *more* unpleasant for some than others, depending upon the nature of their rebellion against God and crimes against humanity.

It is declared by some Christians that *death* is not a fearful enough punishment. Try telling that to the person being executed! Others suggest that termination of *life* (extinction) removes any and all *suffering*. Again, try explaining that theory to the person being executed! "Extinction does *not* exclude the possibility of degrees of punishment" [Dr. Samuele Bacchiocchi, *Immortality or Resurrection? A Biblical Study on Human Nature and Destiny*, p. 240]. Frankly, it seems to *me* that it accommodates that doctrine far *better* than the false notion of endless torture. Those who have committed greater offenses against God and man (like Adolf Hitler, for example) would expect to be shown less mercy in their execution than one who had committed lesser offenses. Yes, *both* are worthy of death, and death will be their eternal destiny, but the nature of the punish*ing* that results in their final punish*ment* may well be quite different in *degree*. On the other hand, if both are to be kept alive (immortal) in the fires of hell for the purpose of endless torture, I seriously doubt that any *fluctuation in Fahrenheit* is going to be perceived by *either* as very significant (never-ending torture at 10,000 degrees Fahrenheit is hardly less severe than never-ending torture at 20,000 degrees Fahrenheit).

Regardless of what the true nature of final punishment proves to be (and I pray none of us will ever experience it), it appears rather certain from the Scriptures that our just and merciful and loving God will punish the wicked in some way that is fair and proportionate to their sins against Himself and their fellow men. As our Lord clearly states: some "will be beaten with *many* blows," whereas others "will be beaten with *few* blows" (Luke 12:47-48). This concept is further perceived in Jesus' rebuke of the inhabitants of certain cities of His day. He told them, "It will be more bearable for Tyre and Sidon on the Day of Judgment than for you ... it will be more bearable for Sodom on the Day of Judgment than for you" (Matthew 11:22, 24). *More* bearable? *Less* bearable? This statement by our Lord clearly suggests *degrees* of punishment. Again, we can only *speculate* as to the exact nature of these degrees, but "here it will suffice to observe that, whatever be its accidents, the essence of eternal punishment is that it will be marked by varying degrees of severity, with each of us by his own use of opportunity providing his own criterion" [Dr. James Hastings, *Dictionary of Christ and the Gospels*, vol. 2, p. 456].

"In this solemn passage (Luke 12:47-48) it is notable that *degrees* or *grades* in punishment are distinctly spoken of" [*Pulpit Commentary*, vol. 16: Luke, p. 338], and that "sinners are not to be cast indiscriminately into some common receptacle, but subjected to a series of graduated punishments of the most carefully adjusted character. According to a person's opportunities will be his doom" [*ibid*, p. 360]. Both this source and Dr. Hastings (see above) have *linked* how one responds to one's God-given opportunities with one's eternal destiny and the nature of the severity or blessedness of that destiny. I believe they are *absolutely correct* in their conclusion. Unto all men our God has given some degree of *"available light"* — a bright light proclaiming His glory, radiating His divine nature, and reflecting unto His creation His will for their daily lives. David, the "poet king," wrote: "The heavens declare the glory of God; the skies proclaim the work of His hands. Day after day they pour forth speech; night after night they display knowledge. There is no speech or language where their voice is not heard. Their voice goes out into all the earth, their words to the ends of the world" (Psalm 19:1-4). The apostle Paul quite astutely observed that "what may be known about God *is plain*" to the peoples of the earth, "because God has *made it plain* to them. For since the creation of the world God's invisible qualities — His eternal power and divine nature — have been *clearly seen*, being *understood* from what has been made, so that men are without excuse" (Romans 1:19-20).

This biblical truth will be discussed extensively in the next chapter, for the emphasis of this teaching, and this parallels the doctrine of degrees of both punishment and reward, is that there are degrees of revelation, enlightenment and opportunity, thereby necessitating degrees of *accountability*. It is *an eternal principle* that one is only accountable for what one has been given. The two talent man wasn't accountable for five talents, for example, but only for that with which he had been entrusted. *Other* servants would be accountable for *more* or *less* depending upon the nature of that with which they had been entrusted by their master. As Jesus Himself stated immediately following the text being examined in this study, "From everyone who has been given much shall much be required; and to whom they entrusted much, of him they will ask all the more" (Luke 12:48). The apostle Paul informed the brethren in Corinth (and, by extension, us as well) that if a person had a desire to do what was right, the fulfillment of that desire would be judged "acceptable according to what a man *has*, not according to what he does *not* have" (2 Cor. 8:12). Simply stated: final judgment will be based upon what each of us individually have done with what we've been given (insight, ability and opportunity), not upon those things to which we had absolutely no access through no fault of our own. Such truths *infuriate* the legalists, and for obvious reasons, but in the Final Judgment "penalty will be inflicted not as passion dictates, but as principle demands" [Dr. W. Robertson Nicoll, *The Expositor's Greek Testament*, vol. 1, p. 561-562]. The divine principles of love, equity and mercy clearly suggest the need for *individual* assessment in judgment based upon one's own response to available light, as well as God-given ability and opportunity. After all, as Lord Byron (1788-1824) astutely observed, "He who is *only* just is cruel; who upon the earth would live were all judged justly?!" I'm reminded of the cartoon depicting a husband and wife standing in line before the Judgment Throne of the Lord, and the wife is seen turning and whispering to her husband, "Now Fred, don't you dare demand to get everything that's coming to you!" If our God dispensed *only* what we *deserved*, the new heavens and earth would be devoid of any human life! Thank God for the truth that "*mercy* triumphs over judgment" (James 2:13).

   H. Leo Boles opined, "It seems that people will be treated according to their *opportunities* and *the light which they have*. Opportunity and ability measure one's responsibility; some have greater opportunities than others; some have greater ability than others; therefore the responsibilities *vary*; so it seems that the reward and punishment will vary according to the responsibilities" [*A Commentary on the Gospel According to Luke*, p. 262]. Paul spoke of this principle that will be applied by our *gracious* Father at the Final Judgment in Romans 2:14ff. If punishment is deemed necessary for offenses committed, such "punishment will be *proportioned* to the powers, gifts, opportunities and knowledge of the offender" [*ibid*]. Adam Clarke declared, "Those who have had *much light*, or the opportunity of receiving much, and have not improved it to their own salvation, and to the good of others, shall receive punishment *proportioned* to the light they have abused. On the other hand, those who have had *little light*, and who had few means of improvement, shall receive few stripes – shall be punished *only* for the abuse of the knowledge they possessed" [vol. 5, p. 445]. "*All* have *some* knowledge of God (Romans 1:20), and God judges according to individual levels of responsibility" [*The Expositor's Bible Commentary*, vol. 8, p. 967].

"In the Final Judgment, each person will be measured, not against the same standard, but against *his own response* to the *light received*. Millions of persons have lived and are living today without the knowledge of Christ as God's supreme revelation and means of salvation. These people may find salvation on account of their trusting response to what they know of God. It is for God to determine how much of His will is disclosed to any person through any particular religion. It is because our God has written certain basic moral principles into every human conscience that every person can be held accountable – 'without excuse' (Romans 1:20) – in the Final Judgment. A *pleasant surprise* will be to meet, *among the redeemed*, 'heathen' who never learned about the Good News of salvation through human agents. Ellen White states this point extremely eloquently: 'Among the heathen are those who worship God ignorantly, those to whom *the light* is never brought by human instrumentality, yet they will not perish. Though ignorant of the written law of God, they have heard His voice *speaking to them in nature*, and have done the things that the law has required (Romans 2:14ff). Their works are evidence that the Holy Spirit has touched their hearts, and they are recognized as the children of God'" [Dr. Samuele Bacchiocchi, *Immortality or Resurrection? A Biblical Study on Human Nature and Destiny*, p. 240].

Some have *mistakenly*, and perhaps even *maliciously*, suggested that this *Doctrine of Available Light* declares that all, indiscriminately, shall be saved. That is not what this doctrine declares. Just the opposite. It is not a form of universalism, but rather based upon the biblical truth that God reveals Himself to all men, thus leaving no one with any excuse whatsoever on the Day of Judgment.

"*Ignorance* is no excuse where knowledge *might* have been obtained. The principle is that the demand of the Master is in *proportion* to the *gifts* dispensed, whether these be temporal or spiritual" [Dr. Paul E. Kretzmann, *Popular Commentary of the Bible*, the NT, vol. 1, p. 338]. Unto *every* man some degree of light has been given, and it is *whether or not*, as well as *in what manner*, they choose to *respond* to that light that will determine their eternal destiny. All men who have ever lived (or ever will live) are responsible for what they have been given, although not all have been given the exact same amount of light, insight, ability and opportunity. Thus, they are accountable for what they *have*, not for what they do *not* have. Just as there are degrees of *revelatory light*, so are there degrees of responsibility and accountability, as, indeed, there will be degrees of both reward and *punishment*. As to the specific nature and application of the latter, "we may well be content to leave *that* question to Him who spake the words (Luke 12:47-48), and in so doing gave the most convincing proof that the Judge of all the earth will assuredly do right" [Ellicott, vol. 6, p. 304].

Chapter 20
Grace and the Caveman

A matter about which reflective disciples of Christ have wrestled throughout the ages pertains to the eternal fate of those persons who, through no fault of their own, never had the opportunity to hear the glorious news of God's grace as revealed in Christ Jesus. Countless men and women over the centuries have lived and died never knowing the name of Jesus. It's not that they willfully *rejected* the Son of God ... they simply had *no knowledge* of His coming. The question thus naturally arises in the hearts and minds of those who serve this risen Savior: What will our Father *do* with such unenlightened souls? Are they all *saved* by virtue of their ignorance? Are they all *lost* by virtue of their ignorance? Are some saved and some lost? If the latter scenario, what *determines* who is saved and who is lost? These are difficult questions, and they have been pondered for centuries.

It is my firm conviction, after much study and reflection on this matter over the years, that our Father has *not* left us uninformed about the eternal destiny of such individuals. I believe His inspired writings give us a glimpse into His divine purpose for those not as blessed as we; those with *lesser light* from above. However, before penning a single syllable of this chapter, I sought the input and insight of the readers of my weekly publication: *Reflections*. I value their perceptions, for "as iron sharpens iron, so one man sharpens another" (Proverbs 27:17).

As in the past, their response to my appeal was overwhelming. I received a *flood* of emails; some sent articles they had published on the issue in years past, and a couple of people even mailed me books that they thought would aid me in my research. For these gifts, as well as the insights provided, I offer my sincere and heartfelt thanks. This chapter will incorporate many of their insights as we seek together to determine the design of our Father regarding those less blessed than we with respect to that *Greater Light* that has come into the world.

Should We Even Care?!

A handful of individuals felt this whole matter to be highly speculative, believing God has offered *no* guidance whatsoever into His dealings with such persons. We all, therefore, should simply "leave it alone, and leave it to Him." One person, who lives in North Carolina, wrote, "You know, this situation ranks right up there with 'Who was Cain's wife?' Honestly, and maybe I'm being too blunt, I really don't care about cavemen and lost tribes in the deepest darkest jungles." A man in Indiana stated, "Why waste time on something that you or I cannot do anything about?"

Along the same lines, some suggested we should forget about these "distant souls" and simply focus on the unenlightened closer to home. A person in Vancouver wrote, "These touchy-feely people who want to hypothesize over something such as cavemen or those in deepest, darkest Africa or you name the location, should have greater concern about their neighbors." I certainly agree, as most reasonable disciples would, that our hearts should feel a burden for the lost right in our own backyards. Most of us will never travel to the far corners of the globe preaching to "cavemen." We *can* proclaim God's grace, however, to our family, friends, and neighbors. And we *should* be doing this far more than we typically do.

There is certainly a danger that we may become so fascinated with the fate of these "cavemen" that we entirely forget about our obligation to let our light shine brightly *right where we are*. We need *balance* in our Christian walk. Let's not shy away from the hard questions, or from deep reflection upon the Word and its application to real life situations. But, at the same time, let's not allow such scholarly pursuits to distract us from our true purpose for being. *Both* serve a purpose in our overall development and maturity as disciples of Christ Jesus.

Should we be discussing such questions? Does it *really matter* what fate befalls those who never had opportunity, through no fault of their own, to hear the gospel of Jesus? I believe the answer to both questions is *Yes*. It matters because these are precious souls that one day will stand before the Creator. We should *care* what happens to them. It also matters because *how* God deals with them will speak directly to His *character*. I believe He has given us insight into the nature of that character, which, if we have perceived it correctly, reveals how He intends to dispense justice and mercy in judgment. The view we take regarding how God will deal with the unenlightened will speak volumes as to our own perception of His divine character. This is no small matter. If we present a false view of His nature, our testimony may well border on blasphemy.

Some, for example, believe God will simply send straight to hell all who have not complied with every tenet and tradition of their denomination or sect. Their view of God is extremely rigid and legalistic, and the thought that grace and mercy might be evidenced in judgment is a concept foreign to them. A church leader in Texas wrote, "You touch upon a very important subject which legalism (relationship based upon law) cannot answer." A fellow New Mexican stated, "I am glad this question came up as I have been asked many times about the people who will not, or never did, have the opportunity to hear the Gospel of Jesus Christ." This reader went on to say in his email, "I personally believe we serve a just God, not a rigid ruler who is out to get us." Another individual from the state of Texas wrote, "Legalists and patternists circumvent God's sovereignty seeking for the 'right and only' pattern, excluding His omniscience and omnipotence, thus belying their neopharisaism."

Scripture makes it clear to us that God "loved the world" (John 3:16), not just the "civilized" portions of it, and that He does not wish "for *any* to perish, but for *all* to come to repentance" (2 Peter 3:9). Thus, one would think that He desires *every* person to come to a saving knowledge of His will. The question is: has He made provision for this? Has *every* man been given opportunity? Or, is salvation for those fortunate few, who through the "luck of the draw," were born in areas of the planet where Bibles are readily available to all, and where the name of Christ is common knowledge? If the latter, then most men are, unfortunately, predestined for wrath, through no fault of their own. *If* this is true, it raises significant questions about the purpose and character of our God. So, *yes*, these are questions that need to be asked; these are questions that need to be taken to God's Word for reflection and resolution.

They Are All Saved

One popular view, and one or two people actually suggested this, is that all who are unenlightened as to the teachings of Christ are thereby *saved*. I suppose this would give credence to the old expression: "Ignorance is bliss." If this is true, then it is argued we do a *disservice* to these "heathen" by preaching the gospel to them. After all, if they are all saved, *why bother*? On the other hand, if we take the gospel to them and they don't respond, then they become lost by that rejection. Thus, the path of wisdom, it is reasoned, is to simply *leave them alone*. R. C. Sproul voiced this view in his book *Reason to Believe*, stating, "Letting him alone would be the most helpful thing we could do for him. If we go to the native and inform him of Christ, we place his soul in eternal jeopardy. For now he knows of Christ, and if he refuses to respond to Him, he can no longer claim ignorance as an excuse. Hence, the best service we can render is silence" [p. 50].

A minister in Tennessee wrote that if these unenlightened souls are all saved, then "why should we go to them and present the gospel, watch them reject it, and thus become lost? They would be better off if we left them alone and allowed them to stay in that ignorant, but safe, condition." A preacher in Texas, who was a missions major at *Abilene Christian University*, stated that he believed "one extremist (postmodern) view was: those who haven't heard the gospel cannot be held accountable for their ignorance, and therefore *they are saved*. However, if we attempt to teach them the truth and they reject it, we condemn them to hell. Therefore, we should not bother to go to them lest we damn them." Another preacher in Tennessee expressed this view as follows: "If those folks can be saved without the gospel then the greatest tragedy of their lives would be hearing the gospel, for it would make the gospel God's power to *damn*, not to *save*. The greatest thing we could do when we have a child born to us would be to deliver that child to a dark, remote village and then pray no missionary ever finds that village."

I personally *reject* this position. I do *not* believe all those who have never heard the gospel of Jesus Christ are thereby saved. That is totally illogical. It would render pointless any and all missionary efforts. Indeed, why would Paul spend years of sacrificial service to the Lord in his missionary journeys if these people were all saved by virtue of their ignorance? It makes no sense. *Ignorance* is *not* the basis of eternal salvation. "In the past God overlooked such ignorance, but now He commands all people everywhere to repent" (Acts 17:30). That certainly sounds to me like ignorance is no excuse. Men are called to *respond* to God's revelation, and to *turn* their lives away from selfish, worldly pursuits to lives of loving service to their Creator. Thus, I don't see ignorance as a "free pass" to eternal life. If it *was*, then any missionary effort on our part, whether local or foreign, would be counterproductive. They would indeed be better off left alone. I simply do not believe such a view is biblical.

They Are All Lost

The opposite extreme, and this is found far more frequently among disciples of Christ, is that these unenlightened ones are all, without a single exception, *lost*. God will cast them all into hell for failing to be immersed into Christ, even though they had never heard of Christ, nor of the command to be immersed. "Ignorance is no excuse!" "It's sad, but too bad!" The fact that untold millions lived and died without ever having the opportunity to hear this good news, through absolutely no fault of their own, is "irrelevant," some will insist. They didn't "obey the gospel," so they are doomed to hell. Period. And, furthermore, *it is our fault*. Why? Because we didn't take the gospel to them like we were supposed to. Thus, their blood will be on *our* heads.

This is an extreme, harsh, and very legalistic theological stance, and it is, unfortunately, held by many of our brothers and sisters in Christ. I was brought up believing this way, but always felt very uncomfortable with it. If this was true, then it seemed to suggest to me something about God's character that was less than just, loving, merciful and compassionate. It simply didn't depict the God I was coming to know through my growing faith and continuing study of His revelation of Himself in the inspired Scriptures. Yet, I kept silent during those early years; after all, to *question* the traditional understandings of one's forefathers in the faith was frowned upon. Those few who dared were quickly "marked." Too many, unwilling to be "marked and maligned," simply mindlessly parroted the party line. I soon chose an alternate route, much to the discomfort of many of my brethren in my faith-heritage. I chose to *ask* those difficult questions; to *challenge* my traditions; to *confront* each of my beliefs, all in light of the Scriptures, and only for the purpose of confirming ultimate Truth. It has been a fascinating spiritual journey, one fraught with danger as well as discovery.

But, I digress. The view that all such persons who have not been blessed with knowledge of Jesus will be eternally lost, *no exceptions*, led naturally to the view that the *blame* for such rests with *each of us*. Had we done our duty – had we preached the gospel to the *whole world* – they would not be in that unenlightened state. Thus, their eternal destruction is not really *their* fault, or *God's*, the blame rests upon *you* and *me*. This argument is often used to promote *Mission-Mindedness* within the church. Guilt, after all, can be a powerful motivating force, and, if we can't go ourselves, we feel "absolved" by writing a fat check to those who do.

A minister in Nashville, TN wrote that the responsibility for these countless souls "rests on the shoulders of the church. It is *our* lack of interest in lost souls, *our* lack of love that will condemn them, not God's. He has prescribed a way to reach them; *we* are the cruel ones for not sharing." This, of course, is a natural *defense mechanism* allowing us to continue our elevated esteem of the Father. Since we can't quite "swallow" the view that a loving, merciful Father would eternally punish a child for a failure to respond to an instruction they had never received, through no fault of their own, we *must of necessity*, to continue our elevated esteem of God, *assign the fault elsewhere*. Thus, the blame falls on *us*. It is *our* fault, not *His*, not *theirs*. This soothes our minds, and helps us "explain" the eternal destruction of countless millions who had the misfortune of living their lives unaware of this greater light with which/whom we are blessed.

The aforementioned missions major at ACU wrote, "Another extremist (modern) view is: those who haven't heard the gospel *cannot be saved*. They will be damned. And *we* may be damned too, if we don't do our best to take the gospel to every one of them (this is largely used as a message to encourage missions)." A dear friend in Texas phrased the concern this way: "Christians should be bound to let there be no stone unturned when delivering the good news. The guilt for those who never hear 'through no fault of their own' becomes the ultimate responsibility of those of *us* who have the treasure and lock it up in our buildings. There are going to be some church leaders that have some hard questions to answer as to why there were so many who never heard the good news of Jesus."

There are many disciples, who hold to this position that these unenlightened ones will be lost, who nevertheless believe this is *God's* doing. Thus, they seek to find some way to justify His action, or even to soften it, so as to make it more personally palatable. One such attempt is to suggest that God will indeed punish these people, but it will be with a *lesser* punishment. This is the doctrine of *Degrees of Punishment, which was examined in the previous chapter.* They appeal to Luke 12:47-48 ~ "That servant who knows his master's will and does not get ready or does not do what his master wants will be beaten with many blows. But the one who does *not* know and does things deserving punishment will be beaten with few blows." There is much uncertainty, speculation and debate as to exactly how this might practically and literally apply on the day of judgment, but it does seem to suggest our Master will be *fair* in dispensing punishment. We would certainly expect no less from our Maker. A man in Alabama wrote, "It appears that, while those who have never heard the gospel message of Christ *will* apparently be found guilty of sin, they may be 'beaten with fewer stripes' because of their lack of knowledge."

We are further "soothed" by the thought that God *knows* those who are searching for Him, and thus will providentially preserve such persons until such time as a preacher of the gospel can get to them, much like the account of Philip being sent to the Ethiopian eunuch (Acts 8) or Peter being sent to Cornelius (Acts 10-11). Thus, those who are ultimately lost will *only* be those God *foreknew* would never receive the gospel if presented with the opportunity; all those who *would* have received it, *will* have the chance. This presents a God more in keeping with our view of His nature and character, declare those who adhere to this position. A woman in Tennessee, for example, wrote, "An all powerful God has the ability to prolong the life of both the preacher and the one in need of teaching. God can grant safety to them both, and time and opportunity, for the gospel to be preached. This is *my* reflection on the subject of those cavemen." There is no question but what this is an emotionally appealing theory, and we would all love for it to be true, but it is unrealistic. The harsh reality is: many who are genuinely seeking to know their Creator, to the best of their ability and opportunity, *do* die never having heard the good news of Jesus Christ. That is simply a *fact*.

All Are Amenable To Available Light
Thus: Some Are Lost, Some Are Saved

The two views given above represent the far left and right *extremes* of the theological spectrum on this issue of the eternal destiny of the unenlightened. I do not believe either of them truly represents the biblical perspective, although they each contain elements of truth. It is *my* studied conviction, after a good number of years of prayerful reflection and research into God's revelation of Himself, that there is a far more rational, not to mention more biblical, position. Simply stated, this view holds that *all* men, who ever have lived or ever will live, are amenable to whatever available light God has given unto them. Those who genuinely *respond* to that light with fullness of faith will be judged fairly and benevolently by our Father; those who willfully *reject* that light will be rejected by God. I believe this not only to be consistent with the nature and character of our God, but consistent with the teaching of Scripture. I was also pleased to discover that the vast majority of those who contacted me embrace this same conviction.

The foundational principle of this teaching is that our God has revealed Himself to *all* men, although the methodology may vary dramatically. There were times, for example, when God revealed His will to certain men via dreams and visions. These persons then became responsible for *complying* with the truths and tenets contained therein. God also spoke through prophets. God also speaks through nature (Acts 14:17; Romans 1:20). He speaks through the Scriptures. And He speaks most perfectly through the "word become flesh" ~ Jesus Christ. In each case, God has dispensed *light*, although some lights shine more brightly than others and are thus more easily discerned. The *King James Version* has poetically phrased this truth as follows: "God, who at sundry times and in divers manners spake in time past unto the fathers by the prophets, hath in these last days spoken unto us by His Son" (Hebrews 1:1-2). Some have regarded this as the doctrine of progressive light (or evolution of enlightenment). With each successive revelation of Himself, the Truth became more evident, with the most perfect revelation of that eternal light being Jesus Himself (John 1:1-18).

Those of us blessed with the knowledge of this *Greater Light* should daily seek occasion and opportunity to share it with those about us still seeking to serve their Maker under the guidance of *lesser light*. After all, if we in America enjoy the blessings of electricity and running water, should we not seek to share these blessings with those peoples who live under lesser conditions? We do not share these blessings because we fear these people will *perish* without these blessings, but we share them because we believe they will *prosper* with them. It is an effort to *ennoble* their lives; to bring greater happiness and productivity. It is not so much that we *save* their lives, as we *enrich* them.

There are people in this world, and there always have been, who have *lesser light* than that with which *we* have been blessed by God. The "caveman," for example, knows nothing of Jesus Christ, the Light of the world. He has never held a Bible; never heard a preacher of the gospel; has no clue what "baptism" is, or the "Lord's

Supper." However, he is *not* without revelation. God has revealed Himself to *all men*. The light available to this caveman, or some primitive person living beyond the parameters of civilization, may well only be that of *Nature*. That then becomes *his* available light "coming down from the Father of lights" (James 1:17). This man is therefore responsible for seeking to understand that revelation to the best of his ability, and also for ordering his life according to the truths perceived therein. Those who perceive God in this revelation, and who seek to live as He would have them to live, as best they perceive it, have indeed *responded* to that revelation of their Creator, and God will judge their hearts and actions accordingly. Those who willfully *reject* this light from above, and choose to continue living for *self*, will be rejected by the One who provided them that guidance in that revelation. Thus, regardless of the brightness or dimness of the light made available, *all* men have a choice; they will either seek and accept, or ignore and reject, and God will judge accordingly, dispensing either life or death based on their choice.

The apostle Paul wrote: "For the wrath of God is revealed from heaven against all ungodliness and unrighteousness of men, who *suppress* the truth in unrighteousness, because that which is known about God is evident within (among) them; *for God made it evident to them*. For since the creation of the world His invisible attributes, His eternal power and divine nature, have been clearly seen, *being understood through what has been made*, so they are without excuse. For even though they *knew* God, they did not honor Him as God, or give thanks" (Romans 1:18-21). This passage clearly declares that God *can be known* through His creation, and that men *have a choice* based on this lesser light of revelation. Those who choose unwisely are "without excuse." The implication of the passage is clear: some *will* choose wisely to follow what light has been made available and to honor God in their lives. It is my conviction that such persons shall be saved. After all, as David beautifully notes, "The heavens declare the glory of God; and the firmament shows

His handiwork. Day unto day utters speech, and night unto night reveals knowledge" (Psalm 19:1-2). These seekers have *responded* to that knowledge, and for such they will be rewarded.

Thomas Merton (1915-1968), in his work *The Seven Storey Mountain*, made the following astute observation: "There is not a flower that opens, not a seed that falls into the ground, and not an ear of wheat that nods on the end of its stalk in the wind that does not preach and proclaim the greatness and the mercy of God to the whole world." Ralph Waldo Emerson (1803-1882) made the following entry into his journal in April, 1847: "Nature is saturated with deity." Elizabeth Barrett Browning (1806-1861) wrote, "Earth's crammed with heaven, and every common bush afire with God" [*Aurora Leigh*]. These gifted authors have merely echoed, in poetic form, the truths conveyed in Scripture. Also, the Jewish *Talmud*, which contains the early rabbinical writings, boldly asserts, "God fills the universe."

Indeed, He does, and He is always close at hand; *visible* to all His creation. In a unique way, *nature* is His voice. Through the magnificent work of His hands, the Creator proclaims His presence and personality to His creation. "From one man He made every nation of men, that they should inhabit the whole earth; and He determined the times and the boundaries of their habitation, that they should *seek* Him and perhaps *reach out for* Him and *find* Him, *though He is not far from each one of us*" (Acts 17:26-28). Paul spoke these words to the "heathen" of Athens. They apply no less to the "heathen" today. God is as near as His creation; nature proclaims its Creator, and if men choose to listen, they will discover God ... even in and through this *lesser* light. "I will have mercy on whom I have mercy, and I will have compassion on whom I have compassion" (Romans 9:15). The legalists and patternists almost seem upset with God over this, but the reality is that our God is a merciful, loving, compassionate God ... and a *fair* God ... far more so than many of His children seem willing to acknowledge.

Dr. Leroy Garrett, in his essay titled "*The Principle of Available Light*," has provided some much needed, and excellent, insight into this matter. I would encourage the reader to seek out that article on the Internet and evaluate it carefully. He points out that in the world today "*every* person, by virtue of God's abundant grace, receives *some* measure of light (revelation)." This may be either through nature, or by means of "the law written in their hearts" (Romans 2:15), or via the inspired Scriptures. There are no exceptions ... *all* men have *some* light available to them, and "every person is responsible for the light (knowledge) that he/she has, but *only* for the light that he/she has. God is not demonic. He does not condemn one for not knowing or not doing what he/she had no way of knowing or doing."

Does this mean everyone is automatically saved? Of course not. It simply means that one finds favor with God, or disfavor, by their response to, or rejection of, that level of light available to them. As Dr. Garrett clearly points out in his essay, "God may well condemn one for *not* making a faithful *response*" to that form of light "in which He discloses Himself." Man is responsible for *seeking* God, and he is then responsible for *responding* to that revelation God provides to the best of his ability and understanding of that light he has been graciously given. Those who willfully *reject* this revelation, however, will be rejected by God.

Our God judges *hearts*, a fact to which Paul confidently alludes in Romans 2:13-15 ~ "For it is not the *hearers* of the Law who are just before God, but the *doers* of the Law who will be justified. For when Gentiles who do not have the Law do *instinctively* the things of the Law, these, not having the Law, are a law to themselves, in that they show the work of the Law written in their *hearts*, their conscience bearing witness, and their thoughts alternately *accusing* or else *defending* them." Thus, some who had never even *heard* of the Law of Moses (*God's* law), will still find a defense as they stand in judgment before God in that they *perceived* His will from what light they *did* have, and they *responded* to that light to the best of their understanding and ability and opportunity. I believe that principle is no less true today in the Christian era.

A person in Texas wrote, "I agree with the 'available light' position referred to in a recent essay by Leroy Garrett (and also by Edward Fudge). As *Sovereign*, God can and has saved any whom He chooses to save in whatever manner He so chooses. Who are *we* to judge? God is just and loving, searching all men's *hearts*." Speaking of Edward Fudge, he wrote in one of his *GracEmail* articles, "God's judgment will be completely righteous, for He will judge all people by the light they actually possessed, rather than by some standard of which they had no knowledge." Fudge further observes, "The heart which knows only God's revelation in creation, but *rejects* that, would also reject *greater* light if it were available. There is no difference *in principle* between the *hearts* of those who reject God -- only a difference in the quantity and brightness of the light they reject. Similarly, there is no difference between the hearts of those who *seek* God's fellowship and who embrace His light -- regardless of the *measure* of the light they possess (John 3:21)."

A church elder in Missouri wrote, "I think, based on Romans 2 and other similar passages, that there may be room for God to exercise His mercy toward these persons, and to judge them based on the level or measure of law they *have* (i.e., how effective they were in living up to their own understanding)." God has placed an awareness of the eternal within each of us (Ecclesiastes 3:11), and thus it is within human nature to seek God. He would not place within us this desire without also providing available light for us to fulfill that desire. Some are blessed with greater light than others, but *all* have *some* light, and *all* are amenable to that light of revelation which they have. A noted author and speaker in the *Stone-Campbell Movement*, and a dear friend, wrote, "I believe we do have some ground of hope in God's mercy. We do know that God notices when someone lives up to what light they *do* have (Romans 2:14-16). The tenets of the Gospel will be the measuring stick, but it appears that God *is aware* when those tenets are practiced simply out of a good conscience, and His judgment will take that into account." A person in Texas put it this way: "To paraphrase Romans 2:13, it is not those who *hear* Christ's law who will be saved, but those who *do* Christ's law. If they do so *by nature*, then by nature they will be judged."

A gentleman in Michigan observed, "Men are without excuse according to whatever measure of light they have, and are accountable only for that." He then quoted 2 Corinthians 8:12 ~ "For if the willingness of mind is present, it is acceptable according to what a man *has*, not according to what he does *not* have." This man then went on to note, "This was, in fact, the focal point of my funeral sermon for my mother-in-law a couple of months ago. She did the best she could with what she had to work with. God does not expect that which we *cannot* give, and this verse has application to more than just money."

A professor at a major Texas university stated, "Al, I have thought a great deal about this issue and have for some time concluded that God will judge every person according to his response to the light he has." Dr. A. H. Strong, in the year 1909, wrote, "We have the hope that even among the heathen there may be some ... who under the guidance of the Holy Spirit working through the truth of nature and conscience, have found the way to life and salvation" [*Systematic Theology*, p. 843]. Josh McDowell, in his book *Answers to Tough Questions*, which he co-authored with Don Stewart, wrote, "We do believe that every person will have an opportunity to repent, and that God will not exclude anyone because he happened to be born at the wrong place and at the wrong time" [p. 137]. Even the great *Stone-Campbell Movement* leader Moses E. Lard acknowledges this principle of accountability to available light in his commentary on Romans 1:20 ~ "Paul here assumes the great and constantly recurring fact in the divine government, that *knowledge of duty* is the *measure of responsibility*. Had the Gentiles *not* known, they would have been free, but *having light*, they were without excuse" [p. 53]. "This knowledge would constitute the ground of their responsibility" [*ibid*, p. 49].

"If God expects men to know Him, we may be sure that He has given them the *means* of knowing Him. God will judge every man according to the opportunities he has had" [*The Pulpit Commentary*, vol. 18]. In commenting upon Romans 1:18ff, the above source states, "These words describe the condition of those who *reject light* from the standpoint of Him who is the great Searcher of hearts. He makes no mistakes. He makes no uncharitable judgments. In His sight those to whom He has given light, and who have chosen to *reject it*, are 'without excuse.' They have no valid reason for their ignorance about the way of salvation and the path of duty if God has given them light about both" [*ibid*]. "These words describe the condition of those who have *willfully rejected light*" [*ibid*]. "If light has been granted to beings of intelligence and reason and conscience, and they have *deliberately chosen to reject it*, is it not fair and just that they should take the consequences?" [*ibid*]. Notice also that "it is characteristic of man in his sinful state that he knows much more truth than he translates into *fitting response*" [*The Expositor's Bible Commentary*, vol. 10, p. 23].

Why Take The Gospel To Them?

A question that will need to be examined, for it is a *valid* one, is: If the unenlightened may be saved by their response to available light from God, then what purpose is served by taking the Gospel of Jesus Christ to them? As some have suggested, as noted above, wouldn't they be better off if simply *left alone*? The answer is a resounding *NO*. I like the way Dr. Leroy Garrett phrased it in his essay: "No one is ever worse off by hearing the gospel." He correctly observes that if a person is genuinely seeking to know the Creator, "accepting such light as is available, they will accept more light as it becomes available." However, if these persons have no interest in seeking to know the Creator or His will, or, if having perceived it they then *reject* it, "they will reject further light (the gospel)" as well.

When someone only sees "through a glass darkly," what a joy it is, both for proclaimer and hearer, to be able to bring to their view that *Greater Light*. We do *not* do the genuine seeker of ultimate Truth a disservice by sharing with them the way of the Lord more completely, as is clearly seen in the account of Aquila and Priscilla sharing greater light with Apollos (Acts 18:26). Was Apollos "lost" before they took him aside? No, merely unenlightened. From what was Cornelius, a devout, God-fearing man, "saved" (Acts 11:14)? He was "saved" from having to continue his journey through life in a dimmer, lesser light. His prayers to God for greater enlightenment were heard and answered, and Peter came and shared Jesus with Him, thus allowing him to perceive more perfectly than ever before the *Greater Light* of God's matchless grace. In sharing this Light with others we increase their joy, for they are now made even more aware of the loving nature of their God.

Conclusion

A pastor in California wrote, "I think the idea that a loving God would arbitrarily punish individuals who, through no fault of their own, never heard the gospel is totally absurd. I have an unshakable conviction that He will be fair to everyone involved." I have sought to demonstrate, and, admittedly this treatment has been brief and skeletal, that the Scriptures seem to reflect a Creator unwilling to leave *any* of His creation without at least *some* revelation of Himself, however dim that revelatory light might be in comparison to other, greater revelations of His nature and will. A God of justice and fairness will, therefore, hold all men amenable *only* to that available light to which He has exposed them. Those who *respond* to that light, to the best of their understanding, ability and opportunity, will be accepted by God. Those who willfully *reject* that available light, will in turn be rejected by God. This fair; this is just; this is consistent with God's love.

As with the light of the gospel, most men will choose to *reject* it and live for self. Thus, *broad* is the way that leads to destruction. I believe this is no less true with the lesser lights given by God. Most men also *reject* the divine precepts written on their hearts, and thus their conscience will *accuse* them on the day of judgment; most men will also *reject* the voice of nature as it pours forth speech and knowledge, and thus they too are without excuse. In all of these revelations of God, *many* are called, but only a *remnant* choose to respond. We have a gracious Father, however, and He does not demand more of us than we are able to give. God has shed His light upon *all* men, and all men *must* respond in faith to whatever light they have if they hope to be saved.

Let me issue a final challenge to the redeemed of the Lord: "Let the redeemed of the Lord *say so*" (Psalm 107:2). We, who have been blessed with the *Greater Light*, have an obligation ... indeed, a privilege ... to *share* this blessing with others less fortunate; men and women who are living by *lesser light*. Let us therefore seek daily to be "the light of the world" (Matthew 5:14) by taking the *Greater Light*, who is Christ Jesus our Lord, to all corners of this world where He may "enlighten every man" (John 1:9).

Chapter 21
Baptism for the Dead

"Now if there is no resurrection, what will those do who are baptized for the dead? If the dead are not raised at all, why are people baptized for them?" (1 Corinthians 15:29). Paul wrote these words while in the city of Ephesus during his third missionary journey (1 Corinthians 16:8). It was written during the winter of 56 A.D. Paul had established the church in Corinth near the end of his second missionary journey (c. 53 A.D.). The historical account of its origin may be read in Acts 18:1-18. Soon after Paul left the city, Apollos came and worked with them (Acts 18:27 - 19:1). This was a relatively young, spiritually immature congregation of believers. They had many questions, many concerns, and many conflicts. Clearly, they were in need of guidance in several critical areas of belief and practice. One such area was their understanding, or lack thereof, with respect to the resurrection of the dead. They were struggling with this foundational truth, and some of their practices reflected great inconsistency with what they seemingly believed and professed.

In the first century, Corinth was infamous as a locale where people could "have a good time" (in a very *worldly* sense). Here one could find the temple of Aphrodite, which boasted several hundred cult prostitutes. At the time of the apostle Paul's establishment of the church in Corinth, this city had a population of almost 700,000 people, with almost two of every three persons being slaves. It also had a reputation of being one of the most *wicked* cities in existence. "The term 'a Corinthian' meant a profligate, and 'to Corinthianize' meant to engage in prostitution. In the Greek plays of that time Corinthians were usually represented as drunkards" [Dr. D. E. Hiebert, *An Introduction to the Pauline Epistles*, p. 106].

"At night its streets were hideous with the brawls and lewd songs of drunken revelry. In the daytime its markets and squares swarmed with Jewish peddlers, foreign traders, sailors, soldiers, athletes in training, boxers and wrestlers, charioteers, racing-men and betting-men, courtesans, slaves, idlers and parasites of every description ~ a veritable pandemonium" [R. D. Shaw, *The Pauline Epistles*, p. 130].

It was to a band of fairly new converts, struggling to be lights in the darkness of such an environment, that Paul wrote his powerful epistle now known to us as *First Corinthians*. It is thus little wonder that these saints were somewhat confused and conflicted. Many had recently come from paganism, others were still perhaps experiencing some loyalty to previous religious traditions. They had "seen the light," but as "through a glass, darkly" (1 Corinthians 13:12). They were in need of additional insight into the wonders of God's marvelous gift and matchless grace. Thus, Paul sought to clarify some of their misconceptions, address some of their problems, and answer some of their questions.

A Logical Fallacy

To better understand the statement of Paul regarding "baptism for the dead" in 1 Corinthians 15:29, we need to perceive the nature of the problem that prompted his reference to this practice, and then note the *reason* he made reference to such a practice. The basic misunderstanding of the Corinthian brethren was with regard to the resurrection of the dead. Apparently, some were not convinced of the truth of this doctrine. Paul boldly asks these brethren, "How can some of you say that there is *no* resurrection of the dead?" (1 Corinthians 15:12). "Paul saw this as a serious error" [*Holman Bible Dictionary*, p. 151].

The resurrection of the dead was, and *is*, a foundational truth of the Christian faith. To deny the promised resurrection is to deny the very heart and soul of Christianity. Acts 17:18 informs us that the message of Paul created quite a stir among those who heard him, "because he was preaching Jesus and *the resurrection*." One cannot preach *Jesus* without preaching the reality of *resurrection*. Indeed, without a resurrection there is no hope. As Paul appeared before the Jewish Sanhedrin, he created yet another stir by proclaiming, "Brethren, I am on trial because of my hope in the resurrection of the dead" (Acts 23:6). This was no trivial teaching for Paul; it was the core of the gospel. Paul informed the Corinthians that to deny the resurrection is essentially to deny all *hope*. Without resurrection reality we are *lost*. Without resurrection, "our preaching is vain, your faith also is vain. Moreover we are even found to be false witnesses of God, because we witnessed against God that He raised Christ, whom He did *not* raise, if in fact the dead are not raised. For if the dead are not raised, not even Christ has been raised; and if Christ has not been raised, your faith is worthless; you are still in your sins. Then those also who have fallen asleep in Christ have perished. If we have hoped in Christ in this life only, we are of all men most to be pitied" (1 Corinthians 15:14-19).

Paul's point is clear: if there is no bodily resurrection of the dead, as promised by the Lord, then when we die physically *we perish*. Our hope as Christians is *not* in the false doctrine of "immortal soulism," but rather in the divine promise of a physical *resurrection from the dead*. Embracing the former renders unnecessary the latter. Satan has gained quite a solid foothold in Christendom through this original lie: "Thou shalt *not* surely die" (Genesis 3:4). That lie has been perpetuated from that day forward, and the notion that "immortal souls" fly instantly off to heavenly bliss at the moment of physical death has caused countless disciples to abandon the hope of resurrection for the original lie of *inherent immortality*. The Lord "*alone* possesses immortality" (1 Timothy 6:16), which means you and I, *inherently, do not*. However, Jesus Christ has "brought life and immortality to light through the gospel" (2 Timothy 1:10). Thus, those who "*seek for* immortality" (one doesn't "seek for" that which one already *possesses*) shall be *given* "eternal life" (Romans 2:7). Immortality is a gift, and it is *only* to be found "in Christ Jesus." Many today, in effect, deny the worth of resurrection by proclaiming the *inherent* immortality of all men (saved and lost alike), rather than proclaiming the hope of resurrection to everlasting life *only* through Christ (*Conditional Immortality*). It is a subtle seduction by Satan, but it is deadly.

The early Corinthians, like far too many today, had lost sight of the spiritual significance of the resurrection from the dead. Some of them had completely rejected it as a valid doctrine of the Christian faith. Therefore, Paul spends much of chapter 15 seeking to bring them to a better appreciation of this foundational truth of the gospel message. He argues his point from many different angles. Some scholars suggest that in vs. 29 he employs what is known as an "*argumentum ad hominem*." This is a Latin phrase which simply means "argument to the man." It is a device in logic where one attacks the person rather than the idea (the messenger rather than the message). I personally do *not* believe this is what Paul is doing in this passage. It is far more likely he is employing what is known as a "*non sequitur*," another Latin phrase, which means "it does not follow." In other words, Paul's statement in vs. 29 signifies "that what they *said* and what they *did* were inconsistent. Their own practice, therefore, controverted their position" [Carl Holladay, *The First Letter of Paul to the Corinthians*, p. 205].

Paul's point in 1 Corinthians 15:29 was simply this: If there is no hope of resurrection to life for the dead; if the dead are just *dead*, with no hope of resurrection to life, as some were professing in the church at Corinth, then *why* be baptized for such persons? What's the point of such a practice? It just doesn't follow; it is logically fallacious. "If the Corinthians have this practice they destroy their own case against the resurrection" [Dr. C. K. Barrett, *First Epistle to the Corinthians*, p. 363]. Their *practice* (baptism for the dead) "does not follow" their *profession* (in which they insist there is no resurrection of the dead). Thus, it is essentially a charge of *inconsistency* between ritual and doctrine. Somewhat like the disciples in Corinth observing the Lord's Supper (a meal signifying, in part, their *unity* -- 1 Corinthians 10:16-17) while dishonoring that Supper through their disharmony and division (1 Corinthians 11:17-22). By their actions and attitudes they were making a mockery of one of the central truths underlying their ritual, and the inconsistency was glaring. This is more commonly known as a "*Logical Fallacy.*"

Thus, Paul's argument to the brethren in Corinth was that the very practice of performing baptisms for the dead *argues against* their teaching that the dead are devoid of any hope of future life. If the dead are *dead*, never to be raised to *life*, then to be baptized for them is *illogical*. Few scholars would argue that this was *not* the primary purpose of Paul in 1 Corinthians 15:29. Paul's *purpose*, however, is really not where the major hermeneutical difficulty lies; it is with the Corinthians' *practice*.

Pondering the Problem

The problem primarily perceived with Paul's pronouncement in 1 Corinthians 15:29 is two-fold: the nature of the practice itself (what *was* this "baptism for the dead") and Paul's silence with respect to any refutation or rebuke of the practice. The latter has led some to wonder if perhaps Paul actually *condoned* baptism for the dead. Most scholars, however, reject this premise, believing instead that this was merely "a custom which Paul cited for his argument *without approving*" [*Davis Dictionary of the Bible*, p. 75].

"Paul was not advocating the practice of baptizing for the dead. Paul was merely pointing to the inconsistency in the thought of the Corinthians" [*Holman Bible Dictionary*, p. 152]. "We are not to understand that St. Paul gives it his sanction -- he only recalls the fact of the custom, and uses it for the purpose of his argument" [*The Pulpit Commentary*, vol. 19]. There are others, however, who are convicted that Paul would never "stoop to make use of this 'superstition' for 'tactical' reasons, i.e., in order to win a point in an argument" [R. C. H. Lenski, *An Interpretation of First Corinthians*, p. 691]. The most likely view, however, is that Paul was merely *alluding* to this practice, which would have been very *familiar* to the Corinthians, to drive home an important truth regarding resurrection reality, and that he was *not* thereby either approving or authorizing said practice.

The *major* difficulty in the passage involves identifying the practice itself, as well as identifying those who were using it. This has led to literally dozens of differing interpretations. Adam Clarke declared, "This is certainly the most difficult verse in the New Testament" [*Clarke's Commentary*, vol. 6, p. 284]. B. W. Johnson observed, "This passage is difficult, and has received almost as many interpretations as there have been commentators" [*The People's NT with Notes*, vol. 2, p. 123]. "This is confessedly an obscure expression, and has given rise to many and conflicting interpretations, none of which are free from difficulties" [*The Pulpit Commentary*, vol. 19]. "This is a famous *crux interpretum*. Opinion concerning its meaning has been divided since early times, and there can be few verses of Scripture concerning which the views of modern commentators are so bewilderingly diverse" [*Zondervan Pictorial Encyclopedia of the Bible*, vol. 1, p. 469]. Jimmy Allen, in his *Survey of 1st Corinthians*, writes, "One expositor mentioned a work which has thirty-six explanations of this verse. Another said the interpretations of it were too numerous to catalogue" [p. 190]. "This in itself should cause the interpreter to be cautious rather than imaginative" [Carl Holladay, *The First Letter of Paul to the*

Corinthians, p. 205]. For those who want to examine an in-depth account of the history of the interpretation of this passage, it may be found in the book *Die Taufe für die Toten* by M. Rissi [published in 1962].

It is clearly beyond the scope of this present study to examine in-depth each of the many interpretations suggested through the centuries by various scholars. "Many of them are not worth recording, and are only worth alluding to at all as specimens of the willful bias which goes to Scripture, not to seek truth, but to support tradition" [*The Pulpit Commentary*, vol. 19]. Having given this disclaimer, I shall nevertheless list some of the more intriguing interpretations below for the enlightenment, as well as the amusement, of the reader:

The term "dead" is taken metaphorically as a representation of suffering and hardships faced because of one's faith. Paul's personal references in vs. 30-32 are used to help justify this view, as well as Jesus' reference to a baptism of suffering (Mark 10:38-39; Luke 12:50; and Matthew 20:22-23 in the *KJV*). Thus, Paul is speculating as to *why* one would willingly submit to such a "baptism of suffering" if there was no reward (a resurrection to life) following such suffering and possible death.

It means to be baptized out of respect for the feelings of those who are now dead. In other words, if your mother had always wanted to see you baptized into Christ, but you had never done so while she was alive, you would now go ahead and be baptized so that your dead mother could rejoice with the angels over your immersion. They often quote Jesus, who said, "There is joy in the presence of the angels of God over one sinner who repents" (Luke 15:10). Thus, the living are baptized for the dead -- i.e., to bring the dead *joy* in heaven. There is some historical evidence that some ancient disciples were actually baptized *over the graves* of departed loved ones so that they might literally be "baptized *over* the dead" (in 1 Corinthians 15:29 the Greek preposition *huper* is used in this phrase, which, in addition to meaning "for, on behalf of," may also mean "over, above;" it generally only signifies the *latter* meaning, however, when used with the *accusative case*, which is *not* the case used in this text).

Another twist on this is for the living to be baptized so that they might *join* their departed loved ones one day. I want to see grandma or grandpa again in heaven, so I had better go get baptized so that I can go there to be with them. Thus, one is baptized for the sake of *joining* the glorified dead. But, again, as with #2, this immersion would be pointless if there is *no such thing* as a resurrection to life for the dead. Such a practice, therefore, argues against their denial of the doctrine of resurrection, which is precisely Paul's point, regardless of which interpretation one embraces.

A more "here and now" focus is evidenced in the theory that living persons are baptized into Christ to fill the vacancies left by members who have died. "This is the military concept of one soldier taking the place of another who has fallen in battle" [Jimmy Allen, *Survey of 1st Corinthians*, p. 190]. One scholar, in *The Pulpit Commentary*, is quoted as saying it applies to "those who, from pagan darkness, were converted by the gospel and were admitted into the visible Church, there to fill up the place of those who, by martyrdom or otherwise, had been called away by death. The new convert then took the place of the departed saint. Thus, conversions in the Church replenish the losses caused by death."

"Baptism for *the dead*" is a reference to being baptized into Christ Jesus -- "the dead" being interpreted as a reference to the Lord. Thus, our baptism is "for *Him*." But, as Paul says in 1 Corinthians 15, if not even *He* has been raised, then our faith (as well as our baptism) is worthless and futile. A strong argument against this interpretation is the fact that the phrase "the dead" is *plural* in the Greek. Thus, it refers to the "dead *ones*," rather than to a "dead *One*."

Some suggest the practice merely alluded to the washing of a dead body to prepare it for burial. But, again, why wash and clean the body if it was never expected to rise again? Such a practice would appear to be inconsistent with the denial of a physical resurrection of the dead. If the body placed in the ground simply rots, never to be raised, why bother to wash it?

A scholar by the name of Olshausen took the view that the resurrection of the dead on the day of judgment could not occur until a specific number of persons had accepted Christ Jesus. The dead must remain dead and in the graves until that number was reached. Thus, many people were baptized in the hope of drawing ever closer to meeting that magic number (known only to our God) and, in so doing, rescuing the dead from their tombs. It could be said, therefore, that they were being "baptized for the dead" (i.e., to their ultimate benefit). Such a theory, even though rather bizarre, still assumes a *resurrection*, which some in Corinth were denying. The *practice* was simply not consistent with the *profession*.

Some see the phrase denoting a *rite of purification*. We are all "dead" in our sins, but those sins are "washed away" in the "waters of baptism," they suggest. The dead (i.e., each of *us*, since we are all sinners) are raised to life ~ "raised from the watery grave." To be "baptized for the dead," therefore, simply signifies that each one of us, who are dead in our sins, are being immersed (a death and burial) and then raised from the water to newness of life. It is thus merely symbolic of a spiritual reality (Romans 6).

Vicarious Baptism

There are obviously countless other theories that could be listed, but these should suffice to show the diversity of opinion that has been generated by this passage from the pen of Paul. The dominant interpretation of the phrase "baptism for the dead," and this view has endured for many centuries, is that it refers to the practice of an immersion *by proxy* (i.e., a vicarious baptism). This is where one person is immersed in water so that *another* person (in this case, one who is physically *dead*) may receive the benefit of that immersion. Thus, a *living* person is baptized on behalf of a *dead* person.

The Pulpit Commentary states, "This clause can have but one meaning, and that is its obvious one, namely, that, among the many strange opinions and practices which then prevailed was one which was entirely unwarranted ~ but which St. Paul does not here stop to examine ~ of persons getting themselves baptized as it were *by proxy* for others who had died … in the hope of extending to them some of its benefits." "The only tenable interpretation is that there existed amongst some of the Christians at Corinth a practice of baptizing a living person in the stead of some convert who had died before that sacrament had been administered to him" [*Ellicott's Commentary on the Whole Bible*, vol. 7, p. 348]. This was a practice well-known among the early Christian heretical groups, such as the *Marcionites*, the *Montanists*, and the *Cerinthians*, where the living were often baptized on behalf of the dead, so that the latter, who had died without having been baptized, might still be saved. Early *Church Fathers*, such as Tertullian, Epiphanius, and Chrysostom recorded actual occurrences of such vicarious baptisms. It was also practiced by the Egyptian *Copts*. The practice was ultimately forbidden in the sixth canon of the *Council of Hippo* (393 A.D.).

"The *present tense* of 'baptize' suggests that the practice of baptizing for the dead was current and evidently well known to the Corinthians" [*The Expositor's Bible Commentary*, vol. 10, p. 287]. This is *not* to suggest, however, that the Corinthians *themselves* were engaging in this practice. This, by the way, is the source of yet another major interpretive controversy among biblical scholars: were the saints in Corinth actually baptizing for the dead, or were they merely aware of the practice among others? Some suggest the former, others insist on the latter. Those who promote the latter point out that just north of Corinth was the city of Eleusis, a site where pagans practiced a form of baptism for the dead (mentioned by Homer in his *Hymn to Demeter*).

Some argue that Paul has shifted from using the *first person* ("we") and *second person* ("you") in vs. 12-19, to using the *third person* ("they") in vs. 29, but then immediately switches back to the previous construction in the verses following vs. 29. It is argued from the force of this grammatical shift that some of the Corinthians were indeed denying the resurrection, but the practice of "baptism for the dead" was being performed by others. The Corinthians were *aware* of these others, but were not engaging in this practice (or, so goes the argument). This is certainly a strong argument, and a real possibility. However, it does seem to reduce some of the vital force of Paul's argument to the Corinthians themselves if *they* are not the ones engaging in this practice. Paul's whole argument pertains to the inconsistency between practice and profession, but if the profession is by one group and the practice by another, that argument almost seems misdirected. Thus, my own view is that Paul was most likely referring to the fact that some of the saints in Corinth had adopted this heretical practice, but that their practice flew in the face of their denial of the resurrection. They weren't *thinking things through*, and Paul simply sought to generate some much needed reflection on their part about this glaring inconsistency.

Paul's goal at this point was not to condemn the practice of baptism for the dead; perhaps he did this at another time, and that discussion is simply not preserved for us. His goal, rather, was to show the inconsistency between their ritual and their doctrine. His focus was the resurrection, and he employed this false practice only to add force to his argument. It has bothered some disciples greatly that Paul did *not* repudiate the practice of baptism for the dead. However, it was not uncommon to allude to a false teaching or practice to make a point, and yet do so *without* taking the time *on that occasion* to refute the error. Even Jesus did this. In John 9, for example, His disciples, as they passed a man "blind from birth" (vs. 1), asked Jesus, "Rabbi, who sinned, this man or his parents, that he should be born blind?" (vs. 2). Some had the mistaken view that one could sin in a previous existence, prior to birth, and thus be forced to pay for that sin by being given a deformed body at birth. Interestingly, Jesus responded to their question, but He *did not* refute this pagan doctrine. He did not thereby *condone* it, however. The same is true with Paul in 1 Corinthians 15:29 and his employment, for the sake of his argument, of the practice of some being "baptized for the dead."

Current Practice: The Mormons

One does not hear much about baptism for the dead in mainstream Christendom, however this is not to suggest it still does not exist in some fringe movements. A perfect example is the *Church of Jesus Christ of Latter Day Saints* (the *Mormons*). Joseph Smith, Jr., the founder of the LDS movement, taught, "If we can baptize a man in the name of the Father and of the Son and of the Holy Ghost for the remission of sins, then it is just as much our privilege to act as an agent and be baptized for the remission of sins for and in behalf of our dead kindred who have not heard the gospel or the fullness of it" [Scott G. Kenney, *Wilford Woodruff's Journal*, vol. 2, p. 165]. According to B. H. Roberts, the major historian for the Mormon Church, Joseph Smith declared, "A man may act as proxy for his own relatives ... we may be baptized for those whom we have much friendship for ..." [*History of the Church of Jesus Christ of Latter Day Saints*, vol. 6, p. 366].

In 1959, Stephen L. Richards, who was First Counselor in the First Presidency of the Salt Lake Church, wrote, "All men are equal before the law and all are to have the opportunity, *even the dead*, to accept the Gospel and receive the promised blessings, but all must know and understand, and the dead who have gone on into the spirit world without knowledge of the Gospel are to be hereafter given an election to embrace it through vicarious works done for them by their descendants and other friends in the brotherhood of the Church" [*About Mormonism*, p. 11]. Richard E. DeMaris, in the *Journal of Biblical Literature,* noted the view of the Mormons was that "the living were thought to be obligated to help the deceased become integrated into the realm of the dead." This they sought to accomplish via acts of *proxy obedience*, which included baptism for the dead.

One Mormon scholar phrased it this way: "Millions of earth's sons and daughters have passed out of the body without obeying the law of baptism. Many of them will gladly accept the word and law of the Lord when it is proclaimed to them in the spirit world. But they cannot here attend to ordinances that belong to the sphere which they have left. Can nothing be done in their case? Must they forever be shut out of the kingdom of heaven? What then is the way of deliverance? The living may be baptized for the dead. Other essential ordinances may also be attended to vicariously. This glorious truth was hid from human knowledge for centuries" [C. Penrose, *Mormon Doctrine Plain and Simple*, p. 48].

The first recorded public affirmation of this doctrine of baptism for the dead in the Mormon Church came in August, 1840. The occasion was the funeral of Seymour Brunson in Nauvoo, Illinois. Joseph Smith delivered the funeral sermon, in which he stated to a woman, whose son had died without having been baptized, that this doctrine would prove to be for her, and also for the departed lad, "glad tidings of great joy." The first recorded baptisms for the dead were performed in the Mississippi River near Nauvoo.

In the early years of Mormonism, vicarious baptisms were performed only for direct blood relatives who were deceased. They would also baptize for their ancestors, although usually not more than four generations back. Today proxy baptisms are far more sweeping. They will even collect names of persons unrelated, sometimes even unknown, to them, and members of the Mormon Church will be baptized for these dead persons so that they might receive the remission of their sins and be saved. When they began collecting the names of Jewish Holocaust victims a few years ago, and began being baptized for *these* persons, then listing them as

"Mormons" in their *International Genealogical Index*, an outcry arose. Ernest Michel, chairman of the New York based *World Gathering of Jewish Holocaust Survivors*, said the number of names collected by the Mormons, for whom they had performed proxy baptisms, was in "six figures." Michel stated, "We are very hopeful that we will be able to convince the church to stop." In point of fact, the Mormon Church did indeed agree to cease this practice with respect to the Holocaust victims. Mormon Church spokesman Michael Leonard stated that future baptisms of such Holocaust victims would only occur *if* it could be demonstrated the deceased was a direct ancestor of a living member of the Latter Day Saints or if the Mormon Church had written permission from all the living members of the deceased person's immediate family. As one can quickly perceive, not only is this practice a major theological problem, but it can quickly become a delicate social issue as well.

Conclusion

It is almost mind-boggling the depths of theological absurdity to which men plunge themselves when they fail to perceive the beauty and simplicity of God's revealed Truth. Paul's statement in 1 Corinthians 15:29, when examined *in context*, is really not that complicated or complex. The relatively new Christians in Corinth were struggling to understand the concept of resurrection. Some, indeed, had come to believe it was a fallacious doctrine. Paul needed to reaffirm this most basic of Christianity's foundational truths. He approached that task from several tactical and strategic directions, one of which was to point out the inconsistency of that denial with the practice of being baptized for the dead. Paul's goal was not to *refute* the practice, but merely to *refer* to the practice, one with which they were familiar, to spotlight the absurdity of their position. I believe he succeeded admirably.

Although Paul did not address the matter directly, he nevertheless would most certainly agree that "baptism for the dead" (vicarious immersion for the deceased) was, and is, a false doctrine and practice. It is both an abomination and an absurdity. It accomplishes *nothing*, and actually denies some of the core truths of the Christian faith, including the nature of man, the nature of redemption, the purpose of active, demonstrated faith, and the parameters of God's grace. Psalm 49:7 clearly states, "No man can by any means redeem his brother." Yet, the practice of vicarious baptism is an attempt to do just that. It is contrary to Truth. Therefore, it must be rejected.

Chapter 22
A Meeting in the Air

When reviewing passages pertaining to the *Parousia* one is immediately and inevitably drawn to Paul's comforting words directed to the brethren in the city of Thessalonica. He tells them that he does not want them "to be uninformed ... about those who are asleep" (1 Thessalonians 4:13). The reason for this concern is also stated: "so that you may not grieve, as do the rest who have no hope" (vs. 13). Obviously, "sleep" is a figure of speech representing physical death. Even some of our Lord's closest companions misunderstood this figure of speech, and thus Jesus had to explain to them that He was talking of literal, physical *death* (John 11:11-14). In the same way, Paul was speaking of those brethren who had already *died* physically and were "asleep" in the dust of the ground (1 Corinthians 15:18, 20, 51; Daniel 12:2).

The message he was about to impart to them would be information they could then use to "comfort one another" (1 Thessalonians 4:18). It was a message of assurance and hope, even of expectation. The Lord will return one day. The dead in Christ shall arise from their graves (*Hades*). The living will be caught up to the Lord together with those believers who have been resurrected. From other passages we also know that the wicked will experience a resurrection unto judgment. The present heavens and earth shall be burned up with fire, and the wicked will be consumed in this process (2 Peter 3:7). Then the redeemed shall be led to the new heavens and earth where they will dwell forever with their Lord. This is a comforting thought mentioned several times in the Scriptures, and from it we can draw great assurance.

In this passage of Scripture (1 Thessalonians 4:13-18) there are several points that need to receive greater attention exegetically if we would truly perceive the full force of this teaching by the apostle Paul. We will notice each one in turn.

ONE -- "For if we believe that Jesus died and rose again, even so God will *bring with Him* **those who have fallen asleep in Jesus"** (1 Thessalonians 4:14). Traditionally, this has been interpreted to signify that the *souls* or *spirits* of the righteous dead will come back from Heaven or Paradise *with Jesus* when He returns (at the *Parousia*). Thus, when our Lord comes again to "claim His bride," His bride will come with Him. Hmm. Wait a minute. That sounds a bit strange, now doesn't it? The traditional explanation, of course, is that He is bringing these "immortal souls" with Him for the purpose of zapping them back into their resurrected bodies. The righteous dead, according to this theory, were already *with* the Lord in Paradise -- the Bridegroom was already *living with* His bride (sounds like what happens too frequently today) -- but at the *Second Coming* He's just coming for the *bodies*. This leads one to ask the question: Why? If the redeemed are already experiencing the joys of Paradise with the Lord, if the Bride is already at home with the Bridegroom, why bother with coming back for a body? Martin Luther (1483-1546), in his *Table Talk*, observed, "That would be a silly soul if it were in Heaven and desired its body!" This thinking has actually led some to contend it is permissible for couples to live together prior to the wedding; after all, *"Jesus is doing it."* The traditional teaching here is twisted theology at its worst.

Jesus declared, "In My Father's house are many dwelling places. ... I go to prepare a place for you. And if I go and prepare a place for you, *I will come again, and receive you to Myself*; that where I am, there you may be also" (John 14:2-3). This sounds to *me* like we won't get there until He comes for us. That *is* what He says, isn't it? In Matthew 24:30-31 Jesus informs us that at His return His angels "will gather together His elect from the four winds, from one end of the sky to the other." *Traditionalists* teach that the righteous dead are *already there* at the moment of physical death, so there is not much need to come gather them, it would seem. Jesus says He will not lose any who are truly His, but will "*raise him up* on the last day" (John 6:39-40). *Jesus* teaches He will come to *receive them* to Himself at the *Parousia*; that they are *not* already there. He also teaches that He will bring His reward *with* Him. "Behold, I am coming quickly, *and My reward is with Me*, to render to every man according to what he has done" (Revelation 22:12). Yet, the traditionalists teach that men receive their reward at the instant of death. Thus, there is no need for Jesus to bring these rewards with Him at the *Parousia* because *we already have them.* Are we to believe the traditionalists or Jesus? I think I'll choose the latter.

Paul declares exactly the same when he says the victory over death is experienced "at the last trumpet." At that point we shall "*put on* immortality," and "*then* will come about the saying that is written, 'Death is swallowed up in victory'" (1 Corinthians 15:52-55).

The notion that the victory is won at the moment of death, and we are already with the Lord in a "place of sweet repose," flies in the face of clear biblical teaching to the contrary. And yet the language of 1 Thessalonians 4:14 does at first glance appear to be saying that Jesus is bringing "with Him" from glory these redeemed ones who have previously died. So, what exactly *is* being declared in this passage?

The *New American Standard Bible* reads: "God will *bring with Him* those who have fallen asleep in Jesus." These are those who are *asleep* (i.e., who are *dead*). The *New English Bible* renders this passage this way: "God will *bring them to life* with Jesus." *The Message* (which is a translation in contemporary English) reads much the same: "God will most certainly *bring back to life* those who died in Jesus." This is assuredly true (our Lord will "raise them up on the last day"), but it is *not* an accurate translation of the actual text.

The solution to this apparent dilemma posed by this passage can be found in the intent of the "bringing" or "leading away." Unto what location are these "asleep ones" being brought or led? And *from where?* And for what purpose? The traditional teaching on this passage (and it is really only an *assumption*) is that they are coming *from* Paradise, and are being led *back to* the earth to fetch their bodies. This certainly does not fit the "Bridegroom coming for His bride" scenario, however. When the bridegroom left the father's home to fetch his bride and bring her to the father's house for the wedding feast, he didn't bring her *with him* (having been *living with her* for centuries already), rather, he went to *get her*. The traditionalists' theory, however, has the bride coming along *to get the bride*. As an old preacher once said, "That ain't Bible, brother! That don't preach!"

Consider this much more biblically consistent possibility: The Lord returns from heaven in the company of the angels to gather His people, both living and dead, from the four corners of the earth. He first calls the righteous dead forth from their graves, arousing them from their sleep in the dust of the ground. Then the redeemed, those formerly dead and the ones still living, are caught up to a meeting with Him in the air, and then *with Him* they are led away from the earth (which is about to undergo the judgment of fire) and unto/into eternal fellowship with the Father in the new heavens and earth.

In other words, when the passage says "God will bring *with Him* those who have fallen asleep in Jesus," it is a *bringing unto Himself* those who were in their graves (and who are still alive at His appearing), not a *sending unto the earth* those who were already in Paradise. The traditionalists have completely misunderstood this "bringing with Him," and they regard it as a sending *to earth*, rather than a bringing *away from* the earth and *unto*/into eternal fellowship with the Father. *With Him* (i.e., in the company of Jesus), we who have been raised from the dead at the last trumpet, as well as the redeemed who are still alive, will be led away (*brought*) to the glorious future which awaits us, and which our Lord had gone to prepare, and which He returned (was *sent*) to lead us to.

The word "bring" in verse 14 is a Greek verb signifying "to lead away, lead out; drag away." The Lord Jesus will lead us *away from* the judgment about to be poured out upon the earth (we shall be caught up from the earth unto a meeting with Him), and then lead us *unto* the glorious future that awaits us. In other words, being *brought with Him* is actually the *reverse* of what the traditionalists teach (which is: we are *sent with Him*). It is a bringing with Him *up from* the earth *to* Paradise (in the new heavens and earth) rather than a sending with Him *down to* the earth *from* Paradise. This interpretation is entirely correct grammatically in the Greek and has the advantage of being consistent with the remainder of biblical teaching pertaining to the events of the *Parousia*.

"We are not to think of them as brought *from* heaven, for they are viewed in respect of their being in their graves. But we may think of them as joining their descending Lord, and brought with him to earth" [*The Pulpit Commentary*, vol. 21, p. 94]. This, of course, would be the *new* earth and heavens which will be created following the destruction of the old. Revelation 21:1ff tells us that after the destruction of the old heavens and earth there will be "a new heaven and a new earth," and the bride of Christ is gathered up and brought *with Him* to dwell forever in this glorious place.

Thus, they are brought up out of the grave to join with Christ in the air, the *old* is destroyed and they are then, *together in His company*, brought with Him to the *new* heavens and earth. Burton Coffman, in his commentary on this passage, writes that the resurrected redeemed do not dwell with Him in the air, when they meet Him there, "but *then* accompany him *to* the new heaven and the new earth."

The Expositor's Bible Commentary [vol. 11, p. 276] comments, "To be brought with Jesus presupposes rising from the dead as part of the process (vs. 16). This is what had been taught the Thessalonians. Yet their ultimate anticipation is not just that of being raised, but that of being 'with Jesus' (4:14; cf. 4:17; 5:10). Beyond resurrection this is the consummating desire of Christians. But even more is in store for Christians. The words 'God will *bring*' point to a continuing *movement heavenward* after the meeting in the air (vs. 17), until the arrival in the Father's presence." Although this commentary perceives our destination to be "heaven," rather than the new heavens and earth, nevertheless it has correctly perceived the concept of being *brought with Him* to be movement *toward* God's presence, rather than a movement *away from* His presence in the company of Jesus as He leaves the Father's home to claim His bride. It is the going home to the Father's house *with the Bridegroom after* the claiming of the bride that is in view, *not* the bride leaving the Father's house with the Bridegroom to go collect a dead body so some "immortal soul" can be zapped back into it. As this same commentary stated earlier in its exegesis of this verse, "Just as 'Jesus died and rose again,' so will 'those who sleep in Him' be raised *when* God brings them *to* heaven *with* Jesus *at* His *Parousia*" [ibid].

In the *New Commentary on the Whole Bible* (which is based upon the classic work by Jamieson, Fausset and Brown), we find the following statement in its exegesis of this passage: "Disembodied souls are *not* spoken of; the original Greek reference is to sleeping bodies awaking and returning."

TWO ~ "For the Lord Himself will descend from heaven with a shout, with the voice of the archangel, and with the trumpet of God; and the dead in Christ shall rise first. Then we who are alive and remain shall be caught up together with them in the clouds to meet the Lord in the air, and thus we shall always be with the Lord" (1 Thessalonians 4:16-17).

In this passage we behold those "dead in Christ" raised from the dust of the ground, and they are gathered up, along with those believers still living at the *Parousia*, unto an "*apantesis*" (meeting, encounter) with the Lord in the air. This will be the *first* "encounter" or "meeting" of the redeemed (both living and dead) with the Lord. "And *thus* we shall always be with the Lord." The word translated "thus" is "*houtos*" which signifies "thusly, under such circumstances or conditions." The conditions or circumstances by which we shall always be with our Lord are: (1) His coming, (2) our resurrection, and (3) our gathering up. Nothing is said about the dead already being with Him for hundreds and thousands of years. Rather, it is under *these* conditions (coming, resurrection, gathering up) that this *encounter* with the Lord occurs, an encounter which leads to us being with Him *always*. Several of our beloved gospel hymns speak of this blessed promise to the redeemed. Perhaps we should pay greater attention to the words of some of our songs of praise and anticipation, rather than mouthing them mindlessly.

Hallelujah, We Shall Rise

In the resurrection morning, We shall meet Him in the air,
We shall rise, Hallelujah, We shall rise!
And be carried up to glory, to our home so bright and fair,
We shall rise, Hallelujah, in that morning we shall rise!

In The Morning Of Joy

When the trumpet shall sound, and the dead shall arise,
And the splendors immortal shall envelope the skies,
When the angel of death shall no longer destroy,
And the dead shall awaken in the morning of joy.

When the King shall appear, in His beauty on high,
And shall summon His children to the courts of the sky,
Shall the cause of the Lord have been all your employ,
That your soul may be spotless in the morning of joy?

When The Roll Is Called Up Yonder

When the trumpet of the Lord shall sound and time shall be no more,
And the morning breaks eternal, bright and fair;
When the saved of earth shall gather over on the other shore,
And the roll is called up yonder, I'll be there.

When He Comes In Glory By And By

Oh, how sweet 'twill be to meet the Lord,
When He comes in glory, by and by;
What a song of praise will be outpoured,
When He comes in glory, by and by.

I am longing for that happy day,
When He comes in glory, by and by;
For with Him I hope to soar away,
When He comes in glory, by and by.

The word translated "caught up" (vs. 17) is the Greek word "*harpazo*" which means to "snatch away by force, convey away suddenly, seize (as a wild beast grabs its prey)." It appears as a

Future Passive which signifies this has *not yet occurred*, but lies in the future (at the *Parousia*), and it is something that happens *to us* (i.e., we ourselves are not the active agent). We are awakened and called forth from the grave, and then we are "snatched away with great power" unto an encounter with our Lord. He seizes us and lifts us mightily from the earth which is about to experience the full outpouring of the fury of God's consuming fire. The wicked are *not* snatched away, but rather will be consumed along with the old heavens and earth (2 Peter 3:7). When this is accomplished, we will all be *brought with Him* to our dwelling in the new heavens and earth, and the wicked, now destroyed forevermore, will be as "ashes under the soles of your feet on the day which I am preparing" says the Lord of hosts (Malachi 4:3).

Kittel, in his classic *Theological Dictionary of the New Testament*, states that this word means "to take something forcefully ~ firmly, quickly ... forcefully snatch ... with the thought of speed" [vol. 1, p. 472]. He further states that it "always expresses the mighty operation of God" [*ibid*]. This whole event will happen suddenly, quickly, in the "twinkling of an eye." Thus, our gathering up to this encounter with the Lord will be a sudden "snatching away" from the earth, for the judgment of God will delay no longer. We are being taken out of the way so as not to be destroyed in the outpouring of His wrath. The wicked will experience no such gathering up out of harm's way, but will flee to caves to seek protection against the consuming fire. There will be no protection, however, and they shall be destroyed along with the old heavens and earth (from which the righteous will have been safely *snatched away*).

"But according to His promise *we* are looking for a new heavens and a new earth, in which righteousness dwells" (2 Peter 3:13). "And I saw a new heaven and a new earth; for the first heaven and the first earth passed away" (Revelation 21:1). "And I heard a loud voice from the throne, saying, 'Behold, the tabernacle of God is among men, and He shall dwell among them, and they shall be His people, and God Himself shall be among them, and He shall wipe away every tear from their eyes; and there shall no longer be any death; there shall no longer be any mourning, or crying, or pain; the first things have passed away.' And he who sits on the throne said, 'Behold, I am making all things new'" (Revelation 21:3-5).

To sum up, the passage in 1 Thessalonians 4:13-18 does not even begin to teach what the traditionalists claim it does. It merely declares that our Lord will return, raise those who sleep in the dust of the ground, snatch those to be saved away from the earth (along with those believers still living at the time) unto an encounter with Him in the air, and then *with Him*, following the destruction, we shall be brought unto the new heavens and earth where only righteousness will dwell, and we shall thus forever be with our Father and His Son. *"Therefore comfort one another with these words"* (1 Thessalonians 4:18).

Chapter 23
Paradise Regained
The New Heavens and Earth

    A friend from England wrote me asking if I would please consider doing an in-depth study of the concept of the *new heavens* and *new earth*. More specifically: what exactly is *meant* by this phrase which appears only a few times in the inspired biblical record? Does this phrase suggest a concept *contrary* to the traditional teaching regarding the future existence of the redeemed? If so, *what*? For those who may be unaware of the more *traditional* position on this topic, it essentially declares the *physical* universe will be utterly obliterated by fire, and that the "immortal souls" of all the redeemed will be joined to "spirit bodies" in some vast, ethereal "spirit realm" known as "Heaven." Many even envision this "eternal city" as having gates of pearl, a street of gold, and the like. Such a view comes primarily from a literal interpretation of the *Revelation* to John. We have all seen the cartoons of souls floating on clouds strumming harps: a view fostered somewhat by this traditional teaching on the "afterlife."

It might come as quite a surprise to many within the Family of God that such a view is *not* taught in Scripture. It might further surprise many within our own faith-heritage to learn that a good number of the noted leaders in the *Stone-Campbell Movement* totally rejected this traditional interpretation, as do an ever growing number within our movement today. I abandoned this teaching *decades* ago, as I simply could *not* reconcile it with an honest examination of the Word of God. The traditional teaching on the nature of man, the fate of the wicked, and the destiny of the redeemed, is, in a word, *false*. Once we come to perceive the true nature of man, as depicted within the Scriptures, and once we come to better appreciate the nature of our God and His eternal purpose for both the wicked as well as the redeemed, we will quickly discover that not only is the traditional teaching on this entire body of belief totally *false*, but it actually borders on *blasphemy*.

An integral part of this entire area of soteriological and eschatological theology is the significant question as to our God's original intent with respect to the destiny of mankind (more specifically: the *redeemed* of all time) and whether or not Satan was/is capable of eternally *thwarting* that divine design. If, in fact, Satan succeeds in preventing our God from realizing His original desire for man, then Satan achieves a significant victory over our Creator. I wonder if any of us are really prepared to promote such a pernicious position? *I'm not*. Yet, the traditional teaching on the ultimate destiny of the redeemed seems to do just that. For this reason alone, in my view, it should be utterly rejected.

"In the beginning God created the heavens and the earth" (Genesis 1:1). "And God saw all that He had made, and behold, it was *very good*" (Genesis 1:31). As the old country preacher declared, "God don't make no junk." God had created a perfect world, and within it He placed man. His intent was to have sons and daughters; to walk and talk with them in this unblemished paradise; to enjoy an endless, intimate relationship with His loving family. It was never God's intent, never His original design, that death, decay, corruption and disease overwhelm His children and the world He had created for them. The *intent* was an everlasting relationship with mankind, one epitomized by a reciprocated love. This living being fashioned by God was designed to live within this paradise *forever*. Not as some spirit being, but as a *physical* being, one perfect in every way; deathless. *This* was what God desired; it was what He *wanted*; it was what He created. It was the way things were *supposed* to be ... forever.

The Fall changed everything. Sin is a corrupting influence, and it corrupts completely. Not only was man himself subjected to this creeping corruption, but so also was the paradise in which man lived. When sin entered the picture, *everything* began to die. As we examine the world about us, we see a diseased planet. Most scientists agree that it is dying. True, it will take eons to finally accomplish, but, should God allow the earth to exist that long, it *will* at some point become virtually uninhabitable. Men and animals also die. The descent to the grave is inevitable for us all. Was all of this God's *original intent*? Did our Creator *desire* the death of His creation? Of course not. But, sin brought about a *detour*; man departed from the blessed destiny designed by his God. Did such a detour *defeat* God's will for His creation? *Never*. It merely *delayed* it. The desire of our Creator *will be realized*. Nothing will defeat it. The history of mankind, when viewed as a whole, is a story of redemption; of a return to that perfect paradise ~ paradise *lost* and paradise *regained* ~ where the redeemed are given the gift of immortality and dwell in the restored heavens and earth forevermore, enjoying sweet fellowship with their Father. This restoration of His original intent does not come without cost, however: the price that had to be paid was the death of His beloved Son.

What many fail to perceive is that with the redemption of fallen man also comes the redemption of the fallen creation. *Both* shall experience a restoration to God's original intent. *In Christ Jesus* all shall be made new. In other words, the Father's original intent will at last be fully realized. "The creation waits in eager expectation for the sons of God to be revealed. For the creation was subjected to frustration, not by its own choice, but by the will of the One who subjected it, in hope that the creation itself will be liberated from its bondage to decay and brought into the glorious freedom of the children of God" (Romans 8:19-21). In figurative language the apostle Paul is informing us that even the planet itself eagerly awaits this great and glorious day when the redeemed of all ages are restored to the paradise of God. Why? Because it means the planet itself will be restored to its state of perfection which it enjoyed prior to the fall of man. Just as the redeemed will cast off this state of corruption and decay, and put on incorruptibility, so *also* shall the physical heavens and earth. "For this perishable must put on the imperishable, and this mortal must put on immortality" (1 Corinthians 15:53). God will not be thwarted. What He set out to achieve in the beginning *will be achieved* in the end. God never loses! As John Milton (1608-1674) so eloquently phrased it in two of his works: Paradise *Lost* ... Paradise *Regained*. God wins!

The Platonic dualism that has infested the thinking of many within Christendom has led to a diminishing of the true biblical hope of a "restoration of God's creational intent," and has instead promoted "a supra-mundane disembodied heaven" where spirit-beings dwell apart from the physical creation in some spirit-realm. For an excellent development of these thoughts (and from which the above quotes are taken), I would encourage a reading of the very scholarly work "*A New Heaven and a New Earth: The Case for a Holistic Reading of the Biblical Story of Redemption*." This work is by Professor J. Richard Middleton of *Roberts Wesleyan College* and appeared in 2006 in the *Journal for Christian Theological Research* [vol. 11, p. 73-97]. Some may find it a rather difficult read, as it was intended primarily for scholars and theologians, but Middleton has done an excellent job of presenting the biblical evidence (in what he calls a "*creation- fall-redemption* paradigm") for "the restoration of God's creational intent for humanity and the world," as opposed to the "traditional, hybrid idea" (largely fostered by Plato) that the redeemed will experience eternal fellowship with their God in "a non-physical realm." Although I tend to differ with some points of his interpretive analysis of certain biblical passages, I believe, overall, he has done an excellent service to Christendom in his scholarly study.

Other biblical scholars agree; many from within our own *Stone-Campbell* faith-heritage. For example, John Mark Hicks and Bobby Valentine, in a book titled *"Kingdom Come"* (they sent me a complimentary autographed copy after it came out), have done a marvelous analysis of the teaching of David Lipscomb and James Harding on this very subject (as well as a much fuller treatment of their view of the nature of God's eternal kingdom). In this book it is demonstrated, through numerous quotes from these men, that they firmly believed "God purposed to restore creation to its original blessedness, to restore *shalom* upon the earth" [p. 33]. "We groan with creation itself for the revelation of a home in the new heaven and new earth" [p. 35]. "The Father would Himself come to dwell with His people in a new heaven and new earth, a new creation. There not only humanity, but the cosmos itself would be liberated from the bondage of sin and death. *This* is the goal of God's redemptive project. Lipscomb and Harding, along with Alexander Campbell, Tolbert Fanning and Robert Milligan among others, believed that God would reign with His people on a renewed earth forever. When Jesus returns 'again to earth,' according to Lipscomb, He will accomplish the 'restoration of all things to their original relation to God' in a new heaven and new earth" [p. 180]. In other words, they believed, as do I, that God's *original intent* will be fully realized on that great and final day for which we all long.

Contrasting the true teaching of Scripture with the traditional fallacies, the *International Standard Bible Encyclopedia* observed, "The *biblical* hope is separated from surrounding religious expectations by the conviction that man's emancipation could not occur apart from the redemption of the created order" [vol. 2, p. 656]. In other words, just as Paul stated in Romans 8, *both* the redeemed *and* the physical earth upon which we live will be ultimately liberated from the effects of sin and death; *both* will be transformed at the coming of Christ; *both* will be made new, with the former dwelling forever upon the latter. God's redemptive plan, then, is in reality a restoration of His original intent: full fellowship with His children in a perfect paradise. In the *Revelation*, "John's picture of the final age to come focuses not on a platonic ideal heaven or distant paradise, but on the reality of a new earth and heaven. God originally created the earth and heaven to be man's permanent home. But sin and death entered the world and transformed the earth into a place of rebellion and alienation; it became enemy-occupied territory. But God has been working in salvation history to effect a total reversal of this evil consequence and to liberate earth and heaven from bondage to sin and corruption" [*The Expositor's Bible Commentary*, vol. 12, p. 592]. Jesus referred to this time as "the regeneration" (Matthew 19:28, which the *New International Version* renders: "at the *renewal* of all things"). This is a Greek word signifying that which is made new; renovated, restored. Scripture does not depict the utter *annihilation* of the present physical universe, but rather the *restoration* of it to its original state of perfection. It is for this *renewal* that Paul says the physical creation "groans" in anticipation (Romans 8). Peter speaks of this very reality, saying that the ascended Savior "must remain in heaven until the time comes for God to *restore* everything, as He promised long ago through His holy prophets" (Acts 3:21). The *New American Standard Bible* reads: "the period of *restoration* of all things." The fire God will pour out upon the earth will be a *purifying* fire (like that used in the smelting process); it will not utterly destroy the earth itself, but rather remove the dross (all impurity), thus restoring the creation to its former state of perfection. This fire is "designed *not* to annihilate but to cleanse and purify" [*The Zondervan Pictorial Encyclopedia of the Bible*, vol.

3, p. 65]. It is within and upon this *new* heavens and earth ("new" in *quality*, as the Greek word *kaine* depicts) that the redeemed will then dwell.

A noted leader in the *Stone-Campbell Movement*, Moses Lard, wrote, "Under the curse on account of Adam's sin the earth certainly fell; for God cursed it directly and in so many words. The earth, then, I conclude, is among the things to be 'delivered.' From every disability under which it now lies in consequence of sin it will be freed. Not only so, but it will be 'translated' into a state of more than pristine newness and glory. It will undergo a change analogous to that which the bodies of the redeemed are to undergo" [*Commentary on Paul's Letter to the Romans*, p. 269-270]. "The creation itself is to be delivered from the bondage of corruption; from every effect of sin it is to emerge" [*ibid*, p. 272]. Adam Clarke declared that although the present earth will be subjected to God's *fire*, "it will not be *destroyed*, but be *renewed* and *refined*, *purged* from all moral and natural imperfections, and made the endless abode of the blessed. Indeed, it is more reasonable and philosophical to conclude that the earth shall be *refined* and *restored*, than finally *destroyed*" [*Clarke's Commentary*, vol. 6, p. 893].

Dr. Kenneth Wuest, in his classic "*Word Studies from the Greek New Testament*," made this insightful observation: "The non-rational creation, subject to the curse put upon it because of man's sin, is expectantly waiting for the glorification of the saints, that *it also* may be delivered from the curse under which it now exists. The creation shared in man's hope as in his doom. When the curse is completely removed from man, as it will be when the sons of God are revealed, it will pass from the creation also; and for *this*, the creation sighs" [vol. 1, *Romans in the Greek NT*, p. 138]. David Lipscomb, in his commentary on the book of Romans, wrote, "As a result of Adam's sin, the whole creation was cursed and fell away from its original design and became subject to the reign of death. Through the sin of man, not of its own fault or action, mortality and death were brought upon the creation." Nevertheless, "the hope is entertained that when the deliverance comes to the children of God, when they are delivered from the bondage of corruption and from the prison house of the grave, *then* the whole creation will share this deliverance and be freed from the corruption and mortality to which it has been subjected by the sin of man. It shared the corruption and mortality of man's sin, and it will also share his deliverance from it" [p. 153].

"As the body of the believer was made subject to death on account of sin, but is to be raised in glory; so that outward world in which the believer's body resides was cursed (Genesis 3:17-19), but is to be repristinated as a suitable dwelling place for it. There being this connection and correlation between the believer's body and the visible world, it is not unnatural that a yearning for this rehabilitation should be metaphorically ascribed to the latter. As the believer longs for the 'redemption of the body,' so that creation in whose environment he is to dwell longs for deliverance from the 'bondage of corruption.'" Thus, "material nature is metaphorically in sympathy with redeemed man, and shall be restored with him" [Dr. William G. T. Shedd, *A Critical and Doctrinal Commentary on the Epistle of St. Paul to the Romans*, p. 251-252].

"Yes, God's purposes shall be fully accomplished. If *we* wait, and wait in hope, so does the *creation* wait, groan, yearn for the revealing of the sons of God" [*The Pulpit Commentary*, vol. 18, *Romans*, p. 239]. Peter, in Acts 3:21, spoke of this time of the *restoration/renewal* of all things, which God had "promised long ago through His holy prophets." "The idea of a renewed universe is present in substance in many passages" [*The Zondervan Pictorial Encyclopedia of the Bible*, vol. 3, p. 65]. "For behold, I create new heavens and a new earth; and the former things shall not be remembered or come to mind" (Isaiah 65:17). "'The new heavens and the new earth which I make will endure before Me,' declares the Lord" (Isaiah 66:22). Although these passages have a more immediate fulfillment in the coming

Messianic dispensation in which spiritual Israel (the universal *One Body*) will be blessed, such reference to a new order clearly has a further reference to the time of renewal that will occur at the *second* coming of Christ. This phrase "new heavens and new earth" is actually "a technical term in the eschatological language of the Bible to define and describe the final, perfected state of the created universe" [*ibid*]. Both Peter and John make use of this phrase in their writings, and the reference is clearly to the anticipated reality following the *Parousia*.

2 Peter 3:13 reads, "But according to His promise we are looking for new heavens and a new earth, in which righteousness dwells." This will be "paradise regained." It will be returned to it original state of purity. No impurity at all will exist within the new heavens and earth. It has been *refined out* by the purifying fire of God. Only righteousness fills this new universe. The fire has done its work, and all that stands in opposition to our God is forever obliterated from existence. "But the present heavens and earth by His word are being reserved for fire, kept for the day of judgment and destruction of ungodly men" (2 Peter 3:7). The Lord poured out this fire from above on the cities of Sodom and Gomorrah, "reducing them to ashes, having made them an example to those who would live ungodly thereafter" (2 Peter 2:6). What happened to them will happen at the end of the age. The fire will descend upon the earth, all that is wicked and impure (and this means *people also*, as Peter says) will be consumed/annihilated in the fire (this, in my view, is the same as the "lake of fire" depicted in *Revelation*). The fire is simply that which *utterly destroys* all *dross* consigned unto it. When its purging work is accomplished, all that is left is the new heavens and new earth, and the Lord will then lead His redeemed ones to this restored, pristine creation, there to dwell with Him forevermore. "Then I saw a new heaven and a new earth" (Revelation 21:1). When the old has "passed away," the new is all that is left. The rest is ashes.

Malachi 4:1-3 speaks dramatically of this coming day: "'For behold, the day is coming, burning like a furnace; and all the arrogant and every evildoer will be chaff; and the day that is coming will set them ablaze,' says the Lord of hosts, 'so that it will leave them neither root nor branch. But as for you who fear My name the sun of righteousness will rise with healing in its wings; and you will go forth and skip about like calves from the stall. And you will tread down the wicked, for they shall be ashes under the soles of your feet on the day which I am preparing,' says the Lord of hosts."

Many have wondered about the order of events of that great day. What specifically will happen, and when? I believe one of the best portrayals is found in 1 Thessalonians 4:13-18, which was examined in some depth in the previous chapter. Here we have depicted the actual coming of our Lord to take His people to their eternal dwelling place, which we know to be the new heavens and earth. Oh how the redeemed and the physical universe *long* for this time of restoration to perfection! "*Come*, Lord Jesus!" (Revelation 22:20).

Chapter 24
Post-Resurrection Recognition

> "I consider the doctrine of the non-recognition of our friends in heaven a marvelously absurd one; I cannot conceive how there can be any communion of saints in heaven unless there be mutual recognition."
> *Charles H. Spurgeon (1834-1892)*

   On Sunday morning (February 12, 2006) I presented a sermon titled: "Headed For Our Heavenly Home: And Why I Can't Wait To Get There!" I listed eight reasons why Christians typically long for that eternal abode, and, since my sermons are accompanied by a *PowerPoint* slide presentation, these eight motivations were all illustrated with some touching graphics that attempted to depict, albeit imperfectly, the marvelous joys awaiting us there. After each of the points, one of my fellow elders, who happened to be leading singing that day, led the congregation in a hymn that was specifically selected to enhance musically the previous point. The congregation seemed to be genuinely edified by this focused worship/edification experience, and it also provided for a far more participatory phenomenon among those gathered. The sermon had been personally requested a couple of weeks earlier by one of our elderly members who was struggling with cancer and undergoing a series of radiation treatments. We all face many trials and tribulations during our earthly sojourn, all of which, I am convinced, will simply make that great eternal reunion one day all the sweeter. How *wonderful* heaven will be!

Although our Lord has given us *glimpses* into this future abode, there is also much we *don't* know; much that has *not* been revealed to us in the inspired Word. Like you, I have lots of questions. There is much I would *like* to know, but, realistically, probably never will until that Great Awakening on the day of our Lord's return to collect His beloved Bride. One of the questions many ask, and this has been debated for centuries, is: "Will we *recognize* one another in heaven?" Will I know my mom and dad, and will they know me? Will I recognize my dear grandparents? We speak of a wonderful *reunion* that awaits us there, but what if we *don't* know one another? What kind of reunion would that be? Although most disciples of Christ firmly believe we *shall* indeed know one another in the hereafter, there are nevertheless a few who declare such will *not* be the case. Therefore, we ask: "What sayeth the *Scriptures*?"

As already noted, there are some who truly believe there will be *no* recognition of one another in heaven. There are several reasons they suggest this. First, they cite the exchange between Jesus and the Sadducees as recorded in Matthew 22:23-32. These Sadducees, "who say there is no resurrection" (so, obviously, their question posed to Jesus was *not* for the purpose of gaining insight, but hopefully to gain an advantage over Him), presented Jesus with the scenario of a husband who had died without having fathered any children, so his brother took the woman to be his wife ... and then it happened again and again through seven brothers. They all die, and, finally, so does the woman herself. The Sadducees ask Jesus whose wife this woman will be in the next life. Jesus responds, "At the resurrection people will neither marry nor be given in marriage; they will be like the angels in heaven" (vs. 30).

Although this is indeed a very interesting passage, and raises some additional questions about future relationships in that eternal abode, it nevertheless does *not* suggest there will be *no recognition*. To try and move from "no marriage" to "no recognition" is quite an interpretive leap. Jesus says we shall be like the angels. Do angels recognize one another? Well, they seem to have names, or at least some of them do. There is Gabriel. Michael. Do you suppose *these* angels know one another? If they do, and if we are to be *like* them, then will *we* know one another? Of course, the advocates of the doctrine of non-recognition say that the *only* way in which we will be like the angels, according to Jesus in this passage, is in the fact that there will be no marriage. Thus, this passage really doesn't answer our question decisively one way or the other; it could be argued either way from this text, although I still believe it is a completely unwarranted assumption to draw the doctrine of *non-recognition* out of the doctrine of *non-marriage*.

Those who embrace the doctrine of *non-recognition* also suggest that many of the "dearly departed" would simply appear in heaven in a form unknown to us. For example, what about the many infants who die at birth? Will these forever be infants in heaven, or will God transform them into adults? If the latter, how would a mother know her child? How would a deceased infant (or even fetus) recognize its mother? What about the aged? How will my grandma appear in heaven? Will she be the aged woman I remember in my youth, or will she be rejuvenated in her resurrection body? If the latter, how will I recognize her? What about those who go through life with horrible deformities and malformations? For example, if the "Elephant Man" makes it to heaven, what will he look like? Certainly one would think, one would *hope*, he would not retain those deformities for all eternity. Thus, how would we recognize him?

These are valid questions. We know that we shall indeed be *changed* when our bodies are raised from the dead at His coming, or when we, the living, are caught up in the air with Him, yet we also are uncertain as to exactly how we shall appear. The apostle John wrote, "Beloved, now we are children of God, and what we shall be has not yet been made known. But we know that when He appears, we shall be like Him, for we shall see Him just as He is" (1 John 3:2). What exactly will we look like? We don't know. We haven't been told. What we *do* know, however, is that we shall be like *Him*. Was the resurrected Jesus recognizable? Well, there were times He was and times He wasn't. He seemed to have the ability to transform His form to some degree. Some recognized Him, some didn't. There is no question but what *we* shall also be transformed in some way so as to be made fit for that eternal realm. "It is sown a perishable body, it is raised an imperishable body" (1 Corinthians 15:42). "You do not sow the body which is to be" (vs. 37). "It is sown a natural body, it is raised a spiritual body" (vs. 44). "And just as we have borne the image of the earthy, we shall also bear the image of the heavenly" (vs. 49). "We shall all be changed, in a moment, in the twinkling of an eye, at the last trumpet; for the trumpet will sound, and the dead will be raised imperishable, and we shall be changed. For this perishable must put on the imperishable, and this mortal must put on immortality" (vs. 51-53).

We will all be changed, transformed, recreated. What will we be like? We shall be like *Him*. "But our citizenship is in heaven. And we eagerly await a Savior from there, the Lord Jesus Christ, who, by the power that enables Him to bring everything under His control, will transform our lowly bodies so that they will be like His glorious body" (Philippians 3:20-21). And, no, I couldn't give you an exact description of that glorious body if my life depended on it -- thankfully, it *doesn't*. I know it will be wonderful, marvelous, magnificent. I know it will be vastly improved from this present earthly tent. Will I still be *me*? Yes, I believe I will be. Al Maxey will still be Al Maxey when raised and transformed. My hunch is, however, that my *appearance* will be *changed*. This fact, of course, leads some to believe I will not be recognizable to others, and that is certainly, at least on the surface, a seemingly strong argument for the doctrine of *non-recognition*, although the weakness of this argument is that it bases recognition upon purely *outward, physical* traits. There is far more to *who we are* than merely the outward markings of a physical body; our true identity is more *inward*. However, if recognition is purely *physical* in nature, they may have a point.

Another argument *against* the view that we shall know one another in the new heavens and earth is: "How can we truly be happy in heaven if we recognize the fact that some of our loved ones are missing?" If we can recognize each other in the hereafter, then would we also not recognize the fact that some *didn't* make it? Could a mother really be happy if she knew her child had been destroyed in the eternal fire? Therefore, some argue that *lack* of recognition might actually be a great blessing; a comfort. Wayne Jackson sought to deal with this argument in an article that appeared in the October 7, 2003 issue of *Christian Courier*. His conclusion was that this emotional appeal was really *just that*, and it was most certainly not just cause biblically for discounting recognition of one another in the eternal realm. Jackson wrote, "It should not be argued that there will not be recognition in heaven, for that clearly is not the case. Nor is it feasible to suggest that one will have no remembrance of earthly associations." David Padfield, the minister for the *Church of Christ* in Zion, Illinois, answers this objection in the following manner in his little two-page tract titled *"Will We Recognize Each Other in Heaven?"* ~ "When we speak of future recognition, some skeptic will usually ask, 'Would you be happy in heaven knowing some of your friends were not there?' ... Yes, we will be saddened by the loss of some, but I always thought this is why 'God will wipe away every tear from their eyes' (Revelation 21:4)." If in fact we *are* able to notice the *absence* of some (which implies we can recognize the *presence* of others), then I have no doubt that God will heal this hurt in some way. *How?* I don't know. But if He can remove the *tears* from our eyes, He can surely also remove the *cause* for them.

I personally must agree with the great preacher Charles H. Spurgeon (1834-1892) on this issue: "I believe that heaven is a *fellowship* of the saints, and that we *shall* know one another there." He also wrote, "Some have doubted whether there will be recognition in heaven; there is no room for such doubt, for it is called 'my Father's house;' and shall not the family be *known* to each other?" In many respects, the gathering together of the redeemed before their God for the great wedding festivities of the Lamb will be a *family* event: the family of God. Family reunions are not times when *strangers* congregate, but when those *known and loved* come together for sweet fellowship. Heaven will be just such an occasion. Jesus said, "And I say to you, that many shall come from east and west, and recline at the table with Abraham, and Isaac, and Jacob, in the kingdom of heaven" (Matthew 8:11). Our Lord certainly seems to imply *recognition* at this table, doesn't He? In a companion passage (Luke 13:28-29) Jesus states that part of the agony of those cast out from the presence of the Lord on that great day will be the fact that they will "*see* Abraham and Isaac and Jacob and all the prophets in the kingdom of God." Again, He seems to clearly suggest *recognition*.

In the Lord's parable of the rich man and Lazarus (Luke 16:19-31) one also sees *recognition* suggested. Although this is clearly just a *parable*, and one should not take it too literally, nevertheless I think the Lord certainly was operating from a fundamental perception among the Jewish people that there *would* be recognition in the afterlife. The account of Jesus on the mount where He was transfigured (Luke 9:28f; Matthew 17:1f), and the appearance of Moses and Elijah, also suggests retention of one's identity in the eternal realm. These two men were identifiable in some way. And who could fail to be moved by the heartfelt statement uttered by David following the death of his infant son: "I shall go to him, but he will not return to me" (2 Samuel 12:23). David apparently expected to be reunited with his son one day. Throughout the OT writings we find one who has died depicted as being "gathered to his people" or "resting with his fathers." Although this may well be little more than a poetic expression for death, nevertheless it conveys the common perception of a *reunion* at some point, a hope held dear by many peoples throughout the world. Small comfort this would be if there was no ultimate *recognition* of one's people or fathers or loved ones who had preceded one in death.

For example, the ancient Athenian philosopher Socrates (469-399 B.C.) wrote the following: "Since death conveys us to those regions which are inhabited by the spirits of departed men, will it not be unspeakably happy to escape from the hands of mere nominal judges? Is it possible for you to look upon this as an unimportant journey? Is it nothing to converse with Orpheus, and Homer, and Hesiod? Believe me, I could cheerfully suffer many a death on condition of realizing such a privilege. With what pleasure could I leave the world, to hold communion with Palamedes, Ajax, and others." Cicero (106-43 B.C.) wrote, "For my own part, I feel myself transported with the most ardent impatience to join the society of my two departed friends. O, glorious day, when I shall retire from this slow and sordid scene, to assemble with the divine congregation of departed spirits; and not with those only whom I have just mentioned, but with my dear Cato, that best of sons and most valuable of men. ... If I seemed to bear his death with fortitude, it was by no means that I did not most sensibly feel the loss I had sustained: It was because I supported myself with the consoling reflection that we could not long be separated." These two examples, of many that could be cited, clearly show that the hope of *recognition* in the afterlife is a hope common to those of virtually all religious faiths throughout history.

Our Christian hymns are filled with poetic expressions of this hope of seeing our loved ones again one day. In the hymn "O

Think of the Home Over There" we read, "I'll soon be at home over there, For the end of my journey I see; Many dear to my heart, over there, Are watching and waiting for me." We are singing of *recognition*. "We shall meet on that beautiful shore" is the sweet refrain from the inspiring hymn "*Sweet By and By*." One of my very favorite hymns is the old classic: "*Beyond the Sunset*." Note the following words from this beautiful hymn: "Beyond the sunset, O glad reunion, With our dear loved ones who've gone before; In that fair homeland we'll know no parting; Beyond the sunset for ever more." What a glorious *reunion* with loved ones. *Recognition*. And who among us has not often sung the following beautiful chorus from the hymn "*If We Never Meet Again*": "If we never meet again this side of heaven, As we struggle through this world and its strife, There's another meeting place somewhere in heaven, By the side of the river of life." Yes, God's people often sing of heaven, and, when we do so, we sing of that joyful *reunion* with those whom we love. *Recognition*. This is a fundamental aspect of our Christian hope.

In his first epistle to the brethren in Thessalonica, Paul spoke to the concern among many of the disciples as to the disposition of their departed loved ones. "But we do not want you to be uninformed, brethren, about those who are asleep, that you may not grieve, as do the rest who have no hope. For if we believe that Jesus died and rose again, even so God will bring with Him those who have fallen asleep in Jesus" (1 Thessalonians 4:13-14). We have *hope*. Part of the nature of this hope is that we shall one day be *reunited* with those who have preceded us in death. There will be a meeting together with them and the Lord (vs. 17). "Therefore comfort one another with these words" (vs. 18). I believe a significant aspect of this comforting would be that the living would have the blessed assurance that they would see these departed loved ones again.

In summation, we must admit that there is much we don't know about the nature of the afterlife. What will we look like? What exactly will we be doing there? The questions go on and on. The reality is: we have far more questions than answers. However, one thing we can be sure of is that *whatever* God has planned for the redeemed, it will be glorious beyond comparison with anything we have yet experienced. I doubt any of us will have any complaints. Will we know and recognize one another there? Although I am not prepared to be dogmatic about my views on this matter, I am nevertheless convicted that the answer is *Yes*, we *will* know one another. Exactly *how* God will bring this about, I don't know; I leave it in His more than capable hands. My ultimate concern in *this* life is to live in such a way that I may experience the *next* life, and to assist as many others as I can to experience the same eternal joys that await us. I hope to see you there. And whether we recognize one another or not, won't it be wonderful to be in the presence of our heavenly Father, His beloved Son, and the Holy Spirit? All else will truly pale in comparison.

Chapter 25
Whose Wife Will She Be?

The public ministry of Jesus Christ had almost reached its *conclusion*. He had come to Jerusalem for the last time; it was the week of His passion. In just a few days He would be led away to be executed on a cross. Prior to that time of agony, however, He continued to teach the people, and great crowds gathered to hear Him. The religious leaders also sought Him out, but with far *less* noble purposes. The Pharisees and Herodians "went out and laid plans to trap Him in His words" (Matthew 22:15). They wanted to know His position on paying *taxes* to Caesar. They believed that no matter what Jesus answered, they could make use of His words to discredit, and ultimately *destroy*, this "trouble maker." "If Jesus said that they should pay the tax, they could then charge Him with disloyalty to Judaism; if He said no, they could denounce Him to the Romans" [*Ryrie Study Bible*]. It was not unusual to find the Pharisees hounding Jesus, but in these final days we also find the *Sadducees* coming after Him. So, *who were* the Sadducees, and *why* did they find Jesus so offensive?

The Sadducees

According to tradition, the Sadducees derived their name from *Zadok*, who was High Priest during the time of King David and King Solomon of Israel. The family of Zadok held on to the high priesthood, and officiated in the Temple, until the time of the exile (a period of several *hundred* years). This family even formed the chief element of the post-exilic priesthood until the time of the great Maccabean revolt. The Sadducees were a much smaller Jewish sect than the Pharisees, but they had far more political power. They were the politicians, the social elite, the *aristocrats* of their day. Although the Pharisees had come to see themselves as *spiritually* superior to other Jews, the Sadducees regarded themselves as *socially* superior. While just about *anybody* could become a Pharisee, no matter his status in life (as long as he *submitted* to the "party line"), membership in the sect of the Sadducees was by *birth* only: one had to be descended from one of the high-priestly or aristocratic families. No "outsiders" allowed. The Sadducees were, simply stated, "high society" ~ much "too good" for the common man.

During the so-called "Intertestamental Period" of Jewish history, this sect embraced the Greek culture and way of life. The Sadducean high priests became the chief negotiators with the various foreign governments in power over the people of Israel. Therefore, they began to acquire (through their pagan alliances) a considerable amount of political *clout*. As a result of their increasing willingness to *compromise* with foreign powers, the Sadducees found themselves in increasing *conflict* with the Pharisees (who were *separatists*). In 1 Maccabees 1:11-15 the Sadducees are described as *traitors* to the Jewish people and to the Laws of God. They were not well-liked by the common people, nor did they have an abundance of vocal supporters.

Religiously, the Sadducees were the "*liberals*," whereas the Pharisees would be considered the "conservatives," of the day. They accepted the Torah, but rejected the prophetic writings of the OT as being in any way authoritative. They also rejected the existence of angels and spirits, the Platonic concept of "immortal soulism," and even denied the hope of a resurrection from the dead (Acts 23:6-10). They also actively mixed their religion in with politics. One scholar stated, "Theirs was a rational religion, placing high value on *logic* and *reason*, and they were more preoccupied with matters of current expedient interest than in eternal truths." They felt it only logical to compromise with whomever was in power in order to secure a more favorable position for themselves. By intimately associating their religious sect with the government, however, they set themselves up for destruction. When the nation finally fell in 70 AD, so also did the Sadducees. "A lesson of history may be *learned* from the Sadducees. With the destruction of the Temple in A.D. 70, the Sadducee party disappeared. A compromising, temporizing spirit was unable to withstand the shock of political revolution. The disbanding of the priesthood and the slaughter of the aristocracy in the terrible war spelled their doom. The religion of these sophisticated few did not have depth enough to endure crisis." It should be noted that only the Pharisees, of all the prominent Jewish sects, survived the fall of the nation.

The Sadducees are not often discussed in the NT writings; they are only mentioned by name 13 times: 6 in Matthew, 1 in Mark, 1 in Luke, and 5 in Acts. During the early part of Jesus' ministry, the Sadducees largely ignored Him. He was a promoter of "new religious ideas," but not a *political* threat. Therefore, He was not worthy of their attention. With His triumphal entry into Jerusalem shortly before His death, however, this perspective began to change rather significantly. They now regarded Him as a threat to their own security, and they began to formulate plans to *destroy* Him. The Sadducees were not very *popular* with the common people. This was partly due to the fact that in order to physically maintain the Temple, they heavily taxed the Jews. Thus, in effect, they were draining the people dry of their personal finances in order to maintain their own religious/political institution. Some scholars feel John 18:15-16 may indicate that the apostle John was a member of the sect of the Sadducees. If this is true, then it would mean the two men who made the greatest contribution to the writing of the New Testament documents (Paul and John) came from opposing sects within Judaism. It would also show how *in Christ* all "party barriers" can indeed come down, and we can all be *One Body* in Him, regardless of various personal preferences, perceptions or positions.

The Challenge

"That same day (note: several scholars feel this may have been *Tuesday* of the passion week) the Sadducees, who say there is no resurrection, came to Him with a question" (Matthew 22:23; cf. Mark 12:18; Luke 20:27). It is important to note that the primary focus of the encounter that is about to occur between this sect and the Savior is the doctrine of a future bodily *resurrection* of the dead. The Pharisees *accepted* this doctrine, but the Sadducees *did not*, and the two groups were often found in heated debate and conflict over this teaching (a dramatic example of this can be found in Acts 23:6-10, where Paul took great advantage of this theological divide). "The Pharisees leaned toward a belief in resurrection that owed more to Greek ideas than to the OT" writings [*The Expositor's Bible Commentary*, vol. 8, p. 1016], which included the paganistic notions of the inherent immortality of the soul, with the physical body being the "soul's temporary prison" (a concept derived from Plato, not Scripture). The Sadducees, on the other hand, felt that all such teaching was sheer nonsense, even rejecting the reality of angels. Understanding their position will help us better understand the purpose of their question, as well as the nature of our Lord's response.

The challenge they posed to Jesus (which we noticed briefly in the previous chapter) was of a woman who had the unfortunate experience of outliving seven husbands, all of whom happened to be brothers. "Moses told us that if a man dies without having children, his brother must marry the widow and have children for him" (Matthew 22:24). This was known among the people of Israel as the *Law of Levirate Marriage*. This was not unique to the Israelites, but was truly "a *cross-cultural* phenomenon whereby the nearest kinsman of a man who dies without sons marries his widow" [*Eerdmans Dictionary of the Bible*, p. 803]. This rather unusual law is described in Deuteronomy 25:5-6 ~ "If brothers are living together and one of them dies without a son, his widow must not marry outside the family. Her husband's brother shall take her and marry her and fulfill the duty of a brother-in-law to her. The first son she bears shall carry on the name of the dead brother so that his name will not be *blotted out* from Israel." The strange account of Judah, Tamar and Onan clearly demonstrates that this law *predated* the time of Moses (see: Genesis 38:6-11). Thus, Jesus, and the crowds surrounding Him that day, would have been quite familiar with the theology behind the question of the Sadducees. They would have understood that the *primary* purpose of this law was "to provide the deceased man with a son to inherit his property and thereby establish his 'name' (i.e., his lineage, his memory). A *secondary* purpose of the levirate law may have been to provide the deceased's wife with the economic security and social status of marriage and children" [*ibid*]. This word "levirate," by the way, is derived from the Latin word "*levir*," which means "brother-in-law" or "husband's brother." Also, "within the *Mishnah* the first tractate (*Yabamot*, 'sisters-in-law') of the third order (*Nashim*, 'women') covers the subject of levirate marriage with considerable detail" [*The Expositor's Bible Commentary*, vol. 3, p. 150].

It should probably be noted at this juncture that this law was not rigidly enforced among the Israelites. In fact, even in God's Law there was a provision for its *circumvention*. This can be found in Deuteronomy 25:7-10. If a deceased man's brother did not want to marry his sister-in-law and have a child by her for her dead brother, he had the option of *refusing*. However, the widow was not without *recourse*. She could file a *complaint* against him at the city gate with the elders of the people. The man would be brought before the elders and encouraged to fulfill his duty. If he persisted in his refusal, however, the widow "shall go up to him in the presence of the elders, take off one of his sandals, spit in his face and say, 'This is what is done to the man who will not build up his brother's family line.' That man's line shall be known in Israel as *The Family of the Unsandaled*" (vs. 9-10). Therefore, this man and his family would be *shamed*, and even potentially *shunned*, because of his unwillingness to fulfill his *obligation* to his deceased brother. "The OT gives *no* actual *case* of levirate marriage, although levirate law stands behind the account in Ruth 1:11-13; 4:1-22." It's very probable that "in Jesus' day the law was little observed: the younger brother's *right to decline* taking precedence over his *obligation*" [*The Expositor's Bible Commentary*, vol. 8, p. 461]. There are additionally hints of the *principle* of this law perceived in Numbers 27:1-11.

"Now there were seven brothers among us. The first one married and died, and since he had no children, he left his wife to his brother. The same thing happened to the second and third brother, right on down to the seventh. Finally, the woman died. Now then, at the resurrection, whose wife will she be of the seven, since all of them were married to her?" (Matthew 22:25-28; cf. Mark 12:20-23; Luke 20:29-33). "This case is so ludicrous it may have been a well-known Sadducean joke used for poking fun at the Pharisees' doctrine of the Resurrection" [*ibid*, p. 735]. "There's a levity and a coarseness in the question which is simply revolting" [*The Pulpit Commentary*, vol. 15, pt. 2, p. 362-363]. The Sadducees weren't really interested at all in trying to determine whose wife this woman would be. In fact, "some of the rabbis had already decided the question: a woman who had been married more than once would, they thought, be the wife of the first husband in the world to come" [*ibid*, p. 372]. These querists, however, did not believe in a world to come, thus whose wife she would be was irrelevant to them. In their mind, she, as well as her many husbands, would all remain *dead* in the *dust*. The Sadducees merely sought to use this question to *malign* the Lord and to further *mock* the Pharisees, who were undoubtedly looking on. Or, phrasing it in the words of Dr. Craig Keener, "The Sadducees are interested neither in moral nor in legal questions here, but endeavor to illustrate the impossible dilemmas they believe the doctrine of resurrection creates" [*A Commentary on the Gospel of Matthew*, p. 527].

It would also be well to inform the reader here that such a scenario as these religionists posed to Jesus was *not uncommon* to Jewish literature. In the *Book of Tobit*, by way of example, one finds a fairly *similar* story (Tobit 3:7-10). This book, which is part of Jewish apocryphal literature, tells the story of a very righteous man named Tobit, from the tribe of *Naphtali*, who is living in Nineveh after the fall of the northern kingdom to the Assyrians in 722 B.C. This book is regarded as uninspired by most Protestants, but is accepted by the Catholics. It was pronounced part of the biblical canon by the *Council of Carthage* of 397 A.D., and then later confirmed as inspired by the *Council of Trent* in 1546. In the passage referenced above, a young woman by the name of *Sarah*, the daughter of *Raguel*, had been given to seven husbands, but an evil demon named *Asmodeus* killed each of them before she could bear them sons. Again, this would have been a story with which Jesus, as well as the people with Him that day, would have been quite *familiar*. Just in passing, several scholars also see a possible allusion in John 4:16-18 to an unfortunate woman outliving a host of husbands, although there are certainly other possible interpretations of that particular passage.

The Rebuke/Response

Jesus began His response to these Sadducees with a *rebuke*: "You are mistaken, not understanding the Scriptures, or the power of God" (Matthew 22:29; cf. Mark 12:24; Luke *omits* the rebuke in his account). The Sadducees were a lot like too many disciples of Christ today: they had read the Scriptures, they had studied them, and perhaps could quote them extensively, but they *didn't understand them*. Therefore, their perception of God's eternal Truth was limited and/or fallacious, resulting in countless inappropriate applications to one's daily living. The OT writings contained ample teaching about the resurrection of the dead, yet these religious leaders had failed to perceive that Truth. As a result, they denied the very power of God to accomplish that which He declared in Scripture He would do.

Our Lord next makes a statement about the nature of the future existence of the *resurrected* redeemed. Jesus wasn't really attempting to satisfy our *curiosity* about the nature of the eternal realm, and our place within it after the resurrection, but was simply seeking to *counter* the false notions of the Sadducees, who denied *both* the resurrection and the existence of angels. It was for this reason that Jesus Christ spoke of men being *resurrected*, after which He stated that they would resemble in some respects the *angels* of God. Thus, in this one statement, He *affirmed* both doctrines *denied* by His questioners. It's important to note that Jesus did not say the resurrected would *become* angels, but that they would be *as* or *like* the angels. In other words, certain *qualities* and *characteristics* of angels will be shared by the resurrected redeemed. Perhaps the most important and highly sought after quality (Romans 2:7) is that we shall be *immortal*. Immortality is not an *inherent* quality of *mortal man*, but is something that we shall "put on" when we are raised on the last day (1 Corinthians 15:50-54). Luke, in his account of this exchange of Jesus with the Sadducees, makes this new reality very clear: "…neither can they die anymore, for they are like angels, and are sons of God, being sons of the resurrection" (Luke 20:36).

The *other* statement of Jesus on this occasion, however, has generated centuries of speculation and debate. He said, "For in the resurrection they neither marry, nor are given in marriage, but are like angels in heaven" (Matthew 22:30; cf. Mark 12:25; Luke 20:35). The phrase "in the resurrection," which Jesus Christ uses here, does *not* refer to the *act* of resurrection *itself*, but rather refers to the resurrected *state*. It would be much the same as stating, "Within the resurrection *realm*." Angels, it appears, neither marry nor are given in marriage, which Jesus indicates is a quality to be *shared* by the resurrected redeemed. Dr. Charles Ellicott gives voice to our *questions* on this passage: "Will there, we ask, be no continuance there of the holiest of the ties of earth? Will the husband and the wife, who have loved each other until death parted them be no more to each other than any others who are counted worthy to obtain that life? Will there be no individual recognition, no continuance of the love founded upon the memories of the past?" [*Ellicott's Commentary on the Whole Bible*, vol. 6, p. 138]. The thought that we will **not know** one another in that realm, or that our cherished relationships *here* will no longer exist *there*, is very *troubling* to a great many individuals. I firmly believe Scripture teaches that we *will* know one another in that realm, and that we shall retain our memories. "Some have concluded from Jesus' answer that in heaven there will be no memory of earlier existence and its relationships, but this is a *gratuitous* assumption" [*The Expositor's Bible Commentary*, vol. 8, p. 461].

But, will the nature of our relationships be different? Apparently they *will*, although there is tremendous *uncertainty* and great *speculation* as to the exact nature of these changes. Collectively, we (the resurrected redeemed) shall be the *bride* of the Lamb, and we shall all be participants in the eternal *wedding* festivities. Exactly what this means in terms of our activities and relationships is anyone's guess. All we can say with any certainty is that it will be wonderful to experience. I want to be part of it, even though I can't even begin to enumerate the *specifics* of these eternal blessings. I simply know I don't want to *miss out* on them. Will Shelly and I be husband and wife in that realm? It *doesn't* appear that we will be. Will we be in a close, intimate, loving, *everlasting* relationship with one another (and all the other redeemed) that will far exceed anything experienced here on earth? It appears absolutely certain that we will be. Does our God and Father have the power to vastly *enrich* our relationships far beyond anything we've known in this temporal realm? Without doubt. Can I be *satisfied* with that changed reality in the world to come? You had better believe it!

By the way, when Jesus spoke of the redeemed "in the resurrection," saying that they neither "*marry,*" nor are they "*given in marriage,*" He was referring in the first case to men, and in the second case to women. Husbands would "take a wife" for themselves, and fathers would "give in marriage" their daughters to some man. In the new order of things, women will no longer be "possessions" to be "given" to another, and men will no longer "take" a woman to be his wife. "The entire arrangement of sex, marriage, reproduction, and childbirth, and all laws pertaining to these, is intended for the earthly life only, and not for the life to come" [R. C. H. Lenski, *The Interpretation of St. Matthew's Gospel*, p. 872]. "In the Resurrection there will be an entirely new order of existence" [*The Expositor's Bible Commentary*, vol. 8, p. 736].

An individual from Maryland emailed me recently, saying, "When Jesus said there would be no 'marrying or giving in marriage,' He was obviously addressing two separate actions. One would be a man contracting to 'buy' himself a bride, perhaps with a *dowry*, through her father or master. The 'giving in marriage' would refer to the one who had the power over the woman to assign her to a man as his wife. Jesus is saying that this sort of social custom would not be tolerated in the era to come; the woman would be 'free like the angels;' she would not be chattel." I think this brother may be on to something important here. Nobody will *possess* us in that realm but our Lord. We are His, and His alone.

Jesus does *not* declare in this statement to the Sadducees that there will be no recognition of others in that realm, nor does He declare that our relationships will not be intimate. He's just stating that the custom of a man taking a woman as his wife or of a woman being given away in marriage to a man, will no longer be practiced.

The nature of all our relationships with one another will have undergone what might be characterized a *"kingdom change."* No longer will any soul be subservient to another in any way. As one redeemed people (His bride), we will all (and each) be subservient only to Him. Spiritually, that is true even *now* (Galatians 3:28), but it will be true in every aspect of our existence *then*. Many disciples down through the centuries have sought to bring their *earthy* perception of marriage to bear upon this passage. Believing the state of marriage to exist solely for the purpose of providing a "legal outlet" for our fleshly *passions*, and in the process *propagate* the human race (since death kept reducing our number), they felt that "in heaven" we would all finally "be free" of such worldly lusts. Dr. Paul E. Kretzmann opines, "In heaven, Christ tells them, the resurrected believers will be *sexless*, like the angels, since there is no longer any need for marriage, both the procreation of children and all the sexual desires of the body being things of the past" [*Popular Commentary of the Bible*, The NT, vol. 1, p. 125]. "Sexless like the angels?" Is *this* what Jesus said? Not even close! But, such is the *assumption* of those who view *marriage* in such a light. As Dr. W. Robertson Nicoll observes, being "as angels" does "*not* necessarily imply *sexlessness*, as the Fathers supposed" [*The Expositor's Greek Testament*, vol. 1, p. 276]. Our bodies are raised male and female; we retain our identity; we are simply made immortal (like angels we never die), and our relationships are enhanced and ennobled so that never again will any person ever be *over* or *under* another, as is often the case in human relationships (even in marriage). Such pertains to *this* realm, but does *not belong* "in the resurrection."

Dr. Ellicott may have come closest to capturing the vision of the resurrection realm when he wrote, "The old relations may subsist under new conditions" [*Ellicott's Commentary on the Whole Bible*, vol. 6, p. 138]. He went on to speculate, "The saintly wife of two saintly husbands may love both with an angelic, and therefore pure and unimpaired, affection" [*ibid*]. What might seem impossible *here*, due to our human nature, may well be fully possible *there* through the *transformation* of this earthly nature that will take place at the resurrection. To some extent, His Spirit transforms us *now*, but we still await that full transformation. "This difference between our *present* life and that life *to come* does *not* imply that our *bodies* will be *discarded*" [R. C. H. Lenski, *The Interpretation of St. Matthew's Gospel*, p. 872]. This is correct. The resurrection at the last day is a *bodily* resurrection. In the eternal realm (in the resurrection) we will not be "spirit beings." Our bodies will be raised, they'll *put on* immortality, and we shall dwell forever within the new heavens and earth. Life will take on a beauty that we can now only imagine (and that poorly). Relationships we have enjoyed here will be enhanced there. Can I explain every aspect of this new existence? No. Indeed, it would be futile to try. Thus, in the final analysis, all efforts to qualify and to quantify the joys that await us must fail. Instead, we live by faith and await His coming. The apostle John sums it up best: "Beloved, now we are children of God; and it has not yet been revealed to us what we shall be, but we know that when He is revealed, we shall be like Him, for we shall see Him as He is" (1 John 3:2). I suppose we shall have to leave it there.

Chapter 26
Paul's Anticipated Departure

With respect to 2 Corinthians 5:8 it has been declared, "No passage in 2 Corinthians has prompted more discussion than this. As a consequence, the diversity of scholarly interpretation is rather bewildering" [*The Expositor's Bible Commentary*, vol. 10, p. 346]. Dr. Samuele Bacchiocchi observes, "This passage is rightly regarded as the *crux interpretum*, primarily because the figurative language is cryptic and open to different interpretations. Unfortunately, many interpreters are eager to derive from this passage, as from Philippians 1:22-23, precise anthropological, chronological, or cosmological definitions of life after death. Such concerns, however, are far removed from Paul, who is using the poetic language of faith to express his hopes and fears regarding the present and future life, rather than the logical language of science to explain the afterlife. All of this should put the interpreter on guard against reading into the passage what Paul never intended to express" [*Immortality or Resurrection? A Biblical Study on Human Nature and Destiny*, p. 180-181].

A wise word of caution is sounded by Dr. Leroy Edwin Froom, "It is both illogical and unsafe to build any major doctrine on isolated passages, apart from the general tenor of Scripture. It is to be remembered that enormous errors have been built upon isolated verses" [*The Conditionalist Faith of Our Fathers*: The Conflict of the Ages Over the Nature and Destiny of Man, vol. 1, p. 324]. In other words, if one's interpretation of a particular passage is in conflict with the remainder of biblical teaching on that subject, then that particular interpretation becomes suspect. Difficult passages must be interpreted and clarified in light of the entirety of God's Word, not isolated from the whole in order to try and "proof-text" a personal theological preference. "God's message to us is consistent. To put it differently, we should interpret the various parts of Scripture in a way that accords with its central teachings. We may not pit one part of Scripture against another, nor may we interpret a detail of Scripture in a way that undermines its basic message" [Kaiser & Silva, *An Introduction to Biblical Hermeneutics*: The Search For Meaning, p. 24].

There is no question but what some interpreters have taken a couple of statements by the apostle Paul and have tried to use them to promote the pagan concepts of the traditionalist positions on the nature of man and the fate of both the righteous and wicked following physical death. These interpretations, however, stand in clear opposition to the overwhelming bulk of biblical teaching on the *true* nature of man and his ultimate destiny. Thus, to seek to build a theology upon a handful of passages which is contrary to revealed Truth throughout the remainder of God's Word is unconscionable. This is exactly what some traditionalists have done with passages such as 2 Corinthians 5:8 and Philippians 1:23. They have ignored the remainder of biblical teaching and sought to derive a doctrine of "immortal soulism" from these isolated passages which do indeed, when viewed out of context with the rest of God's Word, *appear* to promote what they proclaim.

2 Corinthians 5:6-8 -- Paul declares that "while we are at home in the body we are absent from the Lord." Thus, he "prefers rather to be absent from the body and to be at home with the Lord."

Philippians 1:23-24 -- Paul knew that to one whose life was totally focused on Jesus, death would be "gain" for that one *in Him* (vs. 21). However, to "live on in the flesh" would result in further profitable service to the Lord. Thus, Paul was "hard-pressed from both directions, having the desire to depart and be with Christ, for that is very much better; yet to remain on in the flesh is more necessary for your sake."

Helmut Thielicke correctly points out that the New Testament is not concerned about a "state" which exists between death and resurrection, but for a relation that exists between the believer and Christ through death. This relationship of being with Christ is not interrupted by death because the believer who sleeps in Christ has no awareness of the passing of time [*Living With Death*, p. 177]. In other words, Paul was not anticipating some meeting with Jesus in some so-called "Intermediate State," but rather was confidently looking forward, past the moment of physical death, to the *resurrection* which, for the dead, would be perceived as instantaneous. We close our eyes in death and we open them in victory when we are awakened by the trumpet at the Parousia. We will not be conscious of the passing of any time. It is similar to the "sleep" brought about by the anesthesiologist prior to an operation. We close our eyes and "instantly" we awaken in the recovery room. Those who sleep in the dust of the ground "do not know anything" (Ecclesiastes 9:5), "for there is no activity or planning or wisdom in Sheol where you are going" (Ecclesiastes 9:10).

The Bible is filled with striking imagery, but we should not formulate theology based on literal interpretations of images, figures and symbols. To do so will lead to some unbelievably bizarre doctrine. In figurative language Paul simply declares a struggle to know which is personally preferable: to remain alive, serving the Lord and His people, or to rest from one's labors in death (knowing that the next conscious moment, which will seem but an instant, will place one in the presence of the Lord at His coming). Paul longed to lay aside the flesh (physical death) and to "sleep." It's like the child on Christmas Eve who wants to go to bed earlier "because then it will be morning and Santa will have come." They know that the span of time will be "bridged instantly" by sleep, and they long for sleep to come so they may experience the joys of the morning.

The Expositor's Bible Commentary points out that "not all at Corinth shared Paul's view of the Christian's destiny. There were some who taught that resurrection lay in the past, accomplished spiritually and corporately for all believers at the resurrection of Christ or else personally experienced at the moment of baptism." Thus, Paul had "in mind these 'proto-Gnostics' who denied any future, bodily resurrection but envisaged a disembodied immortality" [vol. 10, p. 347]. Paul's hope, as indeed is the hope of all disciples of Jesus, was in the resurrection on that final day, a day when the dead in Christ shall be called forth from their sleep in the dust of the ground, when this mortal shall "put on" immortality, and when the redeemed of all time shall thusly dwell forever with Him in the new heavens and earth. Paul longed for that day, even though he understood the value of remaining physically alive on earth to continue preaching the gospel; he longed for that day so much that "falling asleep" sounded wonderful, for it would hasten that glorious morning when all would be made new and we would be with Christ Jesus and the Father forevermore.

This is all that is being taught in the above passages. It does not declare, as some think, that immortal souls fly off to some intermediate holding area to await the day when they will be zapped back into their bodies. That is a pagan absurdity nowhere taught in Scripture. *The Interpreter's Dictionary of the Bible* states that the 2 Corinthian 5 passage "cannot with any consistency be interpreted of the moment of death" [vol. 4, p. 52]. I agree whole-heartedly. "Paul's words must be understood in the light of his own uniform and repeated teaching on the nature of man, not on a concept never held either by Paul or by any of the other apostles, much less by any group in the Christian church for nearly two centuries thereafter. This mortal body does not enclose an immortal principle or entity, which is released by the stroke of death, and then flies away in glad release. This is simply thinly disguised Platonism" [Dr. Leroy Edwin Froom, *The Conditionalist Faith of Our Fathers: The Conflict of the Ages Over the Nature and Destiny of Man*, vol. 1, p. 325].

Chapter 27
Paying the Penalty for Sin

"Was the crucifixion of Christ on the cross total or token payment for sin?" How one answers this question will reflect the very core of one's theology! This question and its answer take us to the very heart of faith and the essence of the gospel. It is not a trivial question. Indeed, it is *the* question each of us must at some point prayerfully ponder, with our response determining the nature of our subsequent spiritual journey. Yes, it is *that* important! And it is the very reason I have chosen to end this book with a presentation of a few thoughts that I believe may well dramatically change the character of your Christian sojourn. Please consider them carefully and prayerfully.

Very few people ... *very* few ... will openly declare the passion of our Lord to be in any way a "token" payment for sin. The notion that Jesus only *partially* paid the prescribed penalty for sin is almost unthinkable to discerning disciples. Such a view tends to trivialize the suffering and death of our Lord. Over the years *some* have indeed declared such a doctrine, but they are few, and rarely regarded with any favor by the majority of disciples. In a survey I conducted of the readers of my weekly publication *Reflections on this question*, and I received a *great many* responses (several hundred), *only three people* took the position that the sacrifice of Christ was only a *partial* or *token* payment for sin. Needless to say, I happen to agree with the majority position.

When my Lord went to the cruel cross, the debt was cancelled; it was marked: *Paid In Full*. We sing a well-known hymn titled "Jesus Paid It All" (written by Elvina Hall in 1865). The chorus goes: "Jesus paid it all, all to Him I owe." The thought, obviously, is that at the cross Jesus "paid in full" the penalty for sin; not only for *my* sin, but also for those of *anyone* who is willing to come to Him by faith to receive that free gift. The teaching of this chorus is that the *full penalty* for sin has been met; it was met *once for all* by our Lord's sacrifice. Another lesser known hymn, which has the same title, was written some years later (in 1917) by M. S. Shaffer. It goes, in part: "Gone is all my debt of sin ... Yet the debt I did not pay, Someone died for me one day, Sweeping all the debt away, Jesus paid it all." Again, the message is the same as that of the earlier hymn: the full penalty for sin has been paid; paid by Christ on the cross; paid *in full*.

There is an old American folk hymn titled "He Paid A Debt" that has a marvelous message of God's matchless grace. The first stanza and chorus read as follows: "He paid a debt He did not owe, I owed a debt I could not pay. I needed someone to wash my sins away. And now I sing a brand new song, 'Amazing Grace.' Christ Jesus paid a debt that I could never pay." That tells it just like it *is*, doesn't it? The cost of redemption was too high for *any* of us to pay, either for ourselves or for anyone else. "No man can by any means redeem his brother, or give to God a ransom for him, that he should live on eternally; that he should not undergo decay ~ For the redemption of his soul is costly, and he should cease trying forever" (Psalm 49:7-9). It was a debt *we* could not pay. But, thanks be to God, the debt *has been paid*. It was paid *once for all* by the sacrifice of Jesus Christ on the cross.

Another beloved hymn, "He Bore It All," expresses this truth this way: "My precious Savior suffered pain and agony. He bore it all that I might live. He broke the bonds of sin and set the captive free. He bore it all that I might live. I stood condemned to die, but Jesus took my place. He bore it all that I might in His presence live." This is a classic Stamps-Baxter hymn, written in 1926. For generations our spiritual forefathers have been singing this gospel truth: Jesus "took my place" and "bore it all."

These hymns reflect what I believe to be a timeless truth: the sacrifice of Christ was substitutionary in nature; He "took my place" and He *paid in full* the penalty for sin. Strange as it may seem, this teaching is *rejected* by some of our fellow disciples. Indeed, they find these hymns to be offensive, and some even refuse to sing the words. Such is largely the view of those still steeped in legalistic thinking. This threatens their *works-based* efforts at self-redemption, and thus they reject this gift of grace. Paul informs such persons that they "have fallen from grace" and "have been severed from Christ" (Galatians 5:4). If Jesus, by God's grace, paid the penalty for sin in full, and you *reject* that gift and seek to merit your *own* redemption, you will stand before the judgment seat *outside* of grace and *apart from* Christ. What an unenviable prospect. One individual wrote, "I would much rather sing 'Jesus Paid it All' than to sing 'Will It Do, Precious Lord?'" If we are relying on our *own* effort, the answer is: NO, it will *not* do!

A man in Tennessee observed, "For one who is more interested in what God has revealed than the speculations of some theologian, such statements as that of Isaiah 53:6, 'The Lord has laid on Him the iniquity of us all,' should settle the matter." As noted, Scripture makes it abundantly clear that the Father sent the Son to atone for sin ... *all* sin. It is an *unlimited* atonement in that it is freely offered to all men, for He does not wish "for *any* to perish, but for *all* to come to repentance" (2 Peter 3:9). Thus, He gave His beloved Son, "so that *whoever* believes in Him should not perish, but have eternal life" (John 3:16). Yes, the atonement accomplished by Jesus is *unlimited*; it is offered to *all*. On the other hand, it is clearly a *limited* atonement, in that it will only prove efficacious for those who embrace it. The gift is offered to *all*; it is accepted by only a *few*. Jesus "bore it all" and paid the penalty for sin *in full* only for those willing to *accept* this gift of grace through faith. We can do nothing to merit it, but it will never be ours if we don't embrace it. The Lord *forces* salvation upon no man.

Some have tried to argue that Jesus merely died "on our behalf," but that He did not truly die "in our place." In other words, they reject the doctrine of a "substitutionary sacrifice." The late T. Pierce Brown, a well-known and widely-respected servant of the Lord, and a noted Christian author (who graciously informed me, "You may feel free to use my name as long as you give my actual quotations"), emailed me the following thoughts on this particular aspect of the debate. I think his thoughts are excellent, and I share them with you here: "The following may be of some help to those who want to meditate on what the Bible actually teaches about the matter. In Romans 5:6 when Paul said, 'For when we were yet without strength, in due time Christ died for the ungodly,' he used the Greek word *huper*, which means 'on behalf of.' A person can die 'on behalf of' another and *not* die 'in his stead.' The usual death of a soldier for his country is in that category. However, in the Civil War, it was possible for a person to get another one to enlist 'in his stead,' and if he then died, he would not only die on behalf of, but in the place of, another. So it is true that in most cases, when the death of Christ is mentioned, the word *huper* is used, for the writer wanted to emphasize that Christ died on our behalf. However, in such passages as Matthew 20:28, Mark 10:45, and others, where Jesus gave His life a ransom *for* many, the Greek word *anti* is used, indicating that as a ransom, He died 'instead of' us -- he was a substitute for us." T. Pierce Brown concluded his rather lengthy email to me with this statement, "So, the 'bottom line,' if there is one, is that His payment fully satisfied God's prescribed penalty for sin, so that His death was truly 'substitutionary' in nature, but was also 'on our behalf.'" In a separate email, this Christian gentleman wrote, "I freely confess that it is of vital importance whether or not God accepted the payment of Christ as a full payment for the debt of our sin, for if He did *not*, His plan failed, and *we* still have to make some payment."

Of course, other passages come to mind: "And He died for all" (2 Corinthians 5:15), where the Greek scholar Alford points out that "the *vicariousness* of Christ's sacrifice is necessary" to a correct interpretation. "He made Him who knew no sin *to be sin* on our behalf" (2 Corinthians 5:21). "Christ redeemed us from the curse of the Law, having *become a curse* for us" (Galatians 3:13). In 1 Thessalonians 5:9-10 we learn that the redeemed are "*not* destined for wrath" because our Lord Jesus "died *for* us." Hebrews 9:28 informs us that Jesus Christ was "offered once to bear the sins of many." "For Christ also died for sins once for all, the just for the unjust" (1 Peter 3:18). "He Himself bore our sins in His body on the cross" (1 Peter 2:24). There are, of course, a great many others (and we didn't even list those in the OT writings), but something needs to be said about a passage in Hebrews which the critics of the "paid in full" doctrine often mention as "proof" of their own theory of "partial" or "token" atonement: Hebrews 2:9, which reads: "...by God's grace He might *taste death* for everyone."

To merely "taste" death leads some to believe Jesus did not truly experience death to its fullest, thus His sacrifice should only be regarded as "token," at best. There are several places where this *idiom* is used: Matthew 16:28; Mark 9:1; Luke 9:27; John 8:52. These passages make it clear that the idiomatic phrase signifies the fullness of death. Indeed, the Jews argued with Jesus in the John 8 passage, signifying that Abraham was indeed *dead*, so why was Jesus declaring some would not "taste death"? *They* knew what He was saying, even if some don't seem to today. "The verb means to taste with the mouth, from which the metaphorical sense 'come to know' develops. It means here that Jesus died, with all that that entails" [*The Expositor's Bible Commentary*, vol. 12, p. 25].

Of perhaps even greater significance in Hebrews 2:9 is the textual problem associated with the phrase "by the grace of God." There are several manuscripts, with some very strong *patristic* support, which, in the Greek text, have "*apart from* God" rather than "*by the grace* of God." Thus, the teaching would be that Jesus died "apart from God," which would certainly fit with the idea of our Lord Jesus Christ being "forsaken" as He suffered and died on the cross for our sins. The *Pulpit Commentary* declares this reading to be "the original reading." One of its reasons is because "Origen (185-254 A.D.) testifies to its prevalence in his early day, and accepts it as at least equally probable with the other reading" [*The Pulpit Commentary*, vol. 21].

There is really no scholarly justification, however, for the notion that the idiomatic expression "tasting death" merely denoted some type of "token" or "partial" sacrifice of life. Its common usage clearly denotes just the opposite. John Calvin, in his *Commentary on Hebrews*, said that this means "Christ *died* for us, and that by taking on Himself what was due to us, He redeemed us from the curse of death." R. C. H. Lenski wrote that the phrase "to taste death" means "to undergo all its dread bitterness; it is not a softening but rather a strengthening of the simple verb 'to die.' Jesus tasted death, not by merely sipping, but by fully draining the cup" [*The Interpretation of Hebrews*, p. 77]. Dr. Kenneth Wuest, the noted Greek scholar, observed, "He was made for a little time lower than the angels, in order that He might taste death for the human race. The penalty of sin was paid by Him" [*Hebrews in the Greek New Testament*, p. 58]. Robert Milligan, the late President of the *College of the Bible* at *Kentucky University*, wrote in his commentary on Hebrews [published by *Gospel Advocate Company*, 1973], "To 'taste death' is the same as to *experience* death, or to suffer death. And the phrase 'for every man' is just as plain as it can be made;

clearly indicating that the atonement of Jesus Christ is for every human being" [p. 105].

I think it can be safely concluded that the overwhelming majority of disciples of Christ are fully convicted in their hearts, by virtue of their study of the inspired Word, that Jesus was made to be a curse on our behalf, bore our sins to the cross, and died there *in our place* as the substitutionary, atoning blood sacrifice provided by the grace of our God, and that He *paid in full* the prescribed penalty for sin. Those who *reject* this teaching, or who twist it in some way, have been the cause of several false doctrines which have plagued the Lord's church for many centuries. In the remainder of this closing chapter, I would like to examine these false doctrines, and demonstrate how they depart from the above truth regarding the fullness of our Lord's atonement.

The Penalty Paid In Full: The Wicked and their Wages

Admittedly, some of those surveyed were confused about this whole issue; a handful were even somewhat displeased with me for even bringing the matter up. They felt the whole issue has no relevance to men today. One reader asked, "Al, why would you raise such an issue? It will only create doubt among the weak and unsaved." I suppose such a question could be posed with regard to virtually *any* doctrine or practice. Why would we dare to discuss various misunderstandings concerning baptism, for example? Wouldn't preaching God's Truth on the subject merely "create doubt among the weak and unsaved"? Some thought I was wrong for the stand I took against racism and homosexuality, "taking me to task" for it, worried that racists and homosexuals might be offended by my proclamation of God's Word on the matter. Similarly, on more than one occasion the disciples of Jesus came to Him and informed Him that people were "offended" at His teaching. My response is the same as the Lord's: He kept right on preaching and teaching Truth. So did the apostles when *they* were told to cease and desist. So shall I.

Brethren, I don't apologize for taking a stand on God's Word, nor do I apologize for asking the tough questions which often challenge our comfort zones and force us to examine afresh our beliefs and practices. Saints have been slumbering in pews far too long, and the lost have been largely ignored while factionists fight their foolish feuds with one another. One critic of mine wrote, "Knowing you, Al, you have a hidden agenda with this question." No, my "agenda" is not hidden at all; it is very visible: Jesus paid the penalty for our sins, and yet many, both saved and lost, apparently don't have a clue what that means. Some, indeed, *proclaim* this truth, but then don't *practice* it. My "agenda" is to hold aloft this glorious gift of God's grace and in so doing shed light on the horrendous doctrines and practices that tend to subvert it. Frankly, many disciples of Christ have never even bothered to *think* about all of this ... *ever*. They weren't even aware of the deadly inconsistencies of some of their teachings and practices which are completely contrary to a truth they were publicly professing, but which they were failing to fully perceive. One person wrote me, "Very interesting topic, and one I have *never* considered." Another said, "Just when you think you have heard all questions that could possibly come up, Al Maxey comes up with one you have *never* heard." Brethren, it's one we *need* to hear, and to *prayerfully consider*.

Jesus paid the penalty for sin; He paid it in full. Most of us profess to believe this. However, we need to ask a very vital question: What exactly *is* the prescribed penalty for sin? When we speak of the "wages of sin," do we really understand that concept? We declare that Jesus *paid in full* that penalty for sin, but then many turn right around and declare a much different penalty for sin in their preaching and teaching. And, sadly, most are not even aware they are doing it. What *is* the penalty for sin? It is DEATH. "For the wages of sin is death, but the free gift of God is eternal life in Christ Jesus our Lord" (Romans 6:23). Moses told the people of Israel, in his final words of counsel to them, "I call heaven and earth to witness against you today, that I have set before you life and death, the blessing and the curse" (Deuteronomy 30:19). Those same choices face all men today: life and death, the blessing and the curse. *Jesus became the latter for us.* He paid the penalty for sin, He became a curse for us, and He died in our place. The wages of sin is DEATH, and Jesus paid it *in full*. He was cut off and forsaken by God, darkness came over the land, and He died and was buried. He forfeited LIFE on our behalf that He might fully pay the "wages of sin."

Few would argue with the above analysis, *until* it comes time to discuss the final fate of the unredeemed. Those who refuse to avail themselves of the gift of the substitutionary sacrifice of Jesus Christ *must pay their own debt for their sins*. If they are unwilling to allow Jesus to pay that debt for them, then *they* must pay that penalty. What is that penalty which they must pay? It is the same penalty that Jesus paid, which payment they refuse to accept, and thus must pay themselves: it is the penalty of *death*. This is not what is most often taught in our churches, however. Instead, we preach and teach that the penalty for sin which the unredeemed must pay is *never-ending torture*; burning and screaming in endless agony; zillions and zillions and zillions of years of being eaten by immortal maggots. It is the punishment of "eternal LIFE" lived in *everlasting torment*. God will never, ever be satisfied with their misery; it must continue forever.

Yes, that is the traditional view; we've all heard it, and most have probably never really bothered to think about it too deeply. We just accept it and move on to more pleasant thoughts. But, we need to ask a question: If indeed Jesus PAID IN FULL the actual penalty for sin, then by what rationale do we proclaim an infinitely more horrible penalty for those who do not accept His full payment? Let's face it: if the actual penalty for sin is unending torture, then Jesus didn't even come close to being a substitutionary sacrifice! We cannot proclaim "Jesus paid *it all*," and at the same time proclaim the unredeemed will *pay infinitely more*. This is a theological conflict of cosmic proportions. If Jesus actually *did* pay the penalty for sin in full, then that is the *same* penalty that the wicked will be forced to pay if they fail to avail themselves of His payment on their behalf. On the other hand, if the payment for sin is actually perpetual torture, then Jesus didn't pay it; full payment has *not* been made, and at best His sacrifice was only a "partial" or "token" payment, with the *full* payment to be paid by the unredeemed. Do you begin to see the inconsistency?

It is my strong conviction that the problem primarily lies in a widespread misunderstanding of the biblical teaching on the nature of man, the wages of sin, and the ultimate nature of final punishment. False teaching regarding these matters has so permeated and influenced Christendom for so many centuries that Truth is now virtually viewed as heresy. Thankfully, this is changing dramatically in the church today as more and more begin to realize the horrendous nature of the traditional teaching on these matters. We have a long way to go, however.

To be totally cut off from the Giver of Life; to be abandoned to the darkness of death; to have the Father turn away from you, leaving you to suffer and die: *this* is the penalty for one's sin! On the day of judgment, all men will be raised to face the Lord. Some, who allowed Jesus to pay the penalty for their sins, will receive the gift of LIFE, a life which will endure forever. Others, who did *not* allow Jesus to pay the penalty for their sins, will have to pay that penalty *themselves*. "And the witness is this, that God has given us eternal life, and this life is in His Son. He who has the Son has the life; he who does not have the Son of God does not have the life" (1 John 5:11-12). Those who have rejected the Son will thus experience exactly what Jesus did: forfeiture of LIFE. They will be forsaken by God, He will turn His back on them, they will undergo unimaginable suffering as they die, and they will ultimately experience the "wages of sin" -- *death*; a death from which there will be absolutely no future resurrection to life. Just as the redeemed will be *alive* forevermore, so will the unredeemed be *dead* forevermore. "And these will go away into eternal punishment, but the righteous into eternal life" (Matthew 25:46). It is indeed a punishment that is eternal in nature; once dead, they are dead forever. It is a total removal from the presence of the Giver and Sustainer of LIFE, a removal with no attendant promise of resurrection. For just as long as the redeemed are *alive*, so also will the unredeemed be *dead*; both states are everlasting. Just as the redeemed will be given LIFE, nevermore to DIE, so shall the unredeemed be given DEATH, nevermore to LIVE.

Did Jesus pay that penalty for the sins of the world? YES, He did! He was cut off, He was forsaken, He was separated from the Father, and He suffered and DIED. The *only* difference, and it is significant, is that Jesus was also previously given a promise: Because He was sinless, and because, out of love, He took our place, He would not be *abandoned* to the grave. He would be raised to LIFE. No such promise is given to the wicked. Thus, in the death, burial and resurrection of Jesus Christ, our Lord not only fully paid the penalty for sin (forfeiture of life; cut off from God), but He also fully guarantees us the victory (resurrection to life; restored to God's presence). He paid the penalty, but He also won the victory over that penalty for those who trust in Him. He thus evidences *both* the fullness of the penalty, as well as the fullness of the promise.

A minister in Tennessee wrote, "Those who do not accept this gift of salvation will pay the price for sin, which is *death* -- separation from God." When one is completely cut off from the One who sustains life, the result is death. Jesus paid that penalty for us. However, if one refuses that gift, they must pay it themselves. A man in Canada summed it up this way: "The wages of sin is *Death*, not boiling like a chicken for eternity." A lady in Alabama observed, "What was the price that Jesus paid for our sins? Suffering and death. *Not* eternal, unending torture. Rather, it was one very long day of severe suffering that culminated in His death. Suffering and death was the fully sufficient price paid for the sin of all mankind by Jesus. Why should the price for sin be any greater for any one individual found guilty of sin on the day of judgment than that fully sufficient price paid by Jesus for all mankind?" Indeed, *that* is the question. Did Jesus *pay in full* the *full penalty* for sin? I believe He did. That being true, then that is the SAME penalty which will be faced by those who do not avail themselves of the substitutionary sacrifice of Jesus Christ. He paid it for all of us, but we will pay it ourselves if we refuse that gift.

One additional point should be made here with regard to our Lord's payment and its impact upon all of mankind. Some see in this doctrine the basis for *Universalism*: the view that *all* will be saved, and *none* will be lost. One critic wrote, "The flaw in your thinking is to think that just because Jesus has paid the debt in full, the benefits are imputed to everyone without condition." Another wrote, "If Jesus paid the price for all our sins, then it seems no one would be sent to Hell or destroyed." This assumes the gift of our Lord's atoning sacrifice is *imposed* upon all mankind against their will. That is *not* what the Bible teaches. Jesus died for all, but not all will *avail* themselves of this gift. *It must be received*, and that is accomplished by faith. Just because our Lord fully paid the penalty for sin, and freely offered it to all, does not mean it is imposed upon all against their will. It is for those who want it, and who are willing to receive it by faith.

The Penalty Paid In Full: The Redeemed and their Response

There is a far more serious problem than the above theological dispute, however. Although I believe the above study to be an important one, and the disciples of Christ should not flee from it simply because it is controversial, nevertheless, in the final analysis, what God chooses to do with the wicked is entirely in His hands. I have a personal conviction, based on a great deal of research and reflection, and I will boldly share my views with those who may be interested, as I have done in this book, for I consider it to be extremely important to a more enlightened appreciation of God and His Word.

This next concern, though, is in an entirely different category, and it has long impacted our fellowship with one another. Sin separates a man from His God. That sin must be dealt with; it must be taken out of the way; its penalty must be paid. If it is *not*, we are lost. No man can appear before his God on the day of judgment, still in his sins, and hope to receive the gift of LIFE. The "wages" due, which must be paid, will be *death*. The vital question for mankind, therefore, and for every man, becomes: What must be done to remove this barrier of sin that separates me from my God? The answer, of course, as we all know, lies in God's gift of His Son Jesus Christ. When John saw Jesus coming toward him, he declared, "Behold, the Lamb of God who takes away the sin of the world" (John 1:29).

If, in fact, Jesus took away my sin ... if He bore it in His body to the cross ... if He became a curse on my behalf ... if He suffered and died in my place ... if He paid the debt in full ... if He fully satisfied God's prescribed penalty for sin ... then what must *Al Maxey* pay to stand redeemed before God Almighty? The answer is: **Absolutely Nothing!** If the debt is paid in full, *I owe nothing*. A minister in California wrote, "I have never heard this idea that Jesus did not pay the full price for my sin. What *other* thing of value could *add to* His payment? And *who* would pay it?" A minister in Arkansas wrote, "God paid the full price of redemption in Jesus' death. There is *nothing* we either could or can do to mend our human/personal relationship with God." A minister in Oklahoma wrote, "Of course Jesus paid our debt in full. To suggest otherwise would constitute a 'balance due' to God; that we, in some way, have a price still on our heads that we ourselves must somehow find a way to expunge. If Jesus only took care of a *portion* of the penalty, then *we* must WORK to find a way to build enough credit in our account to pay the balance so God won't send us to hell. When actually said out loud, this idea sounds *ridiculous* and goes against many of our core beliefs. What a sad way to live! That surely doesn't sound like *freedom* in Christ." A minister in Wyoming wrote, "If Jesus did not pay it all, then do *we* pay for part of it? Put simply, this would be a *works* salvation. Jesus is my Savior ... *Period*. I pay nothing!"

Sadly, there are a great many people in Christendom, and a great many even within my own faith-heritage, who, although they *profess* the truth that Jesus paid it *all*, nevertheless *live* as though they believe Christ Jesus only *partially* paid the debt for our sin, and that the remainder is up to *us* to pay. Thus, their actual *practice* is seen in this formula: Jesus' payment + my payment = paid in full. Brethren, this is heresy! "The wages of sin is death, but the *free gift* of God is eternal life in Christ Jesus our Lord" (Romans 6:23). Each of us are "justified *as a gift* by His grace through the redemption which is in Christ Jesus" (Romans 3:24). "For by grace you have been saved through faith; and that *not of yourselves*, it is *the gift* of God; not as a result of works, that no one should boast" (Ephesians 2:8-9). And yet there are countless legalistic men and women who seek daily to *make payment* to God for this "free gift." It is not only absurd, it is an affront to the grace of our God. Paul clearly conveys the truth that those who make such an attempt are "fallen from grace;" indeed, they don't even grasp the meaning of the term. If seeking to make one's *own* payment for justification and redemption causes one to fall from grace and to be severed from Christ Jesus, then this truly constitutes a salvation issue. In speaking of his fellow countrymen, Paul wrote, "My heart's desire and my prayer to God for them is for their *salvation*. For I bear them witness that they have a zeal for God, but not in accordance with knowledge. For not knowing about *God's* righteousness, and seeking to establish *their own*, they did not subject themselves to the righteousness of God" (Romans 10:1-3). They, like many today, sought God's favor through their own effort, and, in so doing, failed to find it.

A sister-in-Christ from Florida wrote, "I think it would feel almost *blasphemous* to take away from the supreme sacrifice that Christ made for us and say that *I* must do something *more* for my salvation." Amen! The legalists, whether they realize it or not, are proclaiming, by virtue of their works-based theology, our Lord's sacrifice on the cross to be merely "partial payment" for sin: *token* atonement. Hebrews 10:29 speaks of those who "count as common" the blood of our Lord Jesus Christ. The writer says this is an "insult to the Spirit of grace," and that the full wrath of God awaits such blasphemers. It is not a small thing to suggest the blood of Christ "didn't do the job," and that it is up to *us* to "take up the slack." May God open the eyes of those ignorant disciples who believe such a doctrine of demons.

A well-known brotherhood author wrote, "I have met those in the past who believed that their salvation is by partial payment. They felt that we just do all that we can do, and then God's grace will make up the rest." A man in Florida said, "This is the old 'bootstrap works' idea, which is impossible for anyone to actually do." "If we have only a partial payment by Jesus, then we are only partially saved by Jesus," writes someone from Texas. "So much for the *gift* of salvation," observed another. An elder in West Virginia wrote, "If Jesus only made a partial payment, then that leaves *me* with the rest of the debt, of which I am truly incapable of doing anything about. *His* payment *is my hope*." A minister in Texas stated, "If He paid less than *all*, then *we* must earn our salvation by our *own* efforts. What a bleak picture this presents. Small wonder that there is so little joy in so many of the churches of our day." A fellow minister here in New Mexico wrote, with respect to "our legalistic friends, they must continue 'day by day' to do the works that 'earn' their salvation. The very fact that they must do these works 'day by day' is proof that their works are ineffective in securing salvation. Only in the *completed* work of Jesus is salvation made 'perfect'."

This same minister from New Mexico additionally observed, "In light of what Paul says about legalists having 'fallen from grace' and having been 'severed from Christ,' can we say that the truly legalistic people among us are really our brothers and sisters?" That is an *excellent* question. Are those who are cut off from Jesus our brethren? Are those outside the parameters of God's grace our brethren? I think the *best* we can say of them is that maybe they were *former* brethren. Frankly, if one is outside of grace and severed from Christ, they are *not* our brethren, no matter what they may *profess* to be. Paul refers to such militant legalists as "*false* brethren" (Galatians 2:4). I think that about sums up the sad reality. They *claim* to be brethren in Christ, but their claim is *false*. By seeking a works-based justification and redemption, they have removed themselves from the family of God. Sadly, such people are *not* our brethren!

"The crux of the matter," writes an individual from Texas, "is that man feels this compulsion to try to pay his own debt for sin." An elder from Florida agrees: "I believe that through the years we have shifted our focus from God's grace to our own works, and we teach salvation by meritorious works rather than salvation by grace. Perhaps this is why there is so much concern among some brethren about doctrinal perfection (as you know, many teach that there must be 100% agreement on all doctrinal issues in order to have fellowship)." This elder then made what I consider an extremely astute and insightful statement: "We are saved by *atonement*, not by *attainment*." It is what *He* did once for all, rather than an accumulation of *my own* deeds, that will ultimately prove redemptive. A minister in Tennessee wrote, "It is difficult for most people to accept a gift, given freely, with no expectation of repayment, and most of our teaching in *Churches of Christ* has hedged on this point. We have *wanted* to believe in Jesus' power to save, but we have feared the effect of not *working*. Hence, we have had teachings that say we must do all we can, and then perhaps God's grace will cover the rest (I have heard this expressed in percentage ranges, like 70% our work and 30% God's grace)." One person wrote, freely admitting, that this was a biblical Truth "that was slow and hard for me to realize because it required me to accept a gift that I do not deserve, did not earn, and cannot pay back. I believed that forgiveness of sins was kind of an initial boost up by God, but that I had to climb the remainder of the way by good works."

"I don't think God, or Christ, or the Holy Spirit, do 'token' acts of substitutionary atonement, or *token* salvation, or *token* love, or *token* anything!" May I say a heart-felt "Amen" to this dear sister from England. What are we *saying* about Deity when we declare His gift of grace was merely "token" atonement? That comes about as close to blasphemy as anything I've heard.

We must be very, very careful here, however, lest we take this too far and fall into the theological traps of *Universalism* or *Calvinism*, both of which I have been accused of by those who have not grasped the intent of my teaching from God's Word on this matter. Yes, Jesus *paid* it all *for all*. But, this does *not* mean all are thereby saved, nor does it imply there is no need for some response on *our* part. The gift of our Lord's atoning sacrifice is for *everyone*, but not everyone will choose to receive it. God does not *force* a sinner to be saved. We have free will; the ability to *choose*. Thus, we must reject the notion of the Universalists that *none* will be lost since Jesus died for *all*. Such is a denial of free will and choice. It also denies *reality*, for most men, sadly, have chosen *not* to receive this gift.

Further, as I just implied in my last statement, a gift may be freely offered, but it must still be *received*. Jesus paid the full penalty for my sins, but I will never actually benefit from the payment until I choose to *accept* that gift. That means I must *respond* to His offer. This response is FAITH. There is nothing you or I can, or ever could, do to merit having the penalty for our sins *paid in full*. That is truly a Gift of Grace. It can only be received by FAITH.

Our Lord has paid the penalty for our sins *in full*. It is a gift. You can't earn it. It is yours for the taking. Do you want this gift? Then respond in faith. From that day forward live your life in grateful acknowledgement of His matchless grace, walk with Him in the light, allow His Spirit to transform you into His image and produce within you the blessed fruit of His nature. Serve Him actively, love Him unconditionally, live for Him daily. In Christ our salvation is assured. We never have to question it. We are secure. Our lives of commitment to His will are merely daily demonstrations of gratitude for His gift of salvation. It earns nothing, it evidences much! Yes, "Jesus paid it all, all to Him I owe!" He gave His life for us, let's live our lives for Him!